WEARING THE CLOAK
Dressing the Soldier in Roman Times

edited by

Marie-Louise Nosch

Oxbow Books
Oxford and Oakville

Published by
Oxbow Books, Oxford, UK

© Oxbow Books and the individual authors, 2012

ISBN 978-1-84217-437-1

This book is *available* direct from

Oxbow Books, Oxford, UK
(Phone: 01865-241249; Fax: 01865-794449)

and

The David Brown Book Company
PO Box 511, Oakville, CT 06779, USA
(Phone: 860-945-9329; Fax: 860-945-9468)

or from our website
www.oxbowbooks.com

A CIP record is available for this book from the British Library

Library of Congress Cataloging-in-Publication Data

Wearing the cloak : dressing the soldier in Roman times / edited by Marie-Louise Nosch.
   p. cm.
  Includes bibliographical references.
  ISBN 978-1-84217-437-1
  1. Rome--Army--Uniforms. 2. Rome--Army--Equipment. 3. Rome--Military antiquities. 4. Textile fabrics, Ancient. I.
Nosch, Marie-Louise.
  UC465.R65W43 2012
  355.1'40937--dc23

    2011044900

Front cover: Illustration © Graham Sumner
Back cover: Figure 7.4. Mummy Portrait of a Roman Soldier found in the Fayum (Egypt),
© Ingrid Geske-Heiden, Antikensammlung, SMB.

Ancient Textiles Series Editorial Commitee:
Eva Andersson Strand, Margarita Gleba, Ulla Mannering
and Marie-Louise Nosch

Printed in Great Britain by
Short Run Press, Exeter

CONTENTS

INTRODUCTION and ACKNOWLEDGEMENTS

In every time period and every region of the world, soldiers must be equipped at least with the basics in terms of clothing, armour, and food supply. The Roman army was no exception, and as it successfully evolved into a more and more professional force stationed both within the Empire and on the borders, an adequate and functioning logistic strategy for provisions in clothing, rations, and equipment became vital. Research on the Roman army has been extensive, even fostering specialist journals. However, these have primarily focused on military strategies and the technicality of weaponry and armour, while the supply of clothing in particular has often been neglected.

Textiles played an important role in the defensive equipment of the Roman soldier. They were used for primary as well as secondary protection of the head, torso and extremities. Defensive armour in Antiquity, like that of today, was intended to protect a soldier's body. The armour could be composed of organic and metallic components: basketry and fabric, leather, metal and even wood were joined and attached for complex functional purposes.

Even though the Roman army demanded large amounts of standardised textiles throughout a long period of time, there are only very few archaeologically preserved cloth remains that can definitely be identified as parts of military equipment. It is therefore a challenge to relate the archaeological remains with the written and iconographical sources in order to answer questions concerning for example the colour of the tunic of the common soldier, or the presence and size of purple *clavi* for senators and knights, serving as officers.

In Roman iconography Roman soldiers are often depicted as fully-armed often grim-looking combatants, wearing helmet and armour and sporting appropriate weapons. There is some logic to such representations, and it is therefore not surprising to find them replicated in modern images and reconstructions. Nonetheless, a survey of the literary, documentary and archaeological evidence in this volume suggests a far more detailed and context-related picture of the Roman soldier's every-day appearance.

In this present volume a number of scholars in the field address these gaps in our understanding of the materiality of the Roman soldier's clothing and the textiles associated with his armour. To this end the elite symbols and insignia of the officers' ranks are investigated in the paper *Late Antique Egyptian Military Garments?* by Annette Paetz gen. Schieck (Reiss-Engelhorn-Museen, Mannheim). The self-representation, and hence the self-awareness, of the Roman soldier and of today's idea of the ideal Roman soldier is discussed by Michael Speidel (MAVORS, Basel) in his paper *Dressed for the occasion. Clothes and context in the Roman army.* His paper is an important key to both the methodology and the interpretation of Roman military dress. The scholar and gifted artist Graham Sumner (UK) in *Painting a Reconstruction of the Deir el-Medineh Portrait on a Painted Shroud and other Soldiers from Roman Egypt* challenges the traditional views of how we can use artistic representations to gain a wider understanding of the Roman soldier and his self-perception.

Using the impressive corpus of epigraphical evidence preserved from Egypt, Kerstin Droß-Krüpe (University of Marburg) investigates the economic contexts in which textiles are made for the Roman army in her paper *Purchase Orders of Military Garments from Papyri of Roman Egypt*. She discusses the existence of the markets and the private/public spheres of the Roman economy influenced by army procurement. The economic impact the presence of the Roman army had on the border regions of the Empire is indeed not to be underestimated.

This trickled through to the outskirts of Empire, all the way to North, where the influence can be detected in dye colours and styles of garments in the archaeological remains. Hence we get a glimpse of military textiles and clothing for non-Roman warriors in the first centuries AD, through the study of textile remains from the weapon deposits in bogs throughout southern Scandinavia and Northern Germany, in *Scandinavian Warrior Costume in the Iron Age Weapon Deposits* by Susan Möller-Wiering (CTR).

Over time the Roman army became a conglomerate of troops who displayed their different origins through particular types of clothing. Not only in the North were the local regiments distinctive. For example, Iberian military units were distinguished by the use of such important elements as the *falcate*, a short sword of extremely good quality, as well as by their special linen cuirasses. Another paper deals with the use, fabrication and symbolism of the origin of linen corselets: *Linen Corselets in Etruscan Culture* by Margarita Gleba (CTR and UCL). She presents convincing evidence of the use of linen as armour drawing on both artistic representations and textual sources.

Linen is evident itself in the archaeological record, for example, at Masada, were some unusually thick linen fragments, including carbonized examples, have been analysed by Hero Granger-Taylor (London) and identified as parts of *pteryges*, "flaps", the narrow hanging elements attached to the shoulders and waists of traditional corselets and breastplates. She presents her results in the paper *Fragments of Linen from Masada, Israel – the Remnants of Pteryges? – and Related Finds in Weft- and Warp-twining including several Slings*. In this context, Masada is an exceptional site yielding various types of textiles used in the army and its dress. The paper also considers the very large number of wool textiles from Masada, among which there are many that can be identified as coming from semi-circular cloaks of the type known in Latin as *paenula* (Greek *phailones*). The distribution of fragments of these brown cloaks suggests an association with the Roman army.

Stefanie Hoss (Universität Köln) explores a particularly prestigious part of the military dress – the belt – and its connotations and functionality in *The Roman Military Belt*. The belt was not only a practical part of a soldier's dress but had double function as social marker as well. The question of how to obtain belts and other markers of this type to enhance the individual's social status is examined in the paper of Jinyu Liu: *Clothing Supply for the Military. A look at the inscriptional evidence*.

We would like to express our thanks to all the participants at the international conference on 'Roman Military and Textiles' held at The Danish Research Foundation's Centre for Textile Research, in Copenhagen. They have contributed to this voyage into the material and immaterial world of the Roman soldier.

The conference was held in collaboration with the European Education, Audiovisual and Culture Executive Agency and its research and exhibition project *Clothing and Identities in the Roman World* on May 20, 2008, in Copenhagen. The positive outcome also owes much to the collaboration within the DressID programme, directed by the Curt-Engelhorn-Stiftung of the Reiss-Engelhorn-Museen in Mannheim, Germany. The conference received generous support from the Danish National Research Foundation, the Danish Research Council for the Humanities, The Italian Culture Institute in Copenhagen, and NATO Science.

Marie-Louise Nosch
Henriette Koefoed

1. DRESSED FOR THE OCCASION. CLOTHES AND CONTEXT IN THE ROMAN ARMY

Michael Alexander Speidel

Modern images and reconstructions of the Roman soldier's appearance nearly always show a fully-armed, often grim-looking combatant, wearing helmet and armour and sporting several weapons. Such images have heavily influenced the way in which we think of Roman soldiers and the Roman army. There is, of course, some logic to these representations, as they immediately reveal the person's military profession. It is therefore not surprising to find them in use already by the Roman soldiers themselves.

Images of fully armed soldiers of all ranks can be found in large numbers on gravestones throughout the first three centuries AD (Fig. 1.1). They supplement the information given by the inscription and add splendour to the tombstone and the memory of the deceased soldier. The context, however, is that of a monument, designed to impress the onlooker. As the design of gravestones was based on choices made by individual soldiers these monuments can therefore serve as a guide for the importance Roman soldiers attributed to the composition of their last appearance as well as for the meaning conveyed by such images.

Several obvious reasons may have led soldiers

Figure 1.1. Fully armed legionary. 1st c. AD (Wiesbaden).

to choose representations of themselves in full battle gear for their gravestones: Such images would show the deceased to have been a professional soldier with the Roman army, which means that during his lifetime he had been an agent of the emperor, representing Roman imperial power, and therefore a person to respect (if not to fear). Such images would also serve to impress the onlooker by the wealth and success the soldier had achieved during his time on earth: a splendid appearance in shining armour, perhaps further embellished by military decorations betraying his bravery on the battlefield.[1] Those who had received promotions could show the insignia of higher ranks, revealing their proven capability to be a leader, trusted by their superiors and respected by their comrades, devoted to duty and ready to fight for the Roman empire.

Surprisingly perhaps, the actual act of killing the enemy was, on the whole, rather unpopular on soldiers' gravestones, as it occurs on only one particular type of image, which shows an armed Roman horseman riding down a barbarian and aiming his spear at the fallen enemy while looking straight ahead (Fig 1.3).[2] This image was chosen primarily (yet not exclusively) by Roman cavalrymen on the northern frontiers. It has recently been recognized, however, that in several cases the enemy, a (half-) naked Germanic warrior, is not necessarily fallen, but has willingly dived beneath the horse to stab it from below.[3] That, of course, makes the fight more equal. Perhaps the original meaning of the scene was to show the Roman horseman and his mount jumping over the Germanic horse-stabber rather than riding him down. If correct, jumping, throwing a spear at the enemy underhoof and concentrating on the foe ahead all at the same time is an image which would serve to prove the impressive skills and the courage of the deceased. However, this image also came in less cruel versions, either without the barbarian, or with military decorations or (since the late second century) a wild boar in his stead (thereby turning the picture into a hunting scene). Hence, the emphasis of the message was not so much focussed on the soldier's professionalism at killing but much rather highlighted his heroic and victorious bravery as well as his extraordinary skills as a horseman.[4] That was what he wanted to be remembered for.

The same message as with full portraits of the armour-clad soldiers could also be transmitted in a less martial setting by displaying only selected items of military equipment or military decorations (Fig. 1.4).[5] Again, this type of image was not restricted to any particular rank within the Roman army or any particular frontier. It is revealing that even images of the emperor could make use of the same set of symbols when they were to emphasize the ruler's role as commander-in-chief of the Roman army.[6] Images of the emperor in military dress or in armour were designed to promote the understanding, that the vigilant ruler successfully used his military power to secure peace and

---

1.   Shining armour and weapons were a soldier's pride and the officers' responsibility: Jos. *BJ* 5, 9, 1. Arr. *Takt.* 38,3. Veg. *Mili.* 2,12. 14. M. P. Speidel 2006a, 35. Experimental archaeology and re-enactment efforts have added much to our understanding of Roman military equipment and of aspects of its use, but, naturally, cannot provide insight into the symbolic meaning of the Roman soldier's dress within any of his contemporary contexts. The following pages therefore primarily intend to contribute to this generally neglected aspect of Roman military dress, rather than to the practical functions of the soldiers' garments and armour.

2.   For such images see Schleiermacher 1984, *passim*. See also the many examples in M. P. Speidel 1994a.

3.   M. P. Speidel 2006b, 151ff.

4.   Dio 75, 9. For hunting boars and other wild animals as a popular show of skill, bravery and manliness amongst soldiers and officers and suiting even for emperors see SHA *Hadr.* 2,1. *ILS* 9241. *RIB* 1041. M. P. Speidel 1994a, 7. *Idem* 1994b, 131. 145. It is certainly telling that although boar-hunting was, since the late second century, a very popular scene on gravestones of the *equites singulares Augusti* at Rome, only one known gravestone bears the scene of a horseman of the emperor's guard aiming his spear at a kneeling enemy warrior: M. P. Speidel 1994a, no. 540 (the warrior in this case is armed with a sword and aiming to hit the guardsman's horse).

5.   For examples cf. Keppie 2003, 31–53. CSIR Carnuntum 319. CSIR Deutschland II 5, no. 134 (Mainz). Etc. North-African examples are quoted by LeBohec 1989, 104. For both weapons and military decorations on one monument: Keppie 1983, pl. I c (Ateste).

6.   Cf. e.g. *RIC* II 582. BMC Trajan 911 for a dupondius showing only Trajan's cuirass on the revers side. *RIC* III 545. 567. 1404 are examples of coins showing on their revers sides the emperor Lucius Verus on horseback aiming his spear at a fallen Parthian enemy. For the same scene with Commodus and a Germanic warrior on a gem from Biesheim cf. M. P. Speidel 2000a, 193–197.

Figure 1.2. Soldier and his wife in civilian clothes. 3rd c. AD (Augsburg).

prosperity for the Roman Empire. Of course, such images were not carried by gravestones but by different media, such as statues, reliefs or coins. Their messages, however, were much the same: Armour and weapons were used as symbolic representations in public displays of a successful, responsible, and heroic military service for Rome and empire-wide peace by all members of the Roman army, including equestrian and senatorial officers and generals as well as emperors.[7]

A second style of images on gravestones, which were also produced throughout the first three centuries AD, shows soldiers without armour, wearing only a belted tunic and a cloak (Fig. 1.2). Weapons and other military attributes could also be added. The character of these images is obviously less martial in its general appearance and was certainly intended to preserve a memory of the soldier in a context which was not battle or war. It was with great disgust that Tacitus described Roman

---

7. For statues of Roman senators *habitu militari* see *CIL* VI 1566. *ILS* 1112. *CIL* VI 41145. *Statua armata*: *CIL* VI 41142 = *ILS* 1098. *CIL* VI 41141 = *ILS* 1326 (this inscription also mentions a *statua loricata*). For equestrian officers Devijver 1989, 416ff. *Idem* 1992, 298ff. 305ff.

Figure 1.3. Auxiliary horseman and horse-stabber. 1st c. AD (Glouchester).

Figure 1.4. Legionary centurion's military equipment, servant and horse. 1st. c. AD (Carnuntum)

soldiers without helmet and body armour in the cities of Syria as sleek money-making traders.[8] Tacitus and other Roman aristocrats may have scorned the peaceful appearance of the army in the provinces,[9] many soldiers, however, consciously chose such images for their gravestones. It is therefore certainly revealing, that the images of soldiers wearing only belted tunics and cloaks became ever more popular and finally, by the third century, clearly outnumbered the representations in full armour.[10] This must surely be taken as a sign of the soldiers' increasing will to be remembered not so much as battle-hardened warriors but rather as fellow citizens, or even, when shown with wife and children,[11] as fathers and family-men.

If soldiers more and more preferred not to be seen, on their gravestones, as heavily armoured, battle-ready fighters, they would still regularly choose to show the insignia of their profession and their power, and thereby remind us of their former importance in society. On principle, these insignia included belt and cape. By contrast, the soldiers' servants are never shown with swords, although they are known to have joined the soldiers in training and battle.[12] Soldiers with higher ranks would

8.   Tac. *Ann.* 35.
9.   Of course, Tacitus was of an entirely different opinon when soldiers in Rome were concerned. Their appearance in armour was a frightful sight to him: Tac. *Hist.* 2,88. Cf. also below.
10. Franzoni 1987, 139. Ubl 2006, 262 with n. 11. Coulston 2007.
11. E.g. CSIR Schweiz III no. 65 (Augst). CSIR Deutschland I,1 no. 31 (Augsburg). Wagner 2001, 454 Abb. 167 (Graz). CSIR Carnuntum 317. Nagy 2007, 117 Nr. 123. CSIR Mogetiana 112. M. P. Speidel 1998, 203f. (Zeugma). Images with belted tunics could even be chosen for gravestones of soldiers who died and were buried during military campaigns: cf. e.g. Facella and Speidel (2011).
12. M. P. Speidel 1992, 345ff. For clothing in the Roman army in general cf. e.g. Sander 1963, 144–166. Fuentes 1987,

also not shy away from showing their badges of office. Such details added information and therefore played an important role in the composition of the images of soldiers. Hence, under-officers and officers, dressed in tunics and cloaks, could be shown holding a set of writing tablets or a scroll in one hand, and either *lanceae*,[13] standards,[14] a *fustis*,[15] a *hastile*,[16] or a *vitis*[17] etc. in the other. The tablets were surely meant to portray the soldiers' writing-skills and therefore appear to indicate that at some stage in their career they had held positions involving administrative tasks.[18] *Lanceae* and standards, however, were carried in battle and during manoeuvers, the *fustis* was a nightstick which was used as a police weapon, the long *hastile* was the typical staff of an *optio*, with which he was to keep discipline and order amongst the soldiers in the battle lines, whereas the *vitis*, a vine cane, was the badge of office of centurions and *evocati* and their sign of authority with which they could beat and punish insubordinate soldiers.[19] In some instances such combinations of writing-material and different types of staffs could serve to illustrate the soldier's rank (*signifer, beneficiarius, optio*, etc.) by showing typical items of their office. Obviously, however, both instruments were never used at the same time. Such cases must therefore serve as a warning, not to interpret these images as snapshots of a former reality. They were not composed as guides to the appearance of Roman soldiers at any particular occasion.[20] We should much rather understand the images on soldiers' gravestones as sources for the symbolic meaning of their (often very accurately shown) military equipment and dress. This has, perhaps, not always been fully appreciated, but the point is worth making, as we need to assume that during the soldiers' life-times, too, their dress was often consciously chosen with the intent to express certain messages.

Obviously, war and battle was the main occasion to wear full battle gear. Military training and manoeuvres, such as the *ambulatio*, were another,[21] although there was also special training equipment occasionally used for weapons-training. Finally, a number of festive parades and military shows could call for full battle gear. The most frequent amongst these was the pay parade, which took place three times per year and which was, at the same time, a weapons and armour inspection. Titus deliberately

---

41–75. Bishop/Coulston 1993. Sumner 2002, 9f. *Idem* 2003, 7ff. Goldsworthy 2003, 118ff.

13.   E.g. the first-century gravestone of P. Flavoleius Cordus from Mainz: cf. M. A. Speidel 1996, 60 Bild 27.

14.   E.g. the first-century gravestones of L. Duccius Rufinus from York and of Oclatius Carvi f. from Neuss: cf. M. A. Speidel 1996, 62f. Bild 29 and 30.

15.   E.g. the first-century gravestone of C. Valerius Valens from Corinth: cf. M. A. Speidel 1996, 59 Bild 26.

16.   E.g. the second-century gravestone of the *optio* Caecilius Avitus from Chester: cf. M. A. Speidel 1996, 61 Bild 28.

17.   E.g. the third-century gravestone of the centurion Vivius Marcianus from London: *RIB* 17. The sign in line 3 of this inscription has been interpreted as a *hedera distinguens* (the only one in this inscription). It was, however, clearly intended to represent the sign for centurion, *7(centurioni) leg(ionis) II Aug(ustae)*, as the rank of the deceased is to be expected before *II Aug.* and would otherwise be missing. The image of the deceased confirms this reading.

18.   This has occasionally been doubted: cf. e.g. Haensch 1997, 124 n. 23 with further literature. However, the symbolic meaning of all other prominently shown items strongly suggests that writing-material, too, was depicted to convey information relating to the military service of the deceased soldier. Any of the countless writing-tasks in the Roman army may have justified the representation of writing-materials. The tablets and scrolls themselves, therefore, cannot be taken to indicate any particular rank. It may even be, that in some instances they relate to administrative responsibilities the deceased soldier had held earlier in his career.

19.   For *lanceae*, standards and the *hastile* see M. P. Speidel 2002, 125–143. For the *fustis*: *idem* 1993, 137–149. The *vitis* as a badge of office: Dio 55,24,8. Euseb. *HE* 7,15. Beating: Tac. *Ann.* 1,23. Dig. 49,16,13,4. Cf. also Apul. *Met.* 9,39 where a civilian was beaten with a *vitis* by a legionary whose rank is not mentioned.

20.   That, however, was the understanding of Sander 1963, 144–166, and others, and still seems to be that of Thorne 2007, 227.

21.   Herod. 6,8,5. Veg. 1,27. SHA *Max*, 6,2. Tert. *Ad Martyras 3*.

held such a parade in view of the enemy for four days during the siege of Jerusalem in order to awe the Jewish defenders with the shine of so much gold, silver, armour and weapons.[22] In AD 14, on the other hand, the mutinous legionary soldiers in Pannonia met Tiberius' son Drusus, according to Tacitus, 'not as usual with glad looks or the glitter of military decorations, but in unsightly squalor'. Thus, the condition of a soldier's dress was understood to reflect the state of his morale and discipline, 'for who would believe a soldier to be warlike, when he carelessly lets his arms get stained with dirt and rust'.[23]

For the performance of certain cavalry shows it was officially recommended not to wear armour, for full battle gear would have taken away from the intended elegance and grace of the manoeuvres.[24] This was also true for the horsemen riding in funerary *decursiones* as the ones shown on the base of the Antonine column.[25] Whether military parades were held in full armour or not, was often a political decision made by the emperor. Vespasian, for instance, had his unarmed soldiers dress in silk for his triumph in AD 71,[26] which put the emphasis of the victory-parade on the peaceful and prosperous times he was promising for the future.[27] Nero, in AD 66, on the other hand, ordered his praetorians to appear on the forum in full and shining armour for Tiridates' coronation. As Nero himself was wearing his triumphal outfit he had obviously (and successfully) set the scene to impress the Armenian king with Rome's military power. Tiridates was duely frightened and the cheering crowds were delighted.[28]

Tiridates' coronation is just one example which shows that the shine of weapons and armour was also intended to 'strike terror' into the enemy.[29] The appearance of fully armed soldiers outside the appropriate contexts must therefore have been a fearsome sight to the civilian population of the empire as well. If we are to believe Apuleius, even a single soldier travelling on his own in the provinces could instil fear into unlucky passers-by, simply by tying his shiny helmet, shield and weapons ostentatiously to the top of his luggage.[30] To Pliny the Younger, for one, it was certainly a truly comforting fact well worth mentioning in his praise for Trajan that this emperor and his soldiers, when entering Rome in 98, were hardly discernible from the inhabitants of the capital due both to their civilian dress and their orderly behaviour.[31] Vitellius, on the other hand, is reported to have entered Rome in quite a different style in the summer of 69: with trumpets sounding and surrounded by the standards of his troops Vitellius, armed with his sword, appeared together with his companions, all wearing their military cloaks. His soldiers are described as a frightful spectacle, as they were fully armed, aggressive, and moving about the city in haste and in large numbers.[32]

Under normal circumstances, the heavy armour and most deadly weapons (apart from daggers

22. Pay parade and inspection: Jos. 5,9,1. Arr. *Peripl.* 6,2. 10,3. Three times per year: M. A. Speidel 2009, 349f. Titus: Jos. 5,9,1.
23. Mutinous legionaries: Tac. *Ann.* 1,24. Dress and morale/discipline: see above n. 1 and Onasander 10,14. 28. SHA *Sev.Alex.* 52,3. Maurice, *Strat.* 1,2,25. 'Dirt and rust': Veg. 2,14.
24. Arr. *Tact.* 34,6. M. P. Speidel 2006a, 9. 14f. 37f. 61ff. 91.
25. Koeppel 1989, 26ff. 60ff. M. A. Speidel 2009, 451–462.
26. Jos. *BJ* 7,5,4.
27. Jos. *BJ* 7,5,6f.
28. Suet. *Nero* 13. Dio 63,4f.
29. Veg. 2,14: *Plurimum enim terroris hostibus armorum splendor inportat.* See also Jos. *BJ* 5.9.1. Ps.Quint. *Decl.mai.* 3,12. Amm. 18,2,16. 27,2,6. 31,10,9 and Veg. 2,12. Amm. 31,12,12.
30. Apul. *Met.* 10,1,2.
31. Plin. *Paneg.* 23,3: *nam milites nihil a plebe habitu tranquillitate modestia differebant.*
32. Tac. *Hist.* 2,88. See also Suet., *Vit.* 11.

and swords) of the Rome cohorts were locked away.[33] Hence, ancient reports of fully armed troops in the streets of the imperial capital are set in narrative contexts which aim to illustrate events of illegal or inappropriate violence.[34] The weapons city-Roman soldiers would normally use within the city were the *fustis*-nightstick, a *virga*-rod, the butt of spears or the bladeless *hastile*, all of which were intended for non-lethal police duty.[35] Only as a last resort were iron weapons used against civilians.[36] Even issuing axes to the city-Roman soldiers for breaking into the houses of suspected criminals was seen as the decision of a tyrant emperor.[37] While on duty within the city, the soldiers of these units normally wore the *toga*, a belted tunic[38] or a *subarmalis*, the felt shirts originally designed to be worn underneath the cuirass.[39] Whereas many reliefs show soldiers wearing belted tunics, images of soldiers wearing just the *subarmalis* do not appear to have been deemed worth recording for eternity. However, the fourth-century Anonymus, *De Rebus Bellicis* recommends wearing a leather shirt over the felt-made *thoracomachus* (his term to describe the *subarmalis*) in bad weather in order to protect it from getting wet and heavy in the rain.[40] The *subarmalis*, therefore, must also have regularly been worn without cuirass. Thick felt was lighter than armour and would yet have offered some protection. A *subarmalis* was therefore an ideal garment for police duty. An incident reported by the *Historia Augusta* can be understood to show that the *subarmalis* was indeed a standard garment of the Praetorian Guard at least on certain occasions:[41] when Septimius Severus reached the gates of the imperial capital in 192, he ordered the praetorians to come out and meet him *cum subarmalibus inermes*, 'wearing only felt-shirts and unarmed'. It was Severus' intention to assemble the guardsmen only to send them home in dishonour for their involvement in the murder of the emperor Pertinax and their disgraceful conduct in the events which followed. As the praetorians were fearing that Severus might punish them, he took great care not to arrouse any suspicion of his true intentions.[42] Had it been entirely unusual for praetorian soldiers to leave their camp unarmed (i.e. without swords) and dressed only in *subarmales* (not tunics), they would surely have recognized the plot immediately.[43] The contrary must therefore be true.

Ovid, while in exile at Tomis, was terrified at the daily sight of local tribesmen entering the city in arms, ever-ready to get into a fight.[44] In Ovid's judgement, therefore, daily life in Rome was, in general, less violent than in some far-away frontier cities. However, with very few exceptions, it was the responsibility of the local magistrates to organize and to equip their own police forces and

---

33.   Tac. *Hist.* 1,38. 80. Cf. SHA *Sev.* 6,11 and Herod. 2,13,2 and 12 with the text to n. 41 below.

34.   E.g. *Tac.* Ann. 14,61. 16,27. Herod. 2,5,1ff. For soldiers in Rome not normally wearing heavy armour cf. also Herod. 4,5,1. 7,11,2.

35.   Suet. *Cal.* 26. Davies 1989, 88. M. P. Speidel 1993, 137–149. *Idem* 1994b, 33f. 130f.

36.   Cf. Tac. *Ann.* 14,8. 14,61.

37.   Herod. 2,4,1. 2,6,10. Juv. 16,7ff. *PMich.* VI 425. Jos. *BJ* 2,306. M. P. Speidel 1994b, 52f.

38.   Toga: Tac. *Ann*, 16,27. Belted tunics: Herod. 7,11,2. Koeppel 1986, 2ff. 21ff. (Anaglypha Traiani. No swords are shown, and only very few daggers). Cf. also SHA *Marcus* 27,3.

39.   *AE* 1998, 839. *Tab.Vindol.* II 184,7. 17. 38. SHA *Sev.* 6,11. SHA *Claud.* 14,8. SHA *Aur.* 13,3. Martianus Capella *De Nupt.* 5,426. Ubl 2006, 262–276. M. P. Speidel 2007, 237–240.

40.   Anon. *De Rebus bellicis* 15. Ubl 2006, 270ff. M. P. Speidel 2007, 238f.

41.   SHA *Sev.* 6,11.

42.   Dio 74,17,3. 75,1,1. Herod. 2,13,1ff.

43.   Cf. above n. 34. Severus Alexander, when speaking to his soldiers, also appears to have had them assemble unarmed, even during expeditions: Herod. 6,9,3f. (cf. above n. 11).

44.   Ovid., *Trist.* 5,7,11f. 5,10,44. It should, however, be remembered that Ovid's account was not free of exaggeration and fiction.

militias.[45] (Ovid was less than enthusiastic when he had to join the militia of Tomis).[46] According to Aelius Arisitides, soldiers of the Roman army were employed as police forces in urban centres of the provinces only 'if anywhere a city is so large that it cannot police itself'.[47] When on duty in such cities as Alexandria, Carthago, Lugudunum, and a few others, or in the provincial hinterland, soldiers would again regularly use wooden rods, clubs or nightsticks for riot-control and for punishing individuals.[48] The normal dress for such duty was again the belted *tunica* with a cloak or perhaps also the *subarmalis*.[49] The latter certainly belonged to a soldier's standard equipment in the provinces by the end of the first century at the latest, as a military document from Carlisle reveals.[50] The same document also shows that the cavalry soldiers at Carlisle each seem to have had at least two *subarmales minores*, perhaps one made of felt, the other of leather.[51] Their description as *minores* makes sense, as one would expect the *subarmales* of horsemen to be shorter than those of footsoldiers. Horsemen may also have worn *subarmales* without cuirass for military training and there may even have been different kinds, either for training, police duty and battle, or for summer and winter. For the countless other non-combat duties of his military service, a Roman soldier would normally just wear a belted tunic and perhaps a cloak. If he carried any weapons at all, he may have been armed with just a dagger or perhaps with a dagger and a sword.[52] On the whole, therefore, soldiers wearing full armour must have been a much rarer sight than suggested by the images on gravestones and other monuments, let alone Hollywood productions or most documentaries on television. And even if soldiers were clad in armour, it might not have been obvious from afar, as weapons and armour were often hidden by protective coverings and coats.[53]

Still, even if unarmed, soldiers could be recognized by their clothing and their behaviour, *habitus atque habitudo*, as Apuleius put it.[54] Thus, the evidence leaves no doubt that the military belt, *balteus* or *cingulum militare* (as it was later called), was considered to be a distinctive mark of military service and it was therefore regularly shown on soldiers' gravestones.[55] Images on gravestones also commonly

45. E.g. *ILS* 6087,103. *CIL* XII 3296. See esp. Apul. *Met.* 9,41,3ff. where even soldiers turn to the local magistrates after having been robbed. The magistrates then sent *lictores ceterique publici ministerii* to search the house of the accused and finally to arrest him. The soldiers, in this incident, took no part in the local police work. Cf. also Plin. *Ep.* 10,19f. *Sel. Pap.* II 254 reports the story of two guards unlawfully flogging a veteran with rods at the orders of the strategus Hierax in the village of Philadelphia in Egypt. Local police in Asia Minor used clubs and maces: M. P. Speidel 1992, 190f. For armouries in provincial cities see e.g. Strabo 14,2,5. Dio Chrys. or. 77/78,12. Tac. *Hist.* 1,57,2. 1,66,1. 2,52,2. See also Brélaz 2005.

46. Ovid. *Trist.* 4,1,71f.

47. Arist. *Or. Rom.* 67.

48. Jos. *BJ* 2,9,4. 2,15,5. Apul. *Met.* 9,39f. Acts 16,22. 22,23ff. *Tab.Vindol.* II 344 (*virgis castigatum esse*). ILS 6870 = Hauken 1998, 2ff. no. 1 II 11ff.: *missis militib(us) / [in eu]ndem saltum Burunitanum, ali/[os nos]trum adprehendi et vexari, ali/[os vinc]iri, non<n>ullos cives etiam Ro/[manos] virgis et fustibus effligi iusse/[rit]*. M. P. Speidel 1993, 141ff. Naturally, whenever an uprising was suspected and Roman control was seen to be threatened, the authorities would order the use of deadly iron weapons. This is well illustrated e.g. in Josephus' account of the events leading to the Jewish revolt of AD 66.

49. Jos. *BJ* 2,12,1.

50. *AE* 1998, 839. *Tab.Vindol.* II 184 i 7. i 17. iii 38.

51. M. P. Speidel 2007, 238.

52. Tac. *Ann.* 11,18. Jos. *BJ* 2,12,1. Amm. 28,2,8. See e.g. also the scenes XCII, XCVII, CIII on Trajan's column, and above n. 38.

53. Plut. *Luc.* 27. Cf. Cras. 23f. Jos. *BJ* 5,9,1. Ubl 2006, 262 with n. 15.

54. Apul. *Met.* 9,39. Cf. Also Petr. *Sat.* 82. Plin. *Paneg.* 23,3. Veg. 1,6.

55. Petr. *Sat.* 82. Tac. *Hist.* 1,57. 2,88. Herod. 2,13,10. Servius *Aen.* VIII, 724: *omnes qui militant, cincti sunt*. *Cod.Just.* 1,1,4,3. Suda, s.v. αὐθεντήσαντα. Isid. *Or.* 19,33,2. Etc.

show soldiers wearing cloaks: either a heavy hooded cloak for cold and rainy weather[56] or a light cape for the warmer seasons.[57] Neither type of cloak, however, seems to have been worn in battle.[58] Still, such cloaks were a distinctive sign of military service, for 'taking the cloak', as a figure of speech, meant 'going to war', just as 'wearing the cloak' was an expression for 'being at war'.[59] Hence, Vitellius and his companions were not forgiven for entering Rome in their military cloaks, whereas the emperor Marcus Aurelius (according to the *Historia Augusta*) was praised because he would not allow his soldiers to wear their military cloaks in Italy.[60] Finally, the hobnailed military footwear was also specifically related to the army. Petronius, in his *Satyricon*, tells the story of Encolpius who, by girding on a sword and putting on ferocious looks, tried to disguise himself as a soldier but was soon unmasked because of the Greek slippers he was wearing.[61]

On rare occasions, soldiers could also be ordered to dress as civilians so they would not be recognized. Thus, Pontius Pilatus fearing an unruly crowd at Jerusalem, once had his soldiers disguise as civilians. Armed with hidden swords and wooden rods they mixed with the locals who were gathering around Pilate and beginning to shout in anger, because he was planning to use the temple treasure to build an aquaeduct for the city. When riots broke out he gave his soldiers a sign to draw their rods and to restore order.[62] Epictetus reports another occasion (from the reign of Domitian?): a soldier in civilian dress sits down next to someone in Rome and starts to revile the emperor. As soon as that person, unaware of his interlocutor's military profession, begins to join in on the abuse, he is immediately arrested.[63] It appears, however, that the use of soldiers disguised as civilians for such sinister purposes was a rare exception. On other occasions, a soldier's public appearance without the insignia of his military service was due to entirely different reasons. For soldiers and officers could be ordered to line up in front of their comrades with unbelted tunics as a form of punishment for cowardice.[64] Extreme disgrace, considered 'worse than death' was Julian's punishment of a cavalry unit which had fled during battle: for such cowardice the soldiers were ordered to march through the camp in women's clothes.[65] Pride, honour and shame played an eminent role in the community of the Roman army.[66] Hence such sentences, which aimed to publically humiliate cowards, reveal the great symbolic importance attached to the soldier's dress and to the insignia of his military service. Belt, cloak, sword and shoes belonged to the official military equipment for which soldiers had to pay.[67] The symbolic act of publicly laying down these insignia or being ordered to hand them in meant leaving or having to leave the army.[68]

---

56.   Dio 57,13,5. SHA *Hadr.* 3.

57.   Cf. SHA *Trig. Tyr.* 23,5.

58.   M.P. Speidel 1994b, 103. Sumner 2002, 15.

59.   For *saga sumere, ad saga ire*, or *in sagis esse* see e.g. Cic. *Ver.* 5,94. Cic. *Phil.* 5,31. 6,9. 8,32. 12,16. 14,3. Vell. 2,16,4. Cf. also Dio 50,4,4.

60.   Suet. *Vit.* 11. SHA *Marc.* 27,3.

61.   Pet. *Sat.* 82.

62.   Jos. *BJ* 2,9,4.

63.   Epict. 4,13,5. Incidentally, the story proves, that a soldier could normally be recognised by his clothes. Contra: Sander 1963, 153.

64.   Suet. *Aug.* 24,2. Front. *Strat.* 4,1,26ff.

65.   Zos. 3,3,4f. Cf. also *BHL* 7599.

66.   Cf. e.g. Lendon 1997, esp. 237ff.

67.   M. A. Speidel 2009, 360ff.

68.   See e.g. Dio 75.1,1f. (weapons, horses, belts). Herod. 2,13,10 (daggers, belts, clothes and other military insignia). Tertullian *De Corona* 1,3 (cloak, sword and shoes). HA *Sev.Alex.* 54,4 (weapons and cloaks). For military equipment

Colours, of course must have played an important role as well, but the evidence is scanty and difficult to interpret. Although we know of striped tunics,[69] for example, it has so far remained impossible to recognize whether the stripes or their colours carried any meaning at all. Next to their normal tunics made of wool or linen, soldiers may also have had a special red battle tunic (*tunica russa militaris*).[70] It is certain, however, that every soldier and officer possessed an additional shining white tunic, a *tunica alba*, which must have been a bleached tunic. Such tunics belonged to the soldiers' standard out-fit, as is shown by a pay-receipt on a papyrus from Masada, where a *tunica alba* is listed among the items for which money was deducted from the soldier's pay.[71] The *tunica alba* was worn by all ranks for special, festive occasions such as victory games or religious ceremonies.[72] The emperor, too, had a *vestis alba triumphalis*.[73] Equestrian officers are also known to have had white capes as well as a special dinner tunic, a *tunica cenatoria*.[74] Its appearance is unknown, but judging by its name, it must have differed from the officer's usual tunic. Caligula was ridiculed by Suetonius, because during his northern expedition he ordered his officers, who had stepped in to report the safe return of a group of soldiers, to join him for dinner immediately, clad in armour as they were.[75] The story implies, that for the officers of the Roman army, it was normal, or generally required, to

have the appropriate dinner dress even when on campaign. Common soldiers also wore tunics for dinner, though whether they differed by name or by looks from those they wore for work is not clear. (It is, however, probably safe to assume, that they did not normally wear the same tunics on both occasions.) The funeral banquet scenes on many gravestones of Roman soldiers show the image of an ideal dining scene, which celebrated the good moments of the soldier's life, moments the deceased was hoping to continuously repeat in his after-life. These scenes show the dining soldier lying on a couch, wearing a tunic and a cloak.[76] That must therefore have been the appropriate dinner dress for a soldier, at least when he was attending an elegant banquet. The *Historia Augusta* adds a curious detail: in the second half of the third century, a Roman general supposedly ordered his soldiers to appear at dinner (*convivium*) in a warm cape (*sagum*) in winter, and in a light one in summer, in order to prevent the lower parts of their bodies from getting exposed.[77] The story is fictitious, and it remains unclear whether the order was issued mainly out of concern for the soldiers' health or to enforce appropriate table manners. At any rate, it is revealing that the funeral banquet scenes on soldiers' gravestones always show legs and hips covered by a cloak.

The evidence leaves no doubt, that it mattered to most soldiers to be wearing what was considered to be dashing dress. Thus, military tunics ordered in Egypt for the Cappadocian army were to be

---

identifying Roman soldiers see also Bishop and Coulston 1993, 196ff.
69.   For the *sticharion* see Sheridan 1998, 76f. For stripes and other decorations cf. also Sumner 2002, 9f. *Idem* 2003, 7ff.
70.   SHA *Claud.* 14,5. SHA *Aur.* 13,3: *tunica russa ducalis*. Isid. *Or.* 19,22,10.
71.   P. Yadin 722. A white belted tunic for the army in Cappadocia is also listed in *BGU* 1564 = *Sel.Pap.* II 395. Hoewever, it is not clear in this case, whether the tunic was simply to be left undyed or whether it was to be bleached.
72.   M. A. Speidel 2009, 455–457.
73.   *ILS* 1763.
74.   Tab. *Vindol.* II 196 with Birley 2002, 138f. Cf. SHA *Max.* 30,5 (*vestis cenatoria*). White capes for the army in Cappadocia are also listed in *BGU* 1564 = *Sel.Pap.* II 395.
75.   Suet. *Cal.* 45.
76.   M. P. Speidel 1994a, 5. *Idem* 1994b, 145.
77.   SHA *Tyr. Trig.* 23,5: *nec inferiora nudarentur*.

'from fine, soft, white wool without any dirt, well-woven and well-edged, pleasing and undamaged'.[78] Egypt is known to have been a major source for military clothing.[79] Gaul, which was also famous for its extensive range of dyestuffs,[80] appears to have been another.[81] With the increasing numbers of soldiers from outside Italy serving in the Roman army on far-away frontiers, the preferences for certain styles of clothing also began to change. In AD 69, the Roman general Aulus Caecina, arriving from the frontier on the Rhine, shocked the toga-clad Roman citizens of Northern Italy by wearing Germanic trousers and a cloak of various colours.[82] It still did not pass unnoticed in the early third century, that the emperor Caracalla preferred to wear the same Germanic outfit when he took the field. That eventually gave him his nickname, as the word *caracalla* denotes a Germanic cloak. Dressing like his soldiers on the northern frontier (or more precisely: like the German soldiers he had raised for his bodyguard from north of the frontier) was a strong message, that he wanted to be seen as their comrade, and by continuing to wear such dress (as well as a blond wig in German hairstyle) in Syria and Mesopotamia, Caracalla may indeed have been the one responsible for making this style of dress popular with soldiers throughout the empire.[83] At any rate, long-sleeved tunics, tight trousers and brightly coloured cloaks, all previously considered effeminate and barbarian, became the new third century dress, worn in all branches of the Roman army.[84]

By the late third century the soldier's taste for luxurious clothes had reached a point where a heavy coloured cape cost more than a fine war horse and the élite soldiers of the emperor's bodyguards would wear capes embroidered with threads of gold and silver called *barbaricae*.[85] Yet even in the preceding centuries, ordinary soldiers would have needed to spend a considerable percentage of their pay for clothing. In the case of one auxiliary soldier in AD 81, the expenses for clothing reached 245.5 drachmae.[86] That was nearly one third of the soldier's annual pay.[87] What type of clothes he bought is not known, but the money would have been enough for nearly ten woollen tunics[88] or nine linen tunics[89] or 12 *sagacia* cloaks.[90] It is true, of course, that the amount of such payments varied, depending partly on personal needs and tastes, but also on the soldier's type of unit and his rank. Pliny

---

78. *BGU* VII 1564 = *Sel.Pap.* II 395.
79. E.g. *BGU* VII 1564 = *Sel.Pap.* II 395. *P.Ryl.* II 189. *P.Oxy.* LXIV 4434. Cf. in general Sheridan 1998.
80. Plin., *NH* 22,2.
81. Fink 1971, 63 ii 18. *Tab. Vindol.* II 255 + add. = III p. 157 with Birley 2002, 101 and *idem* 2007, 320f. Cf. also *Tab. Vindol.* II 154 + add. = III p. 155 with Birley 2002, 79.
82. Tac. *Hist.* 2,20. For a Roman description of Germanic clothes see Tac. *Germ.* 17 (cf. also 6).
83. See esp. Herod. 4,7,3. Caracalla as 'fellow soldier' etc.: Dio 77,13,1. 77,17,4. 78,3.1f. 78,9,1. 78,16,7. 78,24,1. Cf. Herod. 4,4,7f. 4,7,4ff. SHA *Carac.* 2,1. 2,3. 9,3. 11,5. M. P. Speidel 1994b, 65. 104. Caracalla's portraits as sole ruler regularly show him wearing a military cloak. Even his fierce looks (cf. also Dio 78,11,1²f.) should be understood to show him as a soldier. Cf. Petr. *Sat.* 82. Apul. *Met.* 9,39. and esp. Herod. 7,1,12 likening the emperor Maximinus' frightening appearance with that of a barbarian élite warrior. Compare also the facial expressions of the Roman soldiers on the Great Trajanic Frieze. On the subject see Leander Touati 1991.
84. Effeminate and barbarian: cf. e.g. Cic. *Fam.* 9,15,2.6. Verg. *Aen.* 9,615. Gell. *Noct. Att.* 6(7),12,3ff., compare also Suet. *Div. Iul.* 45. Third century dress: M. P. Speidel 1994b, 103f. Even at the end of the third century the pretender Allectus was accused of wearing Germanic dress and long hair: Paneg. *Lat.* 8,16,4.
85. Lauffer 1971: *sagum*: 4,000 *denarii* and *equus optimus militaris*: 3,000 *denarii*. Bullion capes (*barbaricae*) worn by the emperor's bodyguard since Caracalla: Herod. 4,7,3. M. P. Speidel 1997, 231–237.
86. Fink 1971, 68 iii.
87. For soldiers' pay (and stoppages) see M. A. Speidel 2009, 349–379; 407–437.
88. 25 drachmae (= sestertii) each (= 6.25 denarii): *BGU* VII 1564.5.
89. 7 denarii each (= 28 sestertii): *P.Yadin* 722.
90.   5 denarii (= 20 sestertii) 2 asses each: *Tab.Vindol.* II 184.

the Younger, for example, helped out a friend of his who needed 40,000 sesterces to buy a centurion's outfit.[91] That sum would have equalled over 33 annual salaries of a legionary soldier or well over twice the centurion's own annual salary.[92] Soldiers, under-officers and centurions in particular also had to pay for their servants' clothes.[93] Thus, a centurion at Vindolanda ordered six *sagacia*-cloaks, an unknown number of *saga*-cloaks, seven *palliola*-cloaks and five or six tunics for his servants.[94]

The conclusion to be drawn from the evidence presented above is that the Roman soldier's everyday appearance was more varied, more context-related and more capable of expressing symbolic meaning than has so far generally been recognized. Taken together, the evidence clearly shows, that Roman soldiers needed a substantial number and variety of clothes for summer and winter,[95] different weather and various occasions both for themselves and for their servants. It is hardly surprising, therefore, to find clothing playing such a prominent role in both private and official military documents, and to see this particular need of the Roman army leading to the creation of the *vestis militaris* – tax.[96]

91. Plin. *Ep.* 6,25.
92. Cf. M. A. Speidel 2009, 407–437.
93. For soldiers' servants see M. P. Speidel 1992, 342ff.
94. Tab.*Vindol.* II 255. Birley 2002, 101.
95. Cf. *P.Oxy.* LXIV 4434, a receipt from AD 154 (?) issued by Claudius Germanus, *optio legionis III Cyrenaicae* (based at Bostra in the province of Arabia) for 55 Syrian winter cloaks to Theon, the representative of 'the makers of thick garments' at Egyptian Oxyrhynchos, who had previously received, by Claudius Germanus, a public contract for their production.
96. Sheridan 1998. For the importance of supplying the army with clothing see SHA, *Sev. Alex.* 52. Cf. also Veg. 3,2. etc. For earlier imperial contributions towards the soldiers' expenses for clothing (or for demands thereof) cf. e.g. Tac. *Hist.* 3,50. Suet. *Vesp.* 8,3. SHA *Sev.Alex.* 40,5. In general: M. A. Speidel 2009, 360ff. 407–437.

2. PURCHASE ORDERS OF MILITARY GARMENTS FROM PAPYRI OF ROMAN EGYPT

Kerstin Droß-Krüpe

In every time period and every region of the world, soldiers who were supposed to serve loyally and dutifully had to have access to the bare necessities of a soldier's life. These necessities were food and clothing. At the very latest with the conversion of the army from the Roman militia to a standing army that was stationed at the borders of the provinces – a process that was accomplished by the Augustan reforms – the army needed a functioning network of supply lines to provide what was necessary. It is impossible to give an exact number of soldiers that the Roman state had to pay for, but current guesses range from 250,000 to 450,000 people.[1] These troops were spread across the whole *Imperium Romanum:* supplying them required the creation and consolidation of a functional infrastructure, an efficient administration, and arrangements with local suppliers in the regions.[2] The close connection between organizing troop supplies and the creation of economic structures is obvious. Thus, many historians have analyzed the supply of the soldiers to gather information about ancient economy. Special emphasis has been put on the organization of food supplies, while the process of purchasing clothing for the troops had been neglected by historians.[3] This is mostly due to the small number of historical sources which provide information on the supply of fabrics and their distribution to the troops. Ancient military authors as Flavius Vegetius Renatus or Aelinanus Tacticus dealt with recruiting, military training, the organization of the army and battle tactics, but tell us little about the actual processes of supplying the troops.

Texts which allow an immediate insight into ancient matters turn out to be more useful than mere literary texts. The Greek, Latin and Coptic papyri found in Egypt provide a unique insight into the everyday life of people living in this area between the conquest of Alexander the Great and the Arabian conquest. The material encompasses not only private correspondence, but also proof of economic affairs and retailers, legal transactions, verdicts, administrative files, as well as literary and religious writings.

The papyri from Egypt do provide information about the process of supplying the army. In this case, we are especially interested in the necessary fabrics for the army during the Early Roman Empire. The fact that providing the soldiers with clothing was the responsibility of the state is not

---

1. Le Bohec 1998, 24 and 36–37 argues for 250,000 men; 300,000–400,000 seen by Drexhage, Konen, Ruffing 2002, 40–41; 400,000–450,000 seen by Wesch-Klein 1998, 9.
2. For the differences between the supply of a marching and a fortified army see Groenman-van Waateringe 1997, 263.
3. Mittof defines army supply as follows: "Unter Heeresversorgung wird ausschließlich die Versorgung der Soldaten mit Grundnahrungsmitteln und der Reit- bzw. Saumtiere des Heeres mit Futter verstanden" (Mitthof 2001, 4).

in question. *P.Gen.Lat.* 1 col. I shows a calculation of the salary of two soldiers in the years 80 and 81.[4] It also shows subtractions from the salary for the goods these soldiers received. The largest sum of these expenses was 240 *drachmae* per year for food. Subtractions for clothing are only shown for the first and the third *stipendium* and vary in their sum. While one soldier received clothing for 60 *drachmae*, his comrade received fabrics for 100 *drachmae*. The sources do not state whether the difference of the subtractions was due to the fact that these two soldiers held different ranks or whether they had different demands. Without doubt, this source shows that the Roman state of the early principate took care of its soldiers' clothing.

P.Ross.Georg. 5/61, a much later papyrus from the 4th century, which is closely connected to this topic, shows a list of payments made by an office for supplying the troops originating in the Herakleopolites. The largest sum mentioned are the expenditures for clothing, in particular the money for χλαμύδες. Thus, it can be assumed that the Roman state was still responsible for supplying the soldiers with fabrics during the Late Roman Empire.

In the following paragraphs, we will have a look at those texts which provide a basis for forming hypotheses about the Roman troops' provision of clothing during the Early Roman Empire:

The earliest text which shows the administrative side of the Roman state's organization of providing its soldiers with clothing is dated from 128 AD (*P.Ryl.* 2/189). Dionysius, son of Socrates, and a group of men, describing themselves as receivers of public garments (παραληπταὶ δημοσίο(υ) ἱματισμοῦ [l. 1–2]), confirm that the weavers of the Egyptian village Soknopaiou Nesos correctly delivered 19 tunics and 5 cloaks. The receivers of the cloaks are named in the text: they were soldiers in Iudea. Accordingly, the editors of this papyrus suppose that the tunics may be assumed to have been intended for the military guards, but they cannot show any proof to confirm that idea. Which units in Judea were to obtain the cloaks cannot be decided explicitly. It is conceivable that those cloaks were meant for the *legio VI Ferrata*, which was transferred to Judea in 123 AD.[5] The presence of the *cohors I Hispanorum* and the *cohors I Thebaeorum* during those times in Judea is also possible.[6]

Only ten years later a similar transaction was recorded in a small village in the Egyptian Fayum: This papyrus – *BGU* 7/1564, dated September 138 AD – is an order for an advance payment. A group of three men, who called themselves receivers of public garments, asked Heracleides the banker to pay the rate of 28 *drachmae* in advance to the weavers of the village Philadelphia.[7] The fabrics were not to be used in Egypt, but by the soldiers in Cappadocia. Furthermore, some of the fabrics were transported to a field hospital (τοῦ ἐν τῇ Σεβαστῇ παρεμβολ(ῇ) ὑγιαστερίου [l. 7]), but it is unclear whether this place was also situated in Cappadocia or whether it was in Egypt.

Again, shipments for troops outside of Egypt are mentioned in this text. Concerning this matter, some historians supposed that "the placing of these orders in other provinces must be the result of problems in the provinces in which the armies were stationed".[8] However, in the above-mentioned cases no major problems were known in the target provinces. Thus, it is fair to assume that it was a well-established procedure to order supplies for the army. The existence of an excellent infrastructure and of a noteworthy network of trade routes has been widely acknowledged and needs no further

---

4.　For the dates see v. Premerstein 1903, 1–46. For the controversial discussion about the text see Watson 1956, 332–340 and Fink 1971, 243–249.

5.　Campbell 1999, 17.

6.　Spaul 2000, 112–113 and 456–457.

7.　Of these 28 drachmae, 6½% (= 6 drachmae), are deduced as tax for the state.

8.　Alston 1994, 111.

discussion.[9] Thus, the existence of shipments of fabrics across the provincial borders could be an example of Roman trade in general. The ongoing academic controversy between the so-called "Substantivists" and the so-called "Formalists" cannot be discussed at this point. I only want to mention their basic ideas: While the "Substantivists" deny the existence of interdependent markets and economic market regulation policies and postulate a unity of place production and consumption, the "Formalists" postulate the existence of market economy and accordingly use modern methods of economic analysis in their studies. In our examples, however, it has to be emphasised that we deal with interregional transactions, meaning that the place of production was not the place of consumption. These places were even divided by the sea. I will get back to possible reasons for this later.

Another document from Philadelphia is directly connected to the last example (*BGU* 7/1572 = Dupl. *P.Phil.* 10). It depicts a petition which has to be dated 15 months later (December 139 AD). In this text, the weavers of Philadelphia ask the *strategos* not to detach further workers for public services, because they fear that they will not be able to deliver the ordered clothing. Thus, they directly refer to *BGU* 7/1564, because they mention the money paid in advance for army services, so it is probably the same transaction. In total, four weavers were sent to Alexandria, while eight of them stayed in Philadelphia. The order had been given to twelve weavers in total and could not be completed – or only with serious problems – by only eight people. One has to bear in mind that the order says that the textiles (1 tunic, 4 cloaks and a blanket) had to be produced quickly (ἐν τάχει [l. 13]). In the light of this apparent urgency it seems astonishing to see that the weavers announce their inability to complete the order 15 months after the order had been placed. Since it is hard to believe that the production of six pieces of fabric would require such a long time, it could be assumed that, apart from the official order, they were working to produce cloth for sale at the market as well. The public order, which had already been partially paid, does not seem to have had a special priority.

At a first glance, the number of weavers in a comparatively large village like Philadelphia seems to have been relatively small. The population of the town during the second century – the time both documents originate – is usually estimated to have been between 3,000 and 4,000 people.[10] A tax list from Philadelphia from the early 1st century lists 88 weavers [*P.Corn.* 23 (a)]. A later tax list from the year 94 AD shows 38 weavers [*P.Lond.* 2/257 (p. 19)]. Tax receipts from the second century show a further reduction of weavers. *P.Phil.* 23, a text written in 123 AD, only lists 11 people with this profession. A list from the same year records 12 or 13 members of the weavers' guild (*BGU* 7/1591). Thus, the number of 12 weavers in the years 138 and 139 AD shown in the two corresponding documents mentioned above mirrors the image we have of Philadelphia. Considering the much bigger village of Oxyrhynchos, which is supposed to have about 25,000 residents,[11] recently a number of 1,100 weavers has been suggested,[12] which means that almost 5% of the village population were weavers by trade. Applied to Philadelphia, this would mean one could expect 150 to 200 weavers in this village. As the numbers are so much lower, we either face a complete difference in the economic structure or we might have to reconsider the expected quantities of textile workers in Oxyrhynchos.

Comparing the documents from Soknopaiou Nesos and Philadelphia, the comparatively small

---

9.   Rathmann 2002, 1134–1160; Kolb 2000, *passim*.
10.   Eiling 2001, 32 in note 161.
11.   Rathbone 1990, 103–142, especially 120–121; Krüger 1990, 68–69; Alston 2002, 332, table 6.3.
12.   Ruffing 2007, 43–44.

amount of cloth and number of garments ordered attract attention. Even the demand of a small military unit must have been significantly larger. The high demand was probably not restricted to one central producer, but distributed among several ones. A group of 13 texts from the archive of the *strategos* Damarion,[13] dating from 184 to 186 AD, shows that this practice was actually used when supplying the troops. These texts originate in the Hermopolis district and show the process of shipping grain to the troops in Egypt. The largest part of these documents consists of receipts for the public purchase of barley. The administrative procedure can be summarized as follows: The *praefectus Aegypti* ordered the requisition of 20,000 artabs of barley for one year for the *ala Herculiana*, which was a horse cavalry division stationed in Coptos. This order was not restricted to the area were the troops were stationed, but rather distributed among different villages even in districts that were further away. The *strategoi* of these districts were told the amount of provisions they had to gather. The administration of the districts then distributed the weight among the villages in the districts. A total of 12 villages had to produce the amount of barley ordered. The contribution of each village was between 15 and 430 *artabai*. Furthermore, the papyri show that the people who contributed were paid by a commission from the state's treasury. A similar procedure could have been applied to the acquisition of clothing. This would explain why the amount of cloth appearing in our texts is relatively small, even if the total demand of the Roman army for fabrics of all kinds had to be much higher.

A text from the second century shows how large the orders placed by the Roman state could be (*P.Oxy.* 64/4434). In this case, 55 'Syrian' coats were ordered in Oxyrhynchos for the *legio III Cyrenaika* in the adjacent province Arabia and, according to the contract, were handed to *optio* Claudius Germanus. Unfortunately, the value of the clothes was not mentioned. In this context another papyrus from the early third century can be cited (*P.Oxy.* 4/735). In this text, a soldier, who also held the rank of an *optio*, accepted a shipment of wheat for the army.

A papyrus from the British Museum shows that soldiers sometimes had to act independently to acquire necessary goods.[14] The text was written during Trajan's Dacian wars and shows the annual report of a military unit – *the cohors I Hispanorum vetera* – from the province Moesia inferior.[15] This papyrus is quite important for the understanding of organizational structures of the military, because it shows how some soldiers of this troop were travelling in other provinces to gather supplies. Under the headline *ex eis apsentes*, we find a soldier who was travelling through either Gallia or Greece (the actual name of the province cannot be read properly), to acquire clothing and food grain for his *cohors* (II,17–19).

Also other paryri show that the Roman state had to cover a high demand for textiles and thus placed large orders to produce them. *P.Oxy.* 36/2760 from the year 179–180 AD is a petition to the *praefectus Aegypti* by Dionysios Amyntianos who was a member of the *ala Apriana* and transported 775 blankets from the district of Oxyrhynchos to Alexandria on official orders. These blankets were supposed to be given to the *legio II Traiana Fortis*. The text does not state where the blankets had been produced, but the expressions used imply that it was a shipment from several villages in Oxyrhynchos.

Even larger amounts are recorded in *P.Bodl.* 1/16, a papyrus from 342 AD. This is a receipt for

---

13.   These texts are *BGU* 3/807, *P.Amh.* 2/107–109 and 173–178, *P.Bodl.* 1/14, *P.Ryl.* 2/85 and 274–275. See also Mitthof 2001, 43 and 317–319 with further references.
14.   *ChPA* 3/219
15.   For this text see Hunt 1925, 265–272; Fink 1958, 102–116; Gilliam 1962, 747–756.

the payment of an arranged sum of money for the production and shipment of 3,500 tunics.[16] The expressions used show that the order must have been placed by the authorities because it mentions a payment made by a banker who administrated the public finances (παρὰ τῶν τοῦ γομοῦ δημοσίων χρημάτων τραπεζιτῶν [ll. 5–7]). The large number of tunics suggests that they were intended to be given to the soldiers. Furthermore, it can be ascertained that the responsibility for the acquisition of clothing changed during the centuries. At first, the troops participated in the order and provision of the garments needed. Afterwards, direct orders of the government (at nome level) to private entrepreneurs were placed.[17]

A text from Hermopolis (*P.Lips.* 1/57) from the year 260–261 AD has to be mentioned in this context, as it also documents the shipment of a large amount of clothing. In this text, Aurelios Achilleus promises the acquisition and transaction of garments. This is also a task on public behalf. Aurelius Achilleus commits himself to transport 147 tunics, 87 "Syrian" coats as well as an uncertain number of other garments to the responsible authorities. These textiles are not for the Roman army, but for the gladiators of Alexandria. Nevertheless, a similar procedure as seen before was used: Again, a central institution was responsible for the organization of the material needed and, after calculating the demand, gave the order to an entrepreneur – in this case Aurelios Achilleus.

The analysis of the texts mentioned provides an insight into the routines behind the supplies of the Roman troops with textiles during the Principate. The state, which was responsible for the food as well as the clothing of its soldiers, fulfilled the need for clothing by ordering different textiles. Small amounts are recorded as well as very large amounts. One might assume that earlier the acquisition of the garments was in the hands of the troops, who appointed representatives from their own ranks. The papyri might furthermore be interpreted in such a way that later development brought the task of ordering and shipping into the hands of entrepreneurs. It is probable that the orders were given to a central administrative institution which distributed the demand among the districts and villages, as it was the case with the provision of grain. The state paid for the fabrics ordered. Thus, it was no forced tribute paid in natural produce that the weavers had to pay representing their *nomoi*. The small number of historical sources and the lack of comparable numbers do not allow us to say whether the state paid the full market price for the goods. It is possible that the weavers profited from the public orders, because they had a guaranteed income due to a guaranteed sales agreement that was not dependent on the fluctuations of the market. Some papyri suggest the conclusion that the public orders did not have to have a higher priority. In contrast to Lothar Wierschowski's thesis that a principle of regionalism and short trade routes dominated the system – a view that supposes that the supplies for the troops came from the surrounding region[18] – the fabrics were not always produced in the region, but also ordered from different parts of the empire. This observation can lead to two hypotheses: on the one hand, they were trying to find special fabrics that were not available locally. However, the everyday vocabulary we find in the papyri does not provide a basis for this assumption.

One the other hand it stands to reason to take Ronald Coase's theory of transaction costs into consideration.[19] This theory suggests that efficient and rational economic business operations go along with the minimizing of costs referring to initiating and processing a business transaction. Morris

16. Mitthof argues for another reading: instead Γφ (= 3,500) better Αφ (= 1,500). Mitthof 2003, 423 with note 1.
17. See Salomons 1996, 39.
18. Wierschowski 2001, 58.
19. Coase 1937, 386–405.

Silver has shown that this theory of transaction costs can be used for ancient economies as well.[20] Applying this approach to the purchase orders from other provinces, it would simply mean that this kind of transaction was cheaper than producing the required garments in the immediate vicinity. This, in turn, implies accepting a quite modern economic approach that is subject to market-oriented structures and the according ideas of heading for a maximum of profit by reduction of expenditure. Thus, this hypothesis is directly contrary to the substantivists' point of view. Which one of the two hypotheses was in fact true might have been dependent on the single case. An excellent infrastructure and heavily used naval trade routes suggest that relatively cheap and quick transport from the place of production to the place of consumption was in fact possible.[21] Maybe the edition of further papyri will enable us to see things more clearly and to confirm some of the generated hypotheses.

ACKNOWLEDGEMENTS

I would like to thank M. Bode, M. Diedrich and J. Häuser (Marburg) for their comments on the English version of this paper. Remaining errors are my own.

---

20. Silver 1995, *passim*.
21. For the shipping routes and the time needed see *P.Bingen* 77 from the second century. It took only six to seven days from Egypt to Cilicia.

3. CLOTHING SUPPLY FOR THE MILITARY.
A LOOK AT THE INSCRIPTIONAL EVIDENCE

Jinyu Liu

As already mentioned in Kerstin Droß's article in this volume, the supply of military clothing has remained a rather marginal interest in the discussion of the logistics of the Imperial Roman army or military supply in general, the focus of which has, not surprisingly, always been food – especially grains.[1] Granted, the ancient writers hardly informed us of the supply system. Strabo stated that the emperor's procurators of the equestrian rank distributed to the soldiers in Iberia the materials (*ta chrēmata*) that were necessary for the maintenance of their lives. Presumably, these materials included food, clothing, and other supplies. But the organization or process of supply was not mentioned.[2] Vegetius only discussed provisions in the context of siege warfare. According to Vegetius, food, sinews, water, and salt were of tantamount importance for the survival of a besieged city.[3] His attention was directed toward how to improvise when supplies for these goods were running low. Although Vegetius mentioned various protective coverings (*centones*) for military machines and so on,[4] how the army obtained these coverings was not a subject for discussion. The importance of outfitting the military, however, was clearly understood by the Romans: clothes were listed along with armour, shoes, food, and money as the essentials that would keep a soldier content.[5] Indeed, military accounts from the Imperial period show that a large percentage of a soldier's *stipendium* went to clothing.[6] J. P. Wild's (1976) study of *gynaecea*, or state-run establishments for woollen production,[7] and J. A. Sheridan's (1998) investigation of military clothing requisition in Egypt are the only works that are directly relevant to clothing supply. The former focused more on the late antique period (after the 3rd century AD), while the latter focused on Egypt, leaving geographical and chronological gaps to be filled.[8]

This paper looks at the clothing supply for the military during the first three centuries in the

---

1. The literature on military supply is vast. Kehne 2007, 337–38 has a helpful annotated bibliography. The sixth volume of the *Impact of Empire* series (de Blois and Lo Cascio eds, 2007), for example, focuses on the impact of the Roman army (200 BC–AD 476); none of the 30 articles discuss textiles.
2. Strab. 3.4.20.
3. Vegetius 4. 7–11.
4. Vegetius 4. 14,15,17,18.
5. *Miles non timendus si vestitus, armatus, claciatus et satur et habens aliquid in zonula* (SHA, *Alex.* 52).
6. An often cited case is *Rom.Mil.Rec.* 68 = *P. Gen. Lat.* 1 recto (AD 88–90). *Cf.* Sheridan 1998, 82; most recently Herz 2007, 309–310. For various deductions, see also Tac. *Ann.* 1.17; MacMullen 1960, 24; Speidel 1992, 131; Campbell 1994,22, 25–26; Whittaker 2002, 207–208; Rathbone 2007, 159–165.
7. According to Wild (1976, 53), one of the factors that seemed to have determined the siting of the Western *gynaecea* was 'the disposition of military field-forces in the frontier provinces'.
8. See also Wild 2002 on the connection between the textile industry and military supply in Roman Britain.

West from the epigraphic point of view. It must be emphasized from the outset that there are many missing links in our understanding of this issue for the West. Since much of what we know about clothing supply comes from papyri, it would be helpful to summarize the main points that have emerged from the papyrological evidence.

First, clothing was not necessarily supplied locally. Egypt, for example, supplied not only garments, tunics, and blankets, but also raw materials, and not just for local armies, but sometimes also for those in Judaea, Cappadocia, Arabia, and so on.[9] It seems that Egypt mostly served the Eastern provinces. Goods for military were exempt from internal customs in Egypt. Second, in the first three centuries, the main source for military clothing was civilian textile workers, who took orders from the military or the government, rather than tax in kind. Supplies could be obtained in a variety of ways: by requisition, by compulsory purchase, or by purchase at market.[10] The civilian suppliers may be granted exemptions from liturgies.[11] Third, after the third century, the general pattern of military supply experienced significant changes in that direct contact between the military and the producers gradually ceased. A cash tax called *vestis militaris* was introduced, and the burden of supply shifted to the communities.[12] State run establishments such as *gynaecea*, *linyfia*, and *bafia* may also have been closely connected with military clothing supply.[13] Despite increased central planning and control, however, civilian craftsmen remained important suppliers in the fourth century.[14]

Are these observations based on papyri also borne out by the evidence from the Western provinces, where the most relevant evidence comes from inscriptions, and wooden tablets? Before discussing the mechanism of supply, it is quite relevant to take a look at the magnitude of the military's demand for textiles in the West.

Demographically, there was a concentration of armies in the Rhine regions and Britain in the first century AD. A total of about 100,000–120,000 soldiers were stationed in the Germanic provinces and Roman Britain in the first century, and around 55,000 in the second century and third centuries.[15] In the second century, the concentration of military shifted from the Rhine to the Danube, with about 100,000 soldiers being deployed in the Danubian provinces. Apart from the soldiers on the Rhine and Danube frontiers, in the city of Rome, 10,000 strong troops needed to be clothed in the first two centuries AD. This number increased to more than 35,000 in the third and early fourth centuries AD.[16] Whether in times of peace or war, the military's need for clothing would have been staggering. Composed basically of tunics and cloaks (*saga*, *paenulae*), the Roman military costumes lacked uniformity in terms of colour or design. Additionally, they were not always easily distinguishable from civilian clothing.[17] Apart from the regular clothing, there was also a special type of padded or layered garment (*thoracomachus*) worn beneath mail or scale armour to protect the

---

9.   See *P.Ryl.* II.189 (AD 128), *BGU* VII.1564 (AD 138).
10.   Sheridan 1998, eps. 84; *BGU* III. 814; Sheridan 1998, 80, citing *P.Mich.* VIII. 467–468.
11.   *P. Phil.* 1 and 10. See also Kerstin Droß in this volume.
12.   Sheridan 1998; Lee 2007, 94.
13.   Wild 1976, 53–54; Lee 2007, 94.
14.   See, for example, *P.Ryl.* 654, L. 6.
15.   Verboven 2007, 303–304. For different estimations of the military strengths in Britain, see also Breeze 1982: 148; Anderson 1992, 89; Davies 2002, 169.
16.   Busch 2007, 315–16; Southern 2007, 115–20.
17.   For descriptions of the Roman military clothing, see; Sheridan 1998, 73–80; Summer 2003 passim; Bishop and Coulston 2006, 184, 224–225, 253; Southern 2007, 152–55; and Speidel in this volume. After the third century AD, see Southern and Dixon 1996, 121–123; Stephenson 1999, 29–31, 99–101.

body from the friction of the armour, counteract its weight, and help absorb force of blow. Although the *thoracomachus* was only mentioned in *De Rebus Bellicis*, which described many fantasy objects, it is reasonable to think, as do Bishop and Coulston, that such a padded garment would have been worn under the armour in all periods.[18] Apart from outfits, there would also have been demands for a wide range of other textile products such as bedding, arming caps, "felt" socks (*udones*),[19] bags, horse saddles, protective coverings for war machines, and so on. As far as fabrics were concerned, the Western armies tended to use wool more, while linen was more prevalent in the East.[20]

Suppose each solider needed two sets of clothing and two sets of undergarments under their armour each year, and additionally allow for some other textile products, about 440,000–520,000 pieces of textile articles would be needed by the military in the Rhine provinces, Britain and Rome annually in the first century. In the second century, the military in the Danube provinces alone would need at least 400,000 pieces of clothing *per annum*. These are just the bare minimums, based on relatively low estimations of the military strength in these regions and individual demand for textile products. Nor have extraordinary needs for special occasions been taken into account. Although soldiers only constituted perhaps 1% of the total population of the Roman Empire, they represented 'large concentrations of non-producers…whose demand often exceeded the capacity of local producers.'[21] The papyrological evidence seems to suggest that after the end of the third century, Egypt had to supply about 9,000 items of clothing annually.[22] If this is of any guide, then, the demand of the armies in the West must have been satisfied by an area five times the size of Egypt.

Unlike papyri, the writings on wooden tablets, metal, or stone usually lack details in terms of the quantities and qualities of the clothing, and the procedure of clothing acquisition for the military. Although the inscriptional evidence contains nothing contradictory to the information provided by the papyri, the inscriptions usually only provide indirect and circumstantial evidence to the mechanisms of military supply, and leave much room for speculation and interpretation. One thing seems clear, however, that is, supply over long-distance was by no means surprising. Seen from the so-called Hunt's *Pridianum*, the *Coh(ors) I Hispanorum Veterana*, which was stationed in Stobi and had many of its soldiers on detachments in Moesia and other places, sent some soldiers to Gaul or Greece for the purpose of procuring clothing:

> 17 *ex eis apsentes*
> 18 *in Gallia (or Grecia) uestitum.*[23]

The connection between Gaul and military supply may also be seen on a tablet from Vindolanda. The tablet (*T.Vindol.* II. 255) is a letter from Clodius Super, who may have been a centurion (l. 20), to Flavius Cerialis, the prefect of the Ninth Cohort of Batavians. It mentions a person called [V]alentinus who just returned from Gaul and had 'approved' some clothing.

---

18.   *De Rebus Bellicis* 15 (dated to AD 366–378); Wild 1979; Southern and Dixon 1996, 123; Stephenson 1999, 29–31; Summer 2003, 37; Bishop and Coulston 2006, 63, 98, 208. SHA, *Sev.* 6,11.
19.   *P.Mich.* VIII. 468.
20.   L. 9 of *P.Masada* 722 (AD 72 or 75), a soldier's account, mentions *tunica linia (denarii) VII*; Amm. *Marc.* 19.8.8; *P.Bodl. I* 16 (AD 342), a receipt for 3,500 linen tunics doubtlessly destined for the army.
21.   Erdkamp 2002, 9.
22.   Sheridan 1998, 88.
23.   *P.Lond.* 2851=*RomMilRec* 63, col. ii. 18(=Campbell 1994, 114–15 no. 183). The reading of neither Gallia nor Grecia is certain, however. See Fink 1958, 106 for the reading *Gallia* and *uestitum*. Cf. Whittaker 1994, 105; 2002, 212; Elton 1996, 115–116; Sheridan 1998, 82; Roth 1999, 133; Adams 2007, 228.

> [Cl]odius Super Ceriali suo
> salutem
> [V]alentinum n(ostrum) a Gallia reuer-
> sum commode uestem adprobas-
> 5 se gratulatus sum [24]

One may wonder, as does A. Birley, 'whether *adprobasse*, rendered by the editors as "approved", may in fact mean something different, boiling down to "delivered" or "fulfilled the commission for"?'[25] In other words, [V]alentinus may have been sent to Gaul to acquire clothing. He was very likely a soldier, as he was referred to as our [V]alentinus. Later in the letter, Clodius Super asked Cerialis to send him a number of cloaks (*sagaciae, saga, [pallio?]la*), and tunics, because he had had trouble obtaining the clothing for his boys (*pueri*). Here, *pueri* may well have referred to Super's slaves. What we would like to know, but is not clear from the text, is whether the clothing that [V]alentinus 'approved' was designated for the soldiers, and whether the clothing that Super requested was supposed to come from that batch. In any case, the movement of goods from Gaul to Vindolanda can reasonably be suggested. This connection may also be seen in *T.Vindol.* 154, a strength report of the *[Co]h(ors) I Tungrorum*. At the end of line 12, *allia viiii* can be read. Here, *allia* may possibly be restored as *[G]allia*. If that restoration is accepted, nine soldiers were probably sent on some mission in Gaul. The fragmentary nature of this line, however, prevents further speculation. It should be noted, however, that certainly not all the textile products found in Vindolanda came from outside. Fiber-analysis has identified locally woven woollen textiles.[26]

A silver plate (2.5 × 23cm) of unknown provenance, which is now in the Staatliche Antikensammlungen München, also has the potential to shed light on issues of clothing supply over long-distance, and/or Gaul's importance in supplying clothing to the military.[27] The following words are found inscribed at the inner bottom of the plate in two circles:

> VEX.L.I.AD.AEMILIANO.C.AG.IN.GAL. (the outer circle)
> VES.BENE.MERENTI.D.D. (the inner circle)

For a comprehensive discussion of the various aspects of this silver plate, I refer to Kruse's article, which has also proposed to expand the inscription as such:

> Vex(illatio) L(egionis) I Ad(iutricis) Aemiliano c(uram) ag(enti) in Gal(lia)
> vest(iario) bene merenti d(onum) d(edit).[28]

> Translation: The detachment of the First Legion the Helper gave this gift to Aemilianus, a clothes dealer taking care of business in Gaul.

Legio I Adiutrix was perhaps founded under Nero. Because of the absence of the honorary cognomen *P(iae) F(idelis)*, which was awarded to the legion by Trajan, it is possible that the inscription is dated to the late first century AD. This, however, is by no means conclusive, for even after Trajan, the cognomen *P. F.* was often omitted.[29] The size of the detachment in question is unknown to us.

---

24. *Cf.* Birley 1997, 278; 2002, 101; Whittaker 2002, 212, 222.
25. Birley 1997, 278.
26. Wild 1976, 55.
27. It now weighs 540.2g. The original weight may have been about 655g. It was purchased from a private collection (Kruse 2005, 115).
28. Kruse 2005, 127; *AE* 2006. 1827.
29. *E.g.*, *CIL* III. 4289 =*ILS* 3656 (AD 269); *CIL* III. 4297 (under Severus).

We know from epigraphic and literary sources that detachments from a unit had no standard sizes, although vexillations of 1,000 or 2,000 strong may be common.[30] For my purpose, the following questions concerning the content of the inscription are of particular importance: What are the possible alternative expansions for *Gal. and vest.*, and what may have been the implications if they can be restored differently? Was Aemilianus a soldier or a civilian? What was the relationship between Aemilianus and the *vexillatio*? Where was the *vex(illatio) L(egionis) I Ad(iutricis)* stationed at that time?

There is little doubt that Aemiliano was in the dative rather than ablative.[31] If, as Kruse has suggested, *vest.* stood for *vest(iario)*. Then, Aemilianus had no military rank but was a civilian wholesale dealer of clothing. The phrase *c(uram) ag(enti)*, which agrees with *Aemiliano*, is a bit puzzling. As a title, *curam agens*, variably abbreviated as *cur. ag., c. ag., c. a.* and so on, usually referred to a person with military rank placed in charge of a unit or area. The title was usually followed by a genitive or genitives: *frumentarius leg(ionis) I adiutricis agens curam carceris* (*CIL* III. 433= *ILS* 2368 = *IK* XVI. 2244), *centurio curam agens stratorum et peditum singularium consularis* (*AE* 1891. 146), and *age/ntes curam leg(ionis)* (*CIL* III. 10429 = *ILS* 2410 = *AE* 1944. 89), for example. Is it possible that Aemilianus was in fact a *curam agens…vest(timenti)*, that is, a soldier or officer with the responsibility to administer clothing supply for the *vexillatio*? If that were the case, it would have been the first instance of such a title. Although the possibility cannot be safely ruled out, the lack of parallel references prevents us from going further. Another peculiarity is the phrase *in Gal.* that is inserted between *c. ag. and vest. Curam agens in Gal. vest(timenti)* would mean that Aemilianus was assigned the duty to obtain clothing in a specific region. Judging from Hunt's *Pridianum*, several other papyri, and the wooden tablets mentioned above,[32] however, there is nothing surprising about this arrangement.

As for what *Gal.* in the inscription may have referred to, it is entirely possible that it represented *Gal(lia)*. Another possible expansion could be *Gal(atia)*. This was suggested but quickly dismissed by Kruse based on Hunt's *Pridianum*. Traces of the activities of the officers from *Legio I Adiutrix* in Asia Minor, however, are attested.[33] In addition, Galatia was well-known for sheep rearing and textile production.[34] It would not have been surprising if some soldiers were sent to Galatia to acquire clothing. As far as the whereabouts of the *Legio I Adiutrix* is concerned, from the later first century to the third century AD, it was found fighting or being stationed in Italy, Hispania, Batavia, Mogontiacum (Germania Superior, modern Mainz), Brigetio (Pannonia, modern Szöny), or Apulum (Dacia, modern Alba Iulia, Romania). For most of the time, the legion was located in the Rhine or Danube frontiers. That does not mean, however, that the detachment mentioned in the inscription was necessarily stationed in the Rhine or Danube areas. Detachments of *Legio I Adiutrix* have been

---

30.   *CIL* X. 5829; *CIL* VIII 2482; Tac. *Hist.* 2. 18. Gilliver 2007, 196.

31.   It is best to take *bene merenti* as refering to *Aemiliano*. *Aemiliano* can only have been dative here but not ablative. If it were in the ablative, *Aemiliano curam agente* would mean that he took care of preparing this gift, and then *bene merenti* must either go back to *vex.* or *vest.* If it modified *vex(illationi)*, that would making *vexillatio* the recipient of the plate. But the difficulties are that *bene merenti* is too far from *vex(illationi)*, and that the subject of the phrase *d. d.* would have been inexplicit. If it modified *vest.*, which could be expanded as *vest(iario)*, then it is strange that the 'worthy one' had no name but just the occupational designation. Therefore, the best way to construe this sentence is to take Aemeliano as dative rather than ablative.

32.   *P.Oxy.* IV. 735, LXIV. 4434, discussed in Kerstin Droß's article in this volume.

33.   *CIL* III. 265 (Ankara, Galatia): *D(is) M(anibus) / Fl(avi) Audacis | (centurionis) / leg(ionis) I Adiutric(is) / nat(ione) Germanic(us) / vixit annis L / mens(ibus) III diebus / IIII Iulius Fortu/natus collega et procur(ator) eius / amico optimo*; *CIL* III. 433= *ILS* 2368 (Ephesus).

34.   Foss 1977, 30; Levick 2004, 197 citing *Expositio totius Mundi*.

found in Aquileia (Northern Italy) for instance.[35] Soldiers in active service (*milites*) or officers of the legion have been found buried in places such as Seleucia Pieria (Samandagi, Syria), Caesarea (Mauretania Caesariensis), and Ankara (Galatia),[36] and making votive dedications in Salona, Novae, and Burnum (Dalmatia).[37] In Ephesus, a *frumentarius Legi(onis) I Adiutricis agens curam carceris* put up the tombstone for a *frumentarius Leg(ionis) X Geminae*.[38] Regardless of whether Gallia or Galatia is the correct expansion, however, the very fact that the region was specified very likely indicates that it was not the region where the *vexillatio* was stationed. In either case, clothing supply over long-distance can be deduced.

The foregoing discussions do not establish a solid conclusion as to whether Aemilianus was a civilian or a soldier, or whether *Gal.* referred to *Gallia* or *Galatia*, especially since neither the provenance nor the date of the silver plate is known. Nor do we know the location of the *vexillatio* of *Legio I Adiutrix*. Aemilianus may have been a soldier or officer who was responsible for procuring clothing for the detachment of *Legio I Adiutrix*. Or he may have been a civilian clothes dealer who took care of the acquisition and transaction of clothing for the detachment in question. If he were indeed a civilian, it is still not clear whether he himself was the contractor, or if he was head of an association of weavers or clothes dealers. It seems fairly clear, however, that Aemilianus played an important role in the process of clothing supply to a detachment of *Legio I Adiutrix*, which expressed its gratitude by presenting this silver plate to him.

In what follows, we will explore the possible role of civilians in the supply chain as indicated by inscriptions. There may have been big-time merchants who purchased products of all kinds in various places, transported them to the frontier and sold them to the soldiers.[39] Some inscriptions seem to mention merchants with military connections. Titles such as *negotiator castr[e]nsiarius* (Mediolanum) seem to suggest that the merchant was associated with the military.[40] In Vicani Marosallenses (Marsal), Belgica, a *[negotiator] vestiar[ius]* from [Germania] Superior made a votive dedication to Mercury (*CIL* XIII. 4564). Perhaps, he was purchasing clothing in Belgica to sell them to the Rhine armies in Upper Germany. In Augusta Vindelicorum (Augsburg), Raetia, Iulius Clemens, the standard-bearer (*[a]quilifer*) of *Leg(io) III Ita(licae)*, took care of burying his brother, Iulius Victor, a *[n]egotiator [qu]ondam vestiarius* (*CIL* III. 5816). It is possible but by no means certain that Iulius Victor may have had some connection with the military through his brother. Some veterans were known to have gone into business. From Aquileia, we know of a *vestiarius* who had served in the navy, *vet(eranus) ex classe*.[41] Whether such veterans-turned-tradesmen had close connections with the military is not clear. But it is by no means unreasonable to suggest that it might have been easier for veterans to establish business relationships with the military.

Not only individuals but also occupational associations (*collegia*) may have been involved in the

---

35. *CIL* V. 954.

36. *AE* 1977. 819; *CIL* VIII. 21049; *CIL* III. 265.

37. *AE* 1989. 599; *CIL* III. 1909, 1910, 2823.

38. *CIL* III. 433= *ILS* 2368 = *IK* XVI. 2244.

39. *Cf.* Verboven 2007 for the *negotiatores* in Gaul.

40. *T(iti) Ponti / Maioris / negotiatoris / lentiari et / castr[e]nsiari / Maria Iusti / Iacci fil(ia) / coniunx marit(o) / incompar(abili) / et Gratus / Geminae fil(iae) / amic(o).* (*CIL* V.5932 = *ILS* 7563; *cf. AE* 2000. 255 from Mediolanum). The absence of *D M* and the lack of *tria nomina* for two of the three people mentioned in the inscription point to a relatively early date, perhaps mid-first century AD.

41. *CIL* V.774 = *ILS* 3120= *IA* 3490 (cf. *AE* 1972.193): *Domnab(us) / sacrum / Sex(tus) Baebius / Bai f(ilius) vet(eranus) ex classe / vestiarius / v(otum) s(olvit) l(ibens) m(erito).*

supply chain. In the city of Rome, one of the *collegia sagariorum* (dealers of *saga*/outer cloaks) was called *collegium Herculis Salutaris c(o)hortis primae sagariorum*. It may have been closely involved in supplying the Praetorian Guards with clothing, since it took Hercules Salutaris, the patron deity of the *cohors prima* of the Praetorian Guards, as its own patron god.[42] Onomastic analysis points to a close connection between the *collegium Herculis Salutaris c(o)hortis primae sagariorum* and the *collegium centonariorum*. The Octavii seem to have been important in both *collegia*. M. Octavius Carpus was one of the *curatores* of the *collegium Herculis Salutaris c(o)hortis primae sagariorum*. The freedmen of the L. Octavii and M. Octavii and their descendants played important, if not dominant, roles in the *collegium centonariorum* at Rome, at least during the period between the end of the first century BC and the mid-first century AD.[43] The *collegia centonariorum* have often been seen as fire-brigades in the Roman cities.[44] At least as far as the city of Rome is concerned, however, no *collegia* seemed to have been connected with fire-fighting until the fourth century AD, when the *vigiles* were disbanded. It is commonly agreed that *cento* and *centonarius* are cognates. In the ancient literary sources, as woollen materials, *centones* were noted for their insulating and protective qualities including fire-resistant qualities.[45] *Dig.* 33.7.12.18 (Ulpianus *20 ad Sab.*), a passage attributed to the first-century jurist Pegasus listed *centones* along with vinegar (*acetum*), pumps (*sifones*), poles (*perticae*), ladders (*scalae*), mats (*formiones*), sponges (*spongiae*), buckets (*amae*), and brooms (*scopae*) as fire-fighting instruments. The *centonarii* may have played an important role in supplying the *vigiles* with both uniforms and mats made of *centones* as fire-fighting instruments. Since the *vigiles* were a large force of several thousand men,[46] the demand from them alone would have been massive. Some rich *centonarii*, or textile tradesmen and/or workmen, such as L(ucius) Sextilius Seleucus, who could afford to make a handsome gift of more than 5,000 denarii to the *collegium*,[47] may have acquired their wealth as contractors in this business.

Outside of Rome, the epigraphic references to the activities of the *collegia centonariorum* mostly come from Northern Italy, Southern Gaul and the Danubian provinces. An inscription, which preserved an imperial rescript from Severus and Caracalla, and which recorded 93 members of a *collegium centonariorum* was discovered during the excavation in Flavia Solva (modern Wagna) in 1915.[48] The size of the *collegium* is impressive. So is the fact that the rescript confirmed its privileges which may have been granted under Commodus.[49] Judging from the plural form of *collegia* in the Solva inscription, the rescript, though discovered in Solva, likely addressed the phenomenon of the *collegia centonariorum* in general. One of the *beneficia* of the *collegia centonariorum* was specified as *vacatio* (exemption), which is doubtless equivalent to the *immunitas* mentioned in *Dig.* 50.6.6.12. *Privilegia/beneficia* were evidently granted to qualified *collegia* as organizations – in other words, only through membership in these *collegia* could one obtain these special arrangements. However, membership *per se* did not assure access to the benefits. The Solva rescript warned the governor (?)

---

42. *CIL* VI.339=*CIL* VI. 30741=*ILS* 7315. *Cf.* MacMullen 1960, 25 with n. 23.
43. *CIL* VI.339=*CIL* VI. 30741=*ILS* 7315; *CIL* VI. 7861, 7863, 7864, 33837.
44. For a more comprehensive treatment of the *collegia centonariourm*, see Liu 2009.
45. For a fuller discussion of *cento*, *centones*, see Liu 2009, 63–70.
46. Dio Cass. 54.2.3; see also *CIL* VI. 1057 and 1058; Rainbird 1986, 150–151.
47. *CIL* VI. 9254 = *ILS* 7244.
48. *AE* 1916.45; *AE* 1920.69–70; *AE* 1966.277; *ILLPRON* nos. 1450–1458; *RIS* 149, with image; *AE* 1983. 731; Wedenig 1997, 224–29 S 25.
49. Although the Solva rescript dates to AD 205, the wording of the rescript would suggest that the grant of the *beneficia* might have been made by earlier emperor(s), perhaps Commodus, whose name was not to be mentioned.

not to rashly take away the privileges of the *collegia*, and restated who among the members of the *collegia centonariorum* could enjoy privileges including exemption from *munera* (compulsory services) and who could not. Members could be disqualified from such privileges on account of irrelevant occupation, or 'too much' wealth. 'Rich' members in the *collegium centonariorum*, therefore, could not receive the benefits, nor could those who did not practice the *artificium* of the *centonarii*. All this was in line with *Dig.* 50.6.6.12 (Callistratus).[50] Apparently, one of the problems that the governing authorities had to address was how to prevent people from joining *collegia* to escape other duties and/or from taking advantage of the privileges while not providing any of the services to which these privileges were attached. Examined alongside *Dig.* 50.6.6.12, the Solva rescript clearly indicates that the *collegia centonariorum* belonged to those legal *collegia* or corporations in which each member was enrolled on the basis of his craft (*artificii sui causa*) and those instituted to provide services required for public needs (*necessariam operam publicis utilitatibus exhiberent*). Both the Solva inscription and *Dig.* 50.6.6.12 suggest that, just like the title *faber*, *centonarius* was an occupational title, designating an *artifex*, or a craftsman, and that the *centonarii* were people who all practiced a certain *artificium*. There may be outsiders (non-*centonarii*) in the *collegia*, but only the true (*dumtaxat*) *centonarii*, who were not considered rich by prescribed standard, could enjoy the privileges granted by the State in exchange for the *necessaria opera publicis utilitatibus* they provided. Although fire-fighting was one of the possible forms of public services for this type of *collegia*, other possibilities also existed.

As far as Solva is concerned, I propose that this city (*municipium*), which had not been altogether a notable city in the first two centuries and suffered destruction during the Marcomannic War, gained new momentum after being resurrected perhaps under Commodus.[51] The grant and the confirmation of privileges such as exemptions from (other) compulsory public services can possibly be understood in connection with the intensified needs for organizing military supplies in the frontier regions as a result of more frequent occasions of war operations after Marcus Aurelius' reign. After all, the location of Solva in the plains and the slightly hilly country to the east was favorable for sheep rearing and wool production,[52] and the evidence for textile production in the area is beyond doubt.[53] Connecting the *collegium centonariorum* with textile supply to the military better explains the size and the privileges of the *collegium* in Solva. Transportation was available both by water (the nearby Mur river) and by roads: Solva lied on the eastern foot of one of the last ridges known as Koralpe. To the South, a road connected Solva with Poetovio in Pannonia Superior (modern Ptuj, Slovenia). A legionary base in the first century, Poetovio still hosted legionary divisions after the second century. But more importantly, Poetovio was located on one of the main traffic and supply

---

50. *Quibusdam collegiis vel corporibus, quibus ius coeundi lege permissum est, immunitas tribuitur: scilicet eis collegiis vel corporibus, in quibus artificii sui causa unusquisque adsumitur ut fabrorum corpus est et si qua eandem rationem originis habent, id est idcirco instituta sunt, ut necessariam operam publicis utilitatibus exhiberent. Nec omnibus promiscue, qui adsumpti sunt in his collegiis, immunitas datur, sed artificibus dumtaxat. Nec ab omni aetate allegi possunt, ut Divo Pio placuit, qui reprobavit prolixae vel inbecillae admodum aetatis homines. sed ne quidem eos, qui augeant facultates et munera civitatium sustinere possunt, privilegiis, quae tenuioribus per collegia distributis concessa sunt, uti posse plurifariam constitutum est.*

51. For Flavia Solva in general, see Hudeczek 2002, 203–212.

52. It must be noted that due to lack of archaeozoological data, sheep rearing in Noricum is not yet a well-understood subject.

53. Cf. most recently, *Kordula Gostencnik, Commercial textile production or household production for domestic use? The evidence of textile-tools and written sources in Roman Noricum.* Paper presented at DressID: Study Group E Meeting 'Work and Identity: The agents of textile production and exchange in the Roman period', Hallstatt, Austria, June, 2009. Gostencnik notes with caution, however, that although weaving was evidently done at a large scale in Solva, she could not establish a chronology for the loom weights, which has prevented her from determining when the peak in production might be.

routes.[54] To the North of Solva, there was a road leading up through the Mur valley to Ovilavis (modern Wels, Austria), which was an important road junction in North-West Noricum, and the Danube frontier. Therefore, it would not have been difficult to move goods from Solva to either Poetovio or the Danube *limes*.

Not only the origin but also the privileges of the *collegia centonariorum*, therefore, may have been due to their usefulness for military supply. It is, however, by no means my intention to suggest that the formation of *collegia* changed the basic organization of production. Rather, the Egyptian parallels suggest that associations of craftsmen and dealers could help facilitate the communication between the civilian suppliers and the military or governmental officials. It would be more significant to know whether and how the *collegia* divided bulk orders and requisitions among the various independent workshops.[55] Unfortunately, our sources do not provide ready answers.

In Ravenna, M. Caesius Eutyches, a *decurio* of the *collegium centonariorum*, and his wife stipulated a high fine of 30,000 sesterces on violation of their tomb payable to the Imperial *fiscus*.[56] It was by no means rare to designate the recipient(s) of such fines. The designated recipients may range from a *collegium*, a city, the *aerarium*, to the *fiscus*.[57] At least another nine epitaphs from Ravenna stipulated fines ranging from 500 denarii to 50,000 sesterces due to the *fiscus* in case of tomb violations.[58] The language of these nine epitaphs was, however, highly formulaic. The fines were usually imposed if anyone should open the tomb, *si quis hanc / arc(am) struct(am) aperuerit*. M. Caesius Eutyches, however, stipulated that anyone who put or built anything else in front of their tomb should pay a fine of 30,000 sesterces to the Imperial treasury, *fiscus Aug(ustorum) (nostrorum duorum)*. Would it be possible that Eutyches had a direct connection with the Imperial *fiscus* under the joint reign of Marcus Aurelius and Verus, or else that of Septimius Severus and Caracalla? If so, perhaps his connection derived from his being a supplier of clothing and textiles to the fleet and being paid by the Imperial *fiscus*. If that is accepted, the implications of this case are of great significance for our understanding of the public service and business connection of the *centonarii* in Ravenna. The *collegium centonariorum* was divided into at least seventeen *decuriae*, or about 400 members, in the late second century AD. The large size of the *collegium* may be due to the presence of the Imperial fleet, with its *c.* 5,000 marines, at Ravenna.[59] It is quite plausible that the *collegium centonariorum* was used as a framework for supplying clothing and all kinds of textiles to the fleet.

CONCLUSION

The texts on inscriptions and wooden tablets only provide patchy and flimsy evidence of the supply of textiles for the military in the Roman West. What seems clear is that soldiers may have been directly involved in obtaining clothing, that legionary detachments may have needed to take care of their own supply, and that acquisition of clothing from some distance was not unusual. None

---

54.   For Poetovio, see Horvat *et al.* 2003, 153–189. It was a prosperous town on the amber route.

55.   Wilson 2001, 291.

56.   *CIL* XI. 125=*ILS* 8242: *M(arcus) Caesius Eutyches / dec(urio) c(ollegii) c(entonariorum) m(unicipii) R(avennatis) dec(uria) XVII / et Tullia Ferusa / coniux karissima / vivi sibi posuer(unt) / si quis ante hanc arcam quid / aliud posuer(unt) vel condider(unt) / dabit fisco Augg(ustorum) nn(ostrorum) HS XXX(milia) n(ummum).*

57.   Millar 1963, 37–38. In the East, there are quite a few inscriptions that made the penalty for tomb violation to the fiscus.

58. *CIL* XI. 105–107, 119, 147, 191, 198, 349, 6755.

59.   For the number of marines, see Starr 1941, 16; Saddington 2007, 209.

of these observations contradicts what we have learned from the papyrological evidence. As far as the West is concerned, what is more difficult to trace is the civilians' role in supplying the military. Some craftsmen and tradesmen may have had close relationships with the military, as suggested by their occupational titles and social networks. But no details can be retrieved. The role of the organized textile dealers/workers in the clothing supply to the military is even more elusive. Quite often, we have to resort to hypotheses that the *collegium sagariorum* and the *collegium centonariorum* were closely involved in supplying the Praetorian Guards and the *vigiles* with textiles, and that the *collegia centonariorum* may have received their privileges due to their roles in military supply. These hypotheses, however reasonable, must stand up to the test of further evidence found in the future.

There is also the question of whether doing business with the military was always lucrative or desirable. The actuality may have been complicated. We cannot assume, for example, that the payments to the civilian suppliers were always satisfactory or timely. Indeed, *P.Cair.Isid.* 54 from Karanis indicates that the payment for twenty-two tunics and eight cloaks, which constituted the village quota of a requisition of military clothing for the year AD 310/311, was not received by the officials of Karanis until three years later in AD 314. Unfortunately, the incriptions tended to record positive interactions and happy stories, which makes it difficult to use inscriptions as sources for possible discontent.

ACKNOWLEDGEMENTS

I would like to thank Professor Marie-Louise Nosch for inviting me to contribute to this volume. I would also like to acknowledge my gratitude to Dr. Kordula Gostencnik, who read through the draft and made very helpful comments. All mistakes are mine alone.

4. THE ROMAN MILITARY BELT

Stefanie Hoss

How do you recognize a Roman soldier for what he is – when he's on the street, alone and without his weapons and armour? The written sources attest that the soldiers were indeed identifiable: The narrator of Apuleius' satirical novel *The Golden Ass* describes a man as being recognisably *miles e legione* (a soldier and legionary) and he also tells us how he recognized this: Through his *habitus atque habitude* (dress and manner).[1] This and other writings in a similar vein make it quite obvious that soldiers were easily recognizable, even when they were not wearing full armour.[2] In this article, I will not speculate on the 'manner' of the soldiers setting them apart from the average Roman man on the street, but instead concentrate on the dress.[3]

In Rome, a man's dress and his social, cultural and political identity in Roman society were directly connected; the toga was both the prerogative and the iconic symbol of the Roman male citizen.[4] In a similar way, other sartorial choices spoke clearly of the status and station in life of the wearer. What then, was the distinguishing dress of the Roman soldier? We know that in Apuleius' time unarmoured soldiers usually wore a belted tunic, nailed sandals and a long, heavy cloak, fixed on the right shoulder with a fibula.[5] Neither the tunic nor the cloak seem to have differed much from average well-off civilian clothing.[6] The truly distinguishing factor of the military dress were the sandals (*caligae*) and the military belt.

WRITTEN SOURCES

Legally, the wearing of arms – especially a sword – at all times in public defined the soldier as such.[7] By extension, the belt to which the sword was fastened became a distinguishing feature of soldierly dress.[8] It became invested with meaning to such an extent that taking away the military belt of a

---

1. Apul. *Met.* IX, 39.
2. With 'Roman soldier', I would like to indicate all ranks from centurion downwards here.
3. For the manner of the soldiers, see James 2001 and James 2006, 253.
4. Edmonson 2008. The female counterpart of the toga was the *stola*, to which only married (female) Roman citizens were entitled.
5. The tunic was fairly short and had short sleeves, the soldiers having exposed arms and legs. This dress can be observed on most military gravestones. It is likely that soldiers wore this sort of dress most of the time when not on campaign. In Roman military archaeology, it is usually called 'camp dress'. Speidel 1976, 124; Bishop and Coulston 2006, 253.
6. Coulston 2004, 142. See also the article of A. Paetz gen. Schieck in this volume.
7. Brunt 1975. Civilians were allowed weapons to defend themselves in dangerous situations, for instance while travelling.
8. This also had a practical reason: the scabbard was fixed to the belt in a way that was durable (but not completely permanent). If one wanted to take off the sword – and not wear the belt with the empty scabbard – one had to take off the belt (or later on the baldric). This practicality has remained more or less the same until today (for dress swords). It is

soldier in public for hours or days was a humiliation used as a disciplinary measure by their superiors.[9] Taking away the military belt permanently after a capitulation or during a dishonourable discharge from the army seems also to have been practised.[10] The significance of the belt as a symbol of 'being a soldier' continued well into the late empire as is demonstrated by the symbolic act of Christian soldier-saints openly refusing to remain in the army by throwing off their military belt in public.[11]

The military belt of the Roman soldier can therefore be defined as a symbolic object, both an article of clothing and a piece of military equipment, setting the soldier apart from civilian men and marking him as a *miles*.

The term *cingulum* for this belt has become customary in Roman archaeology, but it is unlikely that this was the name of the waist-belt before the third century.[12] Most ancient sources seem to use the noun *balteus* when speaking of the military belt, a term which in Roman archaeology has been used to indicate a different kind of sword belt that was in use from the 2nd century AD onwards.[13] This leather band ran from the right shoulder across the body to the left hip with the sword hanging from the lowest point at the hip (see Fig. 4.8). The use of the term *balteus* for this shoulder belt (or baldric) is undisputed, as is the use of *cingulum militare* for the waist-belt from the 3rd century onwards.[14] It seems likely that the term *balteus* switched from the waist-belt to the shoulder-belt when the sword was carried on the latter instead of the former. This could indicate that *balteus* was the word for a sword-belt while *cingulum* indicated just a regular belt

Interestingly, the waist-belt kept its symbolic meaning even after the sword was carried on the baldric. It is used even more frequently as a 'marker' piece of equipment on funerary monuments of soldiers in the third century than in the previous two. This is confirmed by the name of the belt at that time, *cingulum militare*.

The military belt was decorated with elaborate buckles, metal plates, strap-ends and other attachments, which made it heavy, eye-catching and jingly. Together with the crunch of hob-nailed sandals, the jingling of the metal belt pieces must have given soldiers a distinctive 'sound', announcing their presence.[15]

In addition to that, experimental archaeology has shown the heaviness of the military belt favours a peculiar manner of standing and walking.[16] This was reinforced by the heavy cloak and the sword (either on the waist-belt or later on the baldric). All of the above is commented upon as compelling the wearer to stand upright and move in a characteristic way, as well as hindering violent movement (especially running).[17] From both these modern findings as well as ancient comments on the posture

---

confirmed by the so-called Herculaneum soldier, who carried a sword with a belt wrapped around it while trying to flee the city. Bishop and Coulston 2006, 107.

9.   Livius XXVII, 13, 9; Frontinus, *Stratagemata* IV, I, 26–27, 43; Valerius *Maximus* II, 7, 9; Plutarch *Luc.* 15; Suet. *Octavian* 24.

10.   Herodotus *Hist.* II, 13, 8–10; Festus 104; *Codex Theodosianus* XII, 1, 181 §1.

11.   Woods 1993, 55–60.

12. While the term *balteus* is more common as a noun, the verb-forms derived from the term *cingulum* (*cingere, accingere, discingere*) are used with regularity by the ancient writers. Hoss (forthcoming); Müller 1873, 6.

13.   Bishop 1989, 102–103; Bishop and Coulston 2006, 106.

14.   Bishop and Coulston 2006, 106.

15.   Bishop and Coulston 2006, 110.

16.   Petronius, *Satyricon*, 82; Bishop and Coulston 2006, 254; James 2006, 257.

17.   James concedes that this posture would "go out of the window in combat", but that it was highly influential for the manner of standing and walking affected by Roman soldiers when not wearing arms (James 2006, 257). This stance was also an integral part of the soldier's identity (see James 1999).

and deportment of soldiers, it seems that Roman soldiers were prone to a somewhat swaggering, wide-legged manner of standing and walking.

As to the question of ownership of the belts, papyri and literary sources prove that, at joining the army, one set of standard equipment was given to the soldiers out of a unit stock depot (*armamentarium*).[18] They had to pay for it by deductions from their pay, which probably helped to ensure they took good care of it.[19] A similar system seems viable for the military belts, especially considering that they were made in the camps themselves (see below). As with the other equipment, it was possible to add to this stock and buy your own, perhaps reselling your old equipment to the unit.[20] Tacitus writes about some soldiers who gave their belts in lieu of money, which proves that they must have been both valuable and the personal property of the soldiers in question.[21] The finds of buckles and plates of military belts in graves further proves this point.[22] As the military belts probably were taken away at a dishonourable discharge, having your belt as a veteran might have been one of the outer signs of a honourable discharge.[23]

DEPICTIONS OF ROMAN SOLDIER'S BELTS

One of the main problems posed by the Roman military belt is the reconstruction of the precise form and location of the metal parts on the leather of the belt and of the manner it was worn by the men. Finds of complete sets of military belts from graves are quite rare. Most finds of metal belt pieces were made individually, the pieces having been lost or broken and either thrown away or put aside for recycling in antiquity.[24] Consequently, the reconstruction of the appearance of the belt relies to a great extend on the evidence of representations of military belts.

Soldiers and their belts are depicted regularly on official Roman triumphal 'propaganda' reliefs and on the private funerary monuments of the soldiers.[25] The latter group is the largest by far, including at least some 750 monuments.[26]

While the problems around the accuracy of those depictions of equipment are manifold, it can be said in general that the depictions on the official 'propaganda' reliefs are better executed from an qualitative point of view, but tend to have more stylized depictions of soldier's equipment, even using outdated forms of equipment in a sort of visual conservatism.[27] Equipment was also often depicted smaller than in reality in order to be able to place more emphasis on the body, an important principle in Hellenistic artistic tradition.[28] The private monuments on the other hand place a greater

---

18.   Breeze *et al.* 1976, 93.
19.   Tact. *Ann.* 1,17.
20.   Reselling certainly happened on death or retirement. See Breeze *et al.* 1976, 94.
21.   Tact. *Hist.* I, 57.
22.   Contrary to weapons, belts are sometimes found in graves (see Breeze *et al.* 1976). On belt finds in graves as a sign for veterans see Mackensen 1987, 158–159.
23.   A military diploma in bronze was one of the possible official proofs of a soldier's honourable discharge, but there must also have been records held by his former unit (see van Driel-Murray 2003, 211).
24.   While re-melting old artefacts for their metal was common practice in antiquity (and later), some large military waste dumps prove that the Roman army was not always so thrifty. Examples of such waste dumps are the river dump of Alphen aan de Rijn (NL) and the 'Schutthügel' of Vidonissa (CH). In the latter, almost 500 belt pieces were found.
25.   Bishop and Coulston 2006, 2.
26.   This is a minimum number, as many are unpublished yet and more are found every year. Coulston 2007, 541, note 57.
27.   Bishop and Coulston 2006, 2–9.
28.   Coulston 1983, 24–26, 34.

emphasis on the accuracy of the depiction of the equipment while often being of a lesser quality in workmanship. Here, some symbolic pieces of equipment (sword, decorations, etc.) were sometimes enlarged to make them stand out more.[29] In addition to that, 'shorthand' decorations seem to have been used sometimes. One example is the common depiction of rosettes on belt plates. These are unlikely to be a correct representation of reality, as such belt plates have not been found yet among the ample archaeological finds of 1st century belt plates. It seems viable that these rosettes were a 'shorthand' decoration chosen for the double merits of being fairly simple in execution while conveying an appearance of lavish decoration on the belt plates.

Both 'propaganda' reliefs and funerary monuments have in common that at first glace they impress with the apparent realism of their depiction, but that the viewer is disappointed after a more thorough examination: Almost always, the exact construction of a piece of equipment cannot be reconstructed from the relief.

Apart from non-iconic monuments, the gravestones of the soldiers could depict the deceased either in a relief with a civilian subject (e.g. in the so-called Totenmahlszene) or as a soldier. When a military setting was chosen, cavalrymen usually were depicted in profile on their horses, riding down an enemy.[30] Both the position in profile as well as the proportionality of the composition (requiring a fairly small representation of the person) severely limit the information that can be gained on the belt from these monuments.[31] Infantrymen and marines on the other hand were shown standing frontally, usually unarmoured, but with the belt and sidearms prominently displayed (see Figs 4.1 and 4.2).[32]

This motif first appears in Italy and is transferred with the troops to the Rhineland, where it was very popular in the Tiberian period.[33] From there it spread to Britain and in other provinces, but became rare during the 2nd century AD, when non-iconic monuments and those with civilian subjects were preferred. From the Severan period onwards, funerary monuments depicting the deceased as a soldier again became more common, ultimately even resulting in the fact that the number of funerary monuments depicting soldiers dating from the 3rd century is much larger than the number from both the 1st and 2nd centuries together (see Fig. 4.4).[34] From the late 3rd century onwards, these funerary monuments again became rare. Contemporary triumphal reliefs are even less informative, due to the re-use of older relief pieces, and the depiction of outdated forms of equipment.[35] In both groups of monuments from that period, the quality of workmanship and/or conservation is often too poor to allow any conclusions on the belt beyond it's mere existence. Exceptions are the cuirassed Tetrachs form Venice and two cloaked (*chlamys*) statues from Ravenna and Vienna.[36]

On the other hand, mosaics and wall-paintings from this period do give some important information on the military belt, especially on the possible colours, demonstrating that the belts

29.	Coulston 2007, 532–533.

30.	Hoss 2010.

31.	This changed in the third century, when cavalrymen also preferred *stelae* with full-length depictions of frontally standing men. See Hoss 2010.

32.	See for instance the catalogue numbers 2, 3, 4, 7, 8, 9, 10 in Boppert 1992 and the catalogue numbers 5, 6, 7, 8 in Bauchhenss 1978.

33.	Boppert 1992, 48–50; Coulston 2007, 544.

34.	Coulston 2007, 335–544; 549.

35.	Bishop and Coulston 2006, 6–9; Coulston 2007, 142–143.

36.	Bishop and Coulston 2006, 9, fig. 142.

Figure 4.1. Photo of the funerary monument of Firmus, auxiliary infantryman. Found in Andernach, today at the Landesmuseum Bonn (D). Photo © P. Franzen.

Figure 4.2. Detail of Firmus monument. Photo © P. Franzen.

were often dyed red.[37] The most important of those are the so-called Terentius painting from Dura Europos – a wall-painting depicting an act of sacrifice of a tribune surrounded by his men – and the mosaics of the Villa del Casale at Piazza Amerina, Sicily, which show soldiers catching and loading/unloading wild beasts.[38]

THE METAL BELT PIECES

Metal belt plates have two general uses: The first is to stiffen the belt and prevent curling of the leather, especially with heavy loads worn on the belt. The second is the same as with other decorative items worn on prominent areas of the body and involves a complex set of messages to the viewers which include enhancing the wearer's status and confirming his affiliation to certain groups – both important parts of identity. In ancient societies (as in modern ones), artefacts are not purely functional, but rather "active elements in the very construction of [...] identity, its physical experience, and it's visual signification".[39] The notion that identity is constructed and negotiated through the use and experience of objects has been widely accepted now in theoretical archaeology.[40]

Most of the metal parts of the belt were made from copper alloys.[41] Some were made from silver, gold or ivory, which were more expensive than copper alloys, while the pieces in bone and iron can be seen as cheaper versions. Especially in the 1st century, belt pieces were regularly tinned or silvered, later it is more of an exception.

On the whole, the metal belt pieces were made with two different techniques, casting (lost mould or two-part mould) or embossing, or a combination of both. Ivory or bone would be simply cut. The surface of the metal plates could then be further decorated by engraving and cutting or by using niello or enamel decorations.[42] While many early belts seems to have had metal plates on the entire front side of the soldier, it is thought that there were no plates on the soldier's back.[43]

The military belt of the 'typical' infantryman during the pre-Flavian 1st century consisted of two rather narrow belts worn crossing at mid-body, 'cowboy-fashion' (see Fig. 4.2).[44] The leather was completely covered with metal plates on the front at least. These plates were rectangular and either silvered or both decorated with niello and silvered. A third type had large round boss-like protrusions and a forth was decorated with embossed figurative decorations (see n. 83). The belt plates were fixed to the leather of the belt by rivets driven through pre-drilled holes.

Except for centurions and standard-bearers, the soldier wore one sidearm on each belt: his short sword on the right hip and a dagger on the left.[45] While the sword was fixed to the belt in a durable

---

37.   While most belts pictured in colour in either mosaics or wall-paintings are brown, some are red (Hoss, forthcoming). The Terentius painting shows belts that seem to be dyed on one side only, see James 2006, 61.

38.   Terentius painting: James 2006, 39, fig. 18; Mosaics: Caradini *et al.* 1982, figs 17, 119, 121, 122, 125, 126, 130.

39.   James 2006, 257.

40.   See for instance the section on the identities of Romano-British artefacts in G. Davies, A. Gardner and K. Lockyear (eds) (2001). *TRAC 2000: Proceedings of the Tenth Annual Theoretical Roman Archaeology Conference, University College London, April 2000*, Oxford.

41.   Either called bronze or brass according to the various alloying agents, such as zinc, tin, lead, etc. (see Brown 1976, 25–26). They were used fairly indiscriminately and are all referred to as 'bronze' in Roman archaeology.

42.   Hoss, (forthcoming).

43.   This is confirmed by the find from Velsen (Morel and Bosman 1989) and contradicted by the find from Herculaneum (Bishop and Coulston 2006, 107).

44.   Bishop and Coulston 2006, 106; Hoss, forthcoming.

45.   Centurions and standard-bearers wore their sword on the left hip.

fashion, the dagger was easier to take off the belt, being fixed with leather straps to special attachment plates with protruding buttons, so-called 'frogs', which were fixed with hinges to the belt plates (see Figs 4.2 and 4.3, Velsen belt).

The belts were closed with D-shaped belt buckles, decorated with volutes and also fixed to the first belt plate with a hinge. The belt buckles were usually worn in the area of the belly button or to the right or left of the apron (see below). The strap-ends issuing from the buckle were sometimes decorated with hangers.

But the most intriguing detail of this belt was the so-called 'apron', a set of four to eight leather straps decorated with narrow plates and disc-shaped studs and terminating in leaf-, heart- or moon-shaped hangers.[46] As far as can be seen on the monuments, the straps were fixed (riveted or sewed) to the inside of the lower of the two belts (see Fig. 4.2).[47] This 'apron' has often been argued to have been used as a real or psychological protection of the wearer's lower abdomen and groin area. Experimental archaeology has proven the contrary, namely that during violent movement (e.g. running), the weighted straps swinging between the wearer's legs are apt to form a risk to the groin area.[48] It seems more likely that the apron had no practical use, but has to be interpreted as a mark of status for the soldiers, maximising the characteristic jingling.[49]

A simplification of this set is worn from the Flavian period onwards: a single belt with both the sword and the dagger hanging from it. The apron is wrapped around the belt from behind to the fore, perhaps to shorten it.[50] This manner of wearing the belt continues into the first decades of the second century, the visually most important change being the introduction of enamel decorations, which made the belt quite colourful.

During the Antonine period (138–161 AD), a complete change of the metal decoration of the belt takes place. The carriage of the sword changes from the waist-belt to the shoulder-belt. This may have been occasioned by the change from two belts to one.[51] Another possibility is for the baldric to have become necessary because of the introduction of a longer sword and/or a change of tactics, making it possible to draw the sword across the soldier's front. The latter would indicate, that the soldiers did not fight in as tightly massed ranks as they had before.[52]

The fact that the waist-belt – which no longer gets its significance from the fact that the sword

---

46. With two exceptions, the metal apron plates, rivets and hangers have been found as individual finds, resulting in a lot of discussion as to which types were used on the 'apron' and which on horse harness. One exception is a find from a grave in Tekije (SRB), the other a 19th century find from the Rhine at Mainz, a single apron leather strap (c. 20 cm), decorated with 11 studs with round, flat heads and a leaf-shaped terminal hanging from a rectangular piece of metal encasing the whole strap (see Bishop 1992, 94–96).

47. According to the depictions, the apron was fixed to the lower of the two belts, which at the same time usually was the inner belt and the belt on which the dagger was worn. It seems possible that this was done on purpose to be able to minimize the jingling by simply removing the dagger belt. Because the dagger sheath was fixed to the belt with frogs, it could fairly easily be removed. (Hoss, forthcoming).

48. Bihsop and Coulston 2006, 110.

49. Bishop and Coulston speak of the "impossibility of stealth" while wearing an apron, but stress that a whole legion marching past must have made quite an impressive sound (Bishop and Coulston 2006, 110).

50. See for instance two funerary monuments from Greece (von Moock 1998, no. 85, 241) and the signifer on the left side of the Great Trajanic Frieze on Constantine's arch (Koeppel 1985, cat no. 9, fig. 15).

51. Bishop and Coulston 2006, 83.

52. The shorter 1st century sword was probably drawn with the right hand by dipping the mouth of the sheath forward with the thumb and then extracting the sword with the right hand (Hoss, forthcoming). This was necessary in the tightly massed formations of the 1st century, minimising the danger of the soldier's inadvertently wounding their fellow-soldiers standing in front of them. Drawing the sword with the right hand from the left hip needs more space in front.

Velsen, 1st century (after Morel et al. 1989, fig. 5, 6).

From the Rhine between Altrip and Rheingönheim, 1st century (after Ulbert 1969, pl. 32, 5).

Lyon, 2nd-3rd century (after Bishop/Coulston 2006, fig 101)

Kristein (near Enns), 2nd-3rd century (after Wieser 1996).

Faimingen, 2nd-3rd century (after Müller 1999, pl. 51).

Neuburg an der Donau, 2nd - 3rd century (after Hübner 1963, fig. 4).

Lechinta de Mures, 2nd-3rd century (after Petculescu 1995, pl. 7).

Figure 4.3. Ensembles of waist-belts from the 1st and 2nd centuries found in graves.

is carried on it – continues to characterize the soldier (as proven by the fact that it still features quite prominently on the funerary monuments of soldiers that date from this and later periods) is a testimony to the conservatism of soldiers as a group.

During the same period, the apron vanished and the attachment of the belt buckles to the belt changed: The new buckle type has a key-hole form; with a C-shaped buckle and a roughly triangular, open loop at one end. The buckles were fasted to the belt by passing a metal tongue through this loop and then fixing the tongue on the backside of the belt through the leather to the first belt plate.[53] In a simpler and cheaper version of this method, the leather of the belt itself probably passed through the loop and was then fixed by sewing or riveting it on the belt (in effect forming a leather loop). The dagger fastenings also changed from hinges to a loop. In addition to that, the belt plates were no longer fasted by individual rivets put through pre-drilled holes. Instead, short studs with little round 'feet' were cast onto the belt plate. The belt plates could then be 'buttoned' on to the belt by sliding the 'feet' through little slits in the leather. This also ensured that the plates could be retrieved easily.[54]

The whole 'look' of the belt changed as well. The belt decorations up to then had been solid metal plates, mostly tinned or silvered, completely covering the leather of the belt on the front side of the soldier, giving the belt a shiny, silver look. Now, the design changed to an interaction between 'golden' openwork plates with the tanned (and perhaps coloured) leather visible through them, the whole accented in some types by colourful email.[55] In addition to that, more valuable materials like silver seem to be used more often. But this impression could also be falsely created by the increase of belt finds from inhumation burials from this period [56] Because of their material value, silver belt pieces usually were more carefully recycled than cheaper metals and thus hardly ever turn up from refuse dumps.

In general, it can be said that the styles of this period show great variation, with many different types of belt plates being in fashion at roughly the same time (see Fig. 4.3): Some types of openwork belt plates were still rectangular, but others had more open forms – rounded and inspired by a revival of so-called 'Celtic' motifs, which have been indicated to have been inspired by forms common in the Danubian provinces (see the examples from Kristein and Faimingen, fig. 3).[57]

Another remarkable style of the period is the fashion for belt plates spelling out mottos (see the examples from Lyon, Fig. 4.3). These were usually fairly simple wishes, the most common being *Utere felix* (use in happiness). They were either spelled out on the belt in single letters or worked in openwork into a rectangular belt plate.[58] From the archaeological finds, it seems that belts with mottos are more concentrated in the region of the Middle and Lower Danube and Dacia.[59] But

---

53. See Hoss 2006, 239, fig. 1.
54. Oldenstein 1976, 60.
55. The plates were no longer tinned or silvered as a rule and they were most likely polished to make the bronze shine golden (Hoss, forthcoming).
56. The funerary habit slowly changed from cremation to inhumation during the 2nd century (Toynbee 1971, 40). In an inhumation grave, a belt would stay preserved, while it would usually be burned on the pyre as part of the deceased's dress during cremation.
57. Oldenstein 1976, 204, Anm. 687; James 2006, 247. The most famous of these designs is the so-called 'trumpet'-design. The open forms make it even more difficult to distinguish between belt plates and plates used on other leather items, e.g. bags.
58. Hoss 2006, 244.
59. Hoss 2006, 246–249.

Figure 4.4. Drawing of the depiction on the funerary monument of the praetorian guard M. Aurelius Lucianus (3rd century) found in Rome (after Oldenstein 1976, fig. 13,2).

mottos were a fashion not confined to waist-belts, as the shoulder-belts or baldrics of the same period also had metal plates often bearing mottos in openwork, both belts being most likely conceived as a set. In addition to that, similar mottos were also common on other objects of daily use such as rings, fibulae, spoons and drinking vessels, to name a few.[60]

On most types of belt plate sets of this period, rings pointing downwards were attached to one or two plates, to facilitate hanging a leather pouch, a knife or other utensils on the belt.[61] Another common marker was the long strap-end of the belt, tucked into the belt on the wearer's right side and hanging to the knee. The ends were slit into two long strips and decorated with intricate hangers with hinges in many different forms.[62] These would jangle together when the soldier moved, making a noise comparable to a bunch of keys – less impressive, but analogous to the 'sound' of the 1st century apron.[63] Audible signs of the soldier's approach which had their best effect in large groups – but were also recognizable when a single soldier passed – were thus still very much in favour. While the precise dating of these types generally is difficult, most of them seem to have been in use until the mid-3rd century.[64]

As mentioned above, the number of funerary monuments with depictions of soldiers in military dress ('camp dress') increases enormously at the beginning of the 3rd century (see Fig. 4.4). The depictions are quite stereotypical in content, with infantry and cavalry soldiers dressing the same, even though there are of course many variations in quality. A substantial increase in body-coverage from the 1st century is noticeable: Instead of a short-sleeved and fairly short tunic with naked arms and legs, the soldiers wear a long-sleeved, belted tunic falling to the knees and long tight trousers under it.[65] A cloak is fixed with a fibula on the right shoulder and folded back over the left shoulder, it falls to the knees and is sometimes decorated with a fringe along the lower edge. Not all depictions show the soldier with the sword, but in those that do, the sword is worn on a broad baldric on the left hip. Very often the baldric is covered by the fall of the cloak, but in some rare cases, the baldric decoration

60. Hoss 2006, 237 (footnote 3 and 4), 244; Bishop and Coulston 2006, 162–163, fig. 100, 101
61. See letter E on the Lyon set, fig 2.
62. Bishop and Coulston 2006, 182.
63. James 2006, 61.
64. The exact dating of these belt types is hindered by the fact that the border situation of the Roman empire had consolidated in the second part of the 2nd century. Most forts remained intact until the mid-3rd century, which leaves a large group of types of military equipment dating 'between the mid-2nd and the mid-3rd century' (Hoss, forthcoming).
65. James 2006, 246, 249.

of round and square decorative plates can be distinguished (see Fig. 4.4).

Contrary to the baldric, the waist-belt always figures on the depictions and both this and the fact that it is sometimes enlarged demonstrate that it was still a distinctive piece of equipment, distinguishing the soldier from his civilian counterparts.

Figure 4.5. Reconstruction drawing of a frame buckle (after Oldenstein, 1976, fig. 9).

The fairly wide belt (between 2, 5 and 4 cm) of the 3rd century was closed with a ring-buckle, consisting of a simple ring, worn at the area of the belly button. Rectangular openwork frame 'buckles' with a curvilinear, so-called "Celtic" design in the middle fulfilled the same function as the ring-buckles (see Fig. 4.5). These are depicted on just a few funerary monuments, while ring-buckles are depicted on at least 120 monuments.[66] Interestingly, the archaeological evidence is quite the opposite: Only roughly a dozen ring-buckles have been identified so far, while almost 50 frame buckles from Austria, Britain, Germany, Hungary, Morocco, Romania and Switzerland have been published.[67] It seems very likely that this disproportion is due to the fact that the simple bronze or iron rings were not recognized as ring-buckles.[68]

The leather strap of the belt was passed through the ring or frame from the back on both sides and back along the front. The strap was fixed by sliding fungiform studs fixed to the front of the belt (roughly equidistant between hip and belly button) through slits in the leather strap. While the strap was often (but not always) fairly short on the wearer's left side, almost ending at the stud, the strap was longer and thinner on the right side. It could either fall to the knee from the stud, or – more often – was brought back in a long crescent loop to the belt and tucked behind the broad belt (sometimes this loop can be observed on both sides, see Fig. 4.4). As with the earlier types, the strap-end was often split into two and always decorated with hangers, dangling around the area of the knee. On some 3rd century depictions, the soldiers hold this end in their right hand and seem to play with it; thus directing the viewer's attention to the belt as a distinctive piece of equipment.[69] This gesture may also be the shadow of a familiar sight in that period: soldiers twirling their belt-straps on the streets.[70] The origin of this belt has been previously assumed to have been Danubian or Sarmatian; a relatively new suggestion points to the Eastern provinces of the Empire. These were almost constant theatres of war during the 3rd century, with many troops gathering and coming into contact with the enemy, facilitating the transfer and exchange of belt fashions from the latter and among each other.[71] During the late 3rd century, a larger and more elaborate version of the frame buckle evolved, made from silver with intricate openwork decoration set off with niello.[72]

---

66. Hoss, forthcoming.
67. Hoss, forthcoming.
68. Such rings are common in Roman period finds and were used for a variety of purposes. It is thus quite understandable that buckle rings were missed in loose finds. As rings of a similar size were often used on small caskets, rings found in graves were probably also often missed.
69. See for instance the monument of an unknown soldier from Herakleia Pontica (Coulston 1987, pl. 4) and the monuments of two unknown soldiers from Perinthos (Sayar 1998, cat. nos 86, 87, p. 22, fig. 83, 84).
70. Oral communication Jon Coulston and Simon James.
71. James 2006, 249–250.
72. Fischer 1988; Hoss, forthcoming.

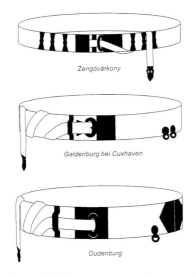

Figure 4.6. Reconstruction drawings of 4th century belts (after Bishop/Coulston 2006, fig. 141).

In the 4th century, the carriage of the sword seems to have reverted to the waist-belt. Unfortunately, not many depictions are known from this period (see above) and most of the information we have about the belts of that time comes from graves, which are very often insecurely dated.[73] In the first half of the century, the belts were closed with belt buckles often decorated with dolphins head-to-head and connected to an openwork belt plate with hinges (see Fig. 4.6). Next to this, so-called 'belt stiffeners' in the form of a propeller were worn and along the lower edge of the belt, small round plates decorated with a rosette were fixed, holding a ring for hanging utensils or a leather pouch. The leather strap-end of the belt usually was decorated with an amphora- or lancet-shaped strap-end hanger.[74] During the second half of the 4th century, the belts became even broader (5–10 cm) and were closed with buckles which were let into large, rectangular or pentagonal belt plates by hinges (see Fig. 4.6). The buckles were often decorated with two animals, but facing towards the hinge rather than towards each other. The actual leather strap passing through the buckle from behind the plate was much less wide than the belt itself.

It was often quite long, though, wrapped around the belt several times and decorated with a strap-end hanger. Belts could have several of the large plates alternating with propeller belt stiffeners and rosette-ring plates. All plates and the hanger were decorated in the geometric, so-called 'chip-carving' style (often enhanced with niello inlay).[75] This type has long been thought to have been brought into the Roman army by German soldiers, who were either serving in the Roman army itself or serving as allied soldier-farmers (*laeti*). Some of the chip-carved belt plates also feature classical motifs which neither occur in the home regions of these German soldiers nor in their graves on Roman territory. Consequently, it seems likely that these must have been in use by the regular Roman army itself.[76] James has lately pointed out that buckles with paired, confronted animals are known from the Iranian region, and that it might be possible that this style also emerged from the East rather than the North, as the East was a regular theatre of war for the Roman army at that time.[77] Another possibility for the origin of this style of belt may have been a combination of Germanic and Iranian influences, by which the Germans in the Roman army influenced the form and the contact with both the Classical world and the Parthian and Sassanid armies had an influence on the decoration of the belt. The type stayed in use until well into the 5th century.

---

73. Bishop and Coulston 2006, 218.
74. Bishop and Coulston 2006, 218–220.
75. Bishop and Coulston 2006, 220–224.
76. Bishop and Coulston 2006, 224.
77. James 2006, 251.

PRODUCTION AND DISTRIBUTION

In the Mediterranean area, the production of the belt pieces was most likely in the hands of private workshops in the cities. When the Roman army conquered areas to the north of the Alps, it moved into a region that did not have an advanced enough bronze production to satisfy the enormous demand. Belt pieces were then produced by the army itself, a side-product along weapons and amour. Finds of moulds, embossing stamps and half-finished products as well as literary, sub-literary and epigraphic evidence prove that the production was done in the army camps by the soldiers themselves – sometimes in large workshops turning out great quantities (*fabricae*), sometimes in a more haphazard fashion.[78] While most evidence for military production comes from the 2nd and 3rd century, evidence for production in the towns and cities (*vici* and *canabae*) that developed around the forts and camps also starts in the 2nd century.[79] It is still a matter of speculation if the latter was military or civil. It seems likely that the veterans settling near their old comrades in the direct environs of the forts and camps continued to work in the trades they had learned in the army.[80] But if their workshops were really private or just moved outside the camp because of the fire hazard is still a matter of dispute. It might also well be that the artisans worked on contract for the army, but could also be approached by private individuals.[81] Another suggestion has been that the essentials of weapons and armour were produced by the army itself, while the decorative elements of the belt and horse's harness were left to private workshops.[82]

Contrary to this, some exceptional pieces were most likely made centrally, in state owned workshops. The prime example is a Flavian type of rivet, decorated with figurative relief, which according to the huge numbers found there (200 rivets), seems to have been made in one workshop in Besançon and – considering the motifs used for the decoration – given to the soldiers as a sort of propaganda.[83] These state-issued decorations probably were not pressed on the soldiers, but on the contrary could have been marks of honour much coveted by them.[84]

Differences in the military belts between the different parts of the Roman army (legions, auxiliary infantry and cavalry and the navy), are difficult to prove, as most camps were occupied by different unit types throughout their history, with vexillations of legions and ancillary cavalry or other auxiliary units being deployed as needed and thus 'muddling' the archaeological record. In addition to that, finds from graves are rare and sometimes also confusing: The famous grave of Chassenard (Dept. Alliers), dating from the Tiberian period, is interpreted as the grave of a local nobleman, buried with his helmet mask (identifying him as cavalryman) and belt with an ornate gilded buckle with decorations of hunting scenes and three gilded belt plates with an embossed decoration depicting the head of Tiberius between *cornucopiae*.[85] At first, this seemed a confirmation of cavalrymen wearing belts decorated with metal plates. Another possible explanation is, that the Chassenard soldier had

---

78. Bishop and Coulston 2006, 233–240, fig. 149.
79. Gschwind 1997, 619–621.
80. Van Driel-Murray 2002, 111–113.
81. Van Driel-Murray 2002, 111.
82. Nicolay 2007, 157. This arrangement seems sensible, but has not been proven.
83. The four main motives are: Victoria *navalis*, Victoria on a chariot, eagle, male head with wreath. Feugère 1985, 123, 125.
84. Bishop and Coulston 2006, 267.
85. See Beck and Chew 1992.

been an infantryman at some point in his life, a career move that is known from other soldiers.[86] It seems more likely though, that he received the belt as a mark of distinction and/or imperial gift. The latter explanation would fit with the interpretation of this grave as belonging to a high-ranking member of the tribal elite who had personally led an auxiliary cavalry unit of his tribesmen in the Roman army.[87]

The best evidence for differences in the belts of different parts of the army come from depictions on funerary monuments announcing the deceased's career and thus affiliation to a certain unit type. These show legionary and auxiliary infantrymen as well as marines with the same type of belts. This is remarkable, because the types of units otherwise differed in many aspects.[88] It seems likely that practical matters were more important here, since the only difference in belt design that can be inferred from the funerary monuments is the one between infantry and navy on the one side and cavalry on the other. As a cavalryman had to sit on a horse, a belt decorated with inflexible metal plates was most likely simply impractical. In addition to that, the belt could not fulfil its secondary function of enhancing the status and confirming the affiliation of the wearer if it was not seen and heard.[89] It seems that – at least until the introduction of the ring buckle belt in the 3rd century – the Roman cavalryman wore a different military belt from the infantryman, namely a belt without metal belt plates and just a simple belt buckle, perhaps with a single belt plate.[90]

Indicators for fashions in units or larger regional groups (*e.g.* the 'Rhine army') have been identified only cautiously up to now, as much of the work to be done is still at an initial stage.[91] One of the strong contenders is a type of belt piece with embossed figurative decoration.[92] The majority of these belt plates were found in Upper Germany, with some coming from along the Rhine in Lower Germany and from the south coast of England (see Fig. 4.7).[93] Their dating and distribution pattern points to their (mainly) being used by the units of Upper Germany, who were part of the army invading Britain.[94]

Fashions in belt decoration probably developed in the lower ranks of the army (that is, from

---

86. An example of this career move from a generation later is the famous Tiberius Claudius Maximus, captor of Decebalus. See M. P. Speidel 1970.

87. Beck and Chew 1992.

88. The legionaries were Roman citizens, while the auxiliaries and marines were not, an important difference in legal status (Vittinghoff 1986). In addition to that, the legionaries received more pay and had a different social status (Speidel 2000b). There is some evidence that these unit types also had different weapons and/or armour (Bishop and Coulston 2006, 254–255). If the military equipment found round the bay of Naples indeed belonged to marines from the naval base at Misenum, their equipment – including the belt – seems not to have differed from the infantry (Ortisi 2002). The same can be postulated for the Rhine fleet's headquarters at Köln-Alteburg, where an assembly of military equipment was found that is familiar from contemporary infantry camps (Cahn *et al.* 2003).

89. But the cavalryman could – and did – use the horse's harness for a display of his wealth, status and group affiliation by fitting it out with decorative plates and hangers, blinking and jingling even more. See Junkelmann 1992, 76–88.

90. See Hoss 2010. The find of a early 2nd century belt with a *spatha* (cavalry sword) and a belt buckle with only one belt plate in Koblenz-Niederberg proves that the belt was still largely without metal plates at that time (Jost 2007, 49–55, Hoss 2010, 320). Of course this does not imply that the cavalrymen's belt had to be completely undecorated. The baldrics from Vimose moor in Denmark (although of a later date) are decorated with embroidery (see Gräff 2010, 133). Decoration by colouring or branding and cutting the leather are also possible.

91. Bishop and Coulston 2006, 260.

92. Four main types of decoration are known for this belt plate: A lotus flower, a hunting scene, the *Lupa Romana* and the portrait of the emperor between *conurcopiae*. The motives of the latter two make it very likely that they were given to soldiers on special occasions as part of imperial propaganda. Künzl 1994, 43; Hoss, forthcoming.

93. Bishop and Coulston 2006, 260; Hoss, forthcoming.

94. Oldenstein 1976, 76; Hoss, forthcoming.

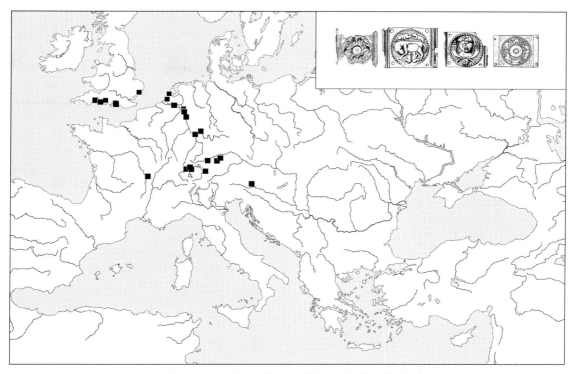

Figure 4.7. Map with distribution of finds of embossed belt plates.

centurion downwards) without conscious organisation. As both the waist-belt and the shoulder-belt had to confirm only to minimum standards of functionality, their decoration probably offered the best opportunity for any individual soldier to express personal symbolism and individualism. This would argue for a wide variety of vastly different belt decorations in use at the same time. In contrast to this, belt fashions exhibit a high amount of homogeneity across the whole Roman empire from Hadrian's Wall to Dura Europos and from Morocco to Romania. This was most likely caused by an abstract idea of the Roman soldiers' identity and worth, which also controlled the choices of belt design.[95] According to a theory developed by Pierre Bourdieu, "[taste] functions as a sort of social orientation, a 'sense of one's place', guiding the occupants of a given [...] social space towards the social positions adjusted to their properties, and towards the practices or goods which befit the occupants of that position".[96] In Bourdieu's theory, symbolic capital (e.g. prestige, honour) is a crucial source of power, enabling the holder to exercise symbolic violence over non-holders. To attain this symbolic power, one must be able to conform to certain social expectations (the 'right' manner of speaking, walking, eating, dressing, etc.). While Bourdieu explored how parents would teach their children to conform to these expectations, it seems convincing that similar mechanisms take place in other social groups than the family. Tight-knit hierarchical groups like army units also constitute a group in which a certain set of rules is passed from a group of older and/or higher ranking men to a group

95.   James 2006, 261.
96.   Bourdieu 1984, 466.

of younger men. This set of rules naturally includes the 'technical' knowledge of the job; knowledge of arms, warfare, camp building and other necessities of army life, but it also includes 'the right way' of walking, talking, eating, dressing, etc. In a outwardly traditional society as the Roman, the older and/or higher ranking soldiers would 'set the tone' in their unit, establishing which fashions were acceptable and which were not, the verdict then being 'executed' by peer pressure.[97] The surprising 'uniformity' of Roman military belts was thus not forced on the soldiers from above, but rather a product of their own desire for conformity.

In a rare interaction between internal pressures to conform to tradition and custom and a desire for novel styles, belt fashions evolved to express the common identity and solidarity of the Roman soldiers.[98] The immense fighting success of the Roman army lay not in the ferocity of its fighters outdoing each other in feats of daring, but in the co-ordinated co-operation of many individuals, making that success – and thus the survival of each individual – dependant on their solidarity and their feelings of communality. The Roman military belt was the outward manifestation of this and a central part of the Roman soldier's identity.

The author wishes to thank the organizers of the conference for the inclusion of this article in the conference proceedings despite the fact that she was unable to attend the conference.

---

97. James 2006, 252.
98. James 2006, 261.

5. LINEN-CLAD ETRUSCAN WARRIORS

Margarita Gleba

Corselets made of linen have been known in the classical world at least since the time of the Homeric poems, yet few modern scholars have confronted the issue of how this type of military attire actually looked and functioned. Unlike other kinds of armour, made of more durable materials such as metal, linen corselets have not survived in the archaeological record and are known primarily from literature. Artistic representations do exist, but have seldom been identified as such. I propose to examine the existing evidence for linen corselets in both Greek textual sources and Etruscan/Italic art.

TEXTUAL SOURCES

Our earliest source is the *Iliad*, where Ajax Oileus and Amphion are λινοθώρηκες, 'linen-corseleted'.[1] The same epithet is also applied to the Argive warriors in the seventh century BC Delphic oracle preserved in the Palatine Anthology, which referred to them as the best men of their day.[2] Slightly later, at the beginning of the sixth century BC, the Lesbian poet Alcaeus included 'corselets of new linen' in his list of armour.[3] Herodotus tells us that in the sixth century, the Egyptian pharaoh Amasis dedicated an elaborate linen cuirass in the Temple of Athena at Lindos and sent another one to Sparta.[4] It has been suggested that these remarkable dedications bore reference to Athena's aegis.[5]

During the Persian Wars in the fifth century BC, linen armour was worn by the Assyrian and other Asiatic troops of Xerxes.[6] The regular armour of the Susan king Abradates was made of linen.[7] Plutarch relates that even Alexander the Great wore an elaborate linen corselet captured from the Persians at Gaugamela.[8] Another interesting reference to this armour type is given by Aeneas Tacticus, who mentions the smuggling of linen corselets into a besieged city, possibly with an implication that superficially they would have looked like regular clothing and thus would have been easy to conceal.[9]

1.   Homer *Iliad* II, 529, 830. Lorimer 1950, 210–211 suggests that the epithet is a seventh century BC interpolation. Strabo (13.1.10) and Pliny the Elder *NH* 19.VI.26 also mention Homer's references to the use of linen corselets during the Trojan War.
2.   *Anth. Pal.* xiv, 73.
3.   Frag. 234; see Page 1955, with comments 215–216.
4.   Herod. II, 182; III, 47. One of the current theories holds that the linen corselet was invented by Egyptians and adopted by the Greeks; see Lorimer 1950, 210, but also Anderson 1970, 23.
5.   Moxon 2000, 125–133.
6.   Herod. IX, 63; Xen. *Anab.* IV. 7.15 and V.4.13. Herodotus (I, 135), also claims that Persians adopted linen amour from Egypt.
7.   Xen. *Cyrop.* VI.4.2.
8.   Plut. *Alex.* 32.5. The armour worn by Alexander the Great on the Alexander mosaic found in Pompeii, has been interpreted as a linen corselet; see Pfrommer 1998, 19–24, who argues that the type was Macedonian and not Persian. See Granger-Taylor in this volume for further discussion and illustration.
9.   Aen. *Tact.* 29.4. It is not known what city is described in the passage.

Like other types of armour, linen corselets were dedicated at sanctuaries. Besides the already mentioned two items sent to Greece by pharaoh Amasis, Gelon of Syracuse dedicated three linen corselets at Olympia, to commemorate his victory over the Carthaginians.[10] Livy also tells us that the linen corselet of Lars Tolumnius, the king of Veii, slain in battle in 437 BC, was dedicated at the Temple of Jupiter Feretrius, where it still could be seen in Augustan times.[11]

Thus, the picture we get from literature is that corselets made of linen were common enough military attire to be mentioned without explanation at least from the eighth century BC onwards. Anna Sacconi has argued that Mycenaean ideograms *162+*KI* and *162+*RI* indicate linen corselet, taking their use even further back in time, although she then assumed that it was worn in combination with bronze armour and could not be used for protection by itself.[12] Archaeological and iconographic evidence however, indicates that linen corselets differed significantly from linen chitons worn under bronze armour. These sources also give us more specific information about how these items were constructed.

LINEN CORSELET CONSTRUCTION

It is clear that, in material, construction and appearance, the linen corselet was distinct from the 'muscle' or 'bell' breastplate, made of large sheets of metal or hardened leather and requiring careful fitting to the individual owner, and from the scale armour, made of many small metal or leather pieces.[13] In most studies on Greek armour, the linen corselet is subsumed under the category of composite or shoulder-piece corselets, which became the most common type of cuirass during the Archaic period, alongside the muscle breastplate.[14] Composite corselets were made of leather or linen. Metal was probably also used in their construction in the form of scales and *laminae*. But the fact that there are no composite corselets surviving in archaeological contexts indicates that they were made mostly of perishable materials. The one unusual example found in the so-called Tomb of Philip at Vergina in northern Greece is made of iron and gold.[15] Peter Connolly has interpreted it as a translation of a linen corselet into metal.[16]

The most characteristic feature of a composite corselet, which appears in Greek artistic depictions by the sixth century BC, consists of two shoulder pieces (*epomides*), which were attached to the back, extended over the shoulders and fastened in front by laces. The corselet itself was made up of many rectangular sections of what was probably thick and stiffened linen fabric, sewn together. The skirt usually had one or two rows of flaps (*pteryges*), or a thick fringe of plaited cords. The corselet was worn wrapped around the waist and fastened on the left side, as is seen in arming scenes depicted in ancient art.[17]

The protective quality of such linen armour had already been questioned during antiquity. Pausanias, who saw them dedicated at various sanctuaries, claims that linen corselets gave protection to hunters against animal bites but were useless against violent blows of a metal weapon, and assumes

---

10. Paus. I.21.7.
11. Liv. IV.20.
12. Sacconi 1971, 49–54, 53.
13. For these and other types of body armour, see Jarva 1995.
14. Jarva 1995, 33.
15. Andronikos 1984, 140–144.
16. Connolly 1998, 59.
17. See, for example, a Greek cup by Brygos painter in the Vatican, *ARV2* 373.48. Also, see reconstruction in Connolly 1998, 58. For reconstructiono experiments, see Aldrete *et al.* forthcoming.

that they were used only in hunting.[18] Arrian however, suggests that linen corselets could be used by cavalry.[19] By Roman times, mail and lamellar armour had replaced for the most part the linen kind but there is little doubt that, in the preceding centuries, linen body armour was ubiquitous. Development of defensive armour always follows the evolution of weapons and it is likely that linen corselets were no longer adequate to counteract the new types of arms.

In fact, there may have been not one but several ways to make linen hard and resistant to weapons. One theory is that the threads were unusually thick, twined of many yarns, which would explain the incredible thread count, 360, mentioned by Pliny the Elder for the corselet dedicated by Amasis.[20] This technique, which makes the fabric much thicker than ordinary weaves, seems to have been used in the few examples of linen armour surviving from antiquity. While not a corselet and quite late in date, the shin guard of coarse undyed linen found at Dura Europos in Syria is of considerable interest in the context of the present discussion.[21] The piece is 44.2 by 27 cm and is warp-twined to shape.[22] The edging and heart-shaped attachments of straps are made of red leather. The remarkable aspect of the fabric is that it is woven of cords, which are plied of six threads in both directions. The guard has three pairs of red leather straps for tying it to the leg and shows both wear (surface felting) and evidence of use in combat (cuts).

Hero Granger-Taylor reports the remains of several different fragments of linen armour at Masada, differing in quality but probably made in the same technique.[23] She convincingly argues that the fragments could be different *pteryges* from the same piece of composite armour.

Many depictions, in fact, show the corselets composed of narrow bands and it has been suggested that band technique or tablet-weaving may have been used to make the early Egyptian corselets.[24] Another theory is that linen corselets were made resistant by the use of many layers. Here we have some archaeological evidence as well, quite early in date, too. A fragment of linen fourteen layers thick was discovered in the nineteenth century in the Bronze Age Shaft Grave V at Mycenae in Greece, which may be a part of a linen corselet.[25]

Sylvia Tørnkvist, on the other hand, brings in evidence from a much later period: Byzantine historian Nicetas Acominatos in a book written *c.* AD 1204–1210 describes the crusader's way of making a linen garment protective against weapons by treating it with a mixture of vinegar and salt.[26] This recipe is in agreement with Pliny the Elder, who mentions that Gauls and Parthians used vinegar for stiffening wool.[27]

---

18.   Paus. I, 21.7. Pausanias' claim is seconded by Bill Cooke: 'Linen is characterized by high tensile strength and low breaking extension relative to most other natural fibres. Thick linen fabrics would therefore be quite resistant to cutting and slashing especially if they were layers with a padding that could be flax tow or wool. These types of fabrics and padding are however less able to resist penetration when laid against the skin, i.e. the point forces the threads and the padding apart to allow penetration' (personal communication 25 May 2002). Contra Pausanias, see Aelian (*De Nat. Anim.* 9.17).
19.   Arrian *Tact.* 4.
20.   Plin. *NH* XIX, II.14. For the discussion of possibility of such thread count, see Granger-Taylor in this volume.
21.   Yale no. 1933.481. See Pfister and Bellinger 1945, 59 no. 292, Pl. XXX; James 2004, 128–129 no. 448, fig. 73. James identifies it as a greave liner rather than a shin guard. I am grateful to Susan B. Matheson at the Yale University Art Gallery for making it possible for me to examine the piece.
22.   More detailed information and the photograph of the piece can be found elsewhere in this volume, in the article by Hero Granger-Taylor, to whom I am thankful for the technical information.
23.   See Granger-Taylor in this volume.
24.   Jarva 1995, 42.
25.   Studniczka 1887, 21–22, fig. 4. It is possible, however, that it was just folded cloth.
26.   Tørnkvist 1969, 81–82.
27.   Plin. *NH* VIII, 192.

Any one of these various techniques or their combination may have made linen quite resistant to weapons and this fact, in addition to it being light, flexible, and not requiring the more valuable metal, would have made it an attractive military garb. The question is, however: what did a linen corselet look like?

ICONOGRAPHIC SOURCES

The earliest representational evidence comes from Greek vase painting, where linen corselets, however, have been identified seldom as such because of the problem of distinguishing them from the leather ones.[28] Eero Jarva points out that while in black-figure vase painting this type of corselet is often painted white and, consequently, has been interpreted as linen corselet, in red-figure painting, similar breastplates are depicted in red and have been identified as leather.[29] The images may reflect more the technique of vase painting or artistic preference than reality and, in most cases, we cannot distinguish the linen corselet in Greek art, as neither sculptures nor vase-paintings indicate the material.

Still, as Anderson notes, the "colour doubtless has a meaning, particularly white".[30] Even if a linen corselet was reinforced with metal or leather, its external appearance nevertheless projected the look and feel of linen. Linen is notoriously difficult to dye, but when naturally bleached, it has a bright white colour, striking by itself, but even more so when decorated with, for example, bright appliqués or by other means. Hence another possible point of departure in the quest to identify linen corselets is their elaborate adornment. Herodotus mentions the luxurious appearance of the corselet dedicated by Amasis at Lindos.[31] It is also the decoration that is emphasized by the artists depicting the garment, even in schematic representations, as attested by Greek vase paintings. Two criteria, colour and decoration, may thus be used to identify linen corselets in Etruscan and Greek art, as I shall now attempt to demonstrate.

Protective garments of the composite variety are found in Etruscan art as early as the sixth century BC: on bronze mirrors, cist urns, statuettes, and stone and terracotta sarcophagi.[32] However, the most important body of evidence comes from the medium of painting and this is where I believe it is possible to identify linen corselets with a high degree of certainty.

One of the most detailed depictions of linen corselets appears on the walls of the fourth-century BC François Tomb at Vulci, the paintings now at the Museo Torlonia, Villa Albani in Rome.[33] The painting depicts a Homeric episode of sacrifice of captive Trojans by Achilles (Fig. 5.1). The Greek heroes in the scene are dressed in various types of armour. The bluish-white colour and the construction of the corselets worn by Ajax Telamonios and Ajax Oileus indicate armour of linen fabric (Fig. 5.11, top left and centre). Contrast to the undoubtedly metal 'muscle' cuirass worn by

---

28. For an exhaustive compilation of depictions of composite corselet in Greek vase painting, see Anderson 1970, 267–269 and Jarva 1995, 33–46.
29. Jarva 1995, 34, and in this volume.
30. Anderson 1970, 44.
31. Herod. II, 182.
32. Mirrors: *Corpus Speculorum Etruscorum* Belgique 1, no. 30; *Corpus Speculorum Etruscorum* Italia 1, I, no. 2 and no. 40; *Corpus Speculorum Etruscorum* Vaticano 1, no. 11; *Corpus Speculorum Etruscorum* USA 1, no. 15; *Corpus Speculorum Etruscorum* USA 3, no. 2; *Corpus Speculorum Etruscorum* Bundesrepublik Deutschland 1, no. 39; *Corpus Speculorum Etruscorum* Bundesrepublik Deutschland 3, no.15; *Corpus Speculorum Etruscorum* Bundesrepublik Deutschland 4 no. 15; *Corpus Speculorum Etruscorum* France 1, I, no. 11; *Corpus Speculorum Etruscorum* Denmark 1, no. 22; *Corpus Speculorum Etruscorum* DDR I, no. 30. For terracotta reliefs and bronze warrior figurines, see a list in Jarva 1995, 46.
33. Buranelli 1987; Moretti Sgubini 2004.

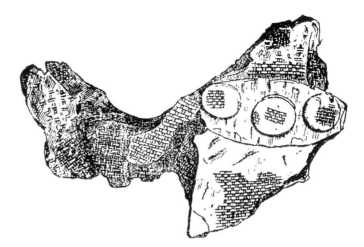

*Figure 5.1. Drawing of a fragment of linen
from Shaft-Grave V, Mycenae, Bronze Age
(After Studniczka 1887, fig. 4).*

Achilles is quite clear. The corselets are made in horizontal bands and in one place the artist has
carefully rendered what looks like stitches connecting them. The decoration is also carefully depicted
(Fig. 5.11 top centre). As in other monuments, to be discussed later, the decorative geometric and
floral patterns are bright red. They may represent leather elements, like the red leather edgings on
the Dura Europos shin guard.[34]

The composition of the scene of the Trojans' sacrifice probably derives from another painted
source, possibly originating in Southern Italy, ancient Magna Graecia, as the same subject appears
on a number of Faliscan vases, Praenestine bronze cistae and Etruscan sarcophagi.[35] Among these is
a painted marble sarcophagus, the so-called Sarcophagus of the Priest, found in Tarquinia and dated
to the second half of the fourth century (Fig. 5.2).[36] The paint is badly worn but enough details
remain to reveal the linen corselets, identified by Horst Blanck, who published the paintings on the
sarcophagus.[37] The garments are of composite type, white with occasional red decoration. One of
the long sides shows the sacrifice of the Trojans with five Greek warriors depicted in linen corselets.
In contrast to the François Tomb paintings, here even Achilles wears one, and I will return to the
significance of this difference shortly. The other long side of the Sarcophagus of the Priest shows a
scene of Amazonomachy with four warriors wearing linen corselets as well.

The Amazonomachy theme also appears on the so-called Amazon Sarcophagus from Tarquinia,
dated to the second half of the fourth century BC (Fig. 5.3).[38] This is probably our most informative
iconographic source on linen corselets because of the relatively good preservation of paint and high
degree of details in the painting. Warriors clad in linen corselets appear on all four sides of the
sarcophagus. In two cases the artist carefully showed the fastening on the left side (Fig. 5.4). The
decoration of each corselet is individualized (Fig. 5.5, 5.6, 5.11 bottom), possibly reflecting the real
life practice. Buttons and the ends of shoulder pieces are rendered in yellow paint, as are the helmets,
greaves and other bronze panoply of the warriors. These details are especially important because the

34.   I am grateful to Hero Granger-Taylor for this suggestion.
35.   Holliday 1993, 179.
36.   Now in the Archaeological Museum at Tarquinia (inv. RC 9871).
37.   Blanck 1982, 11–28, and Blanck 1983, 79–84.
38.   Now in the Archaeological Museum of Florence. See Bocci 1960; Bottini and Setari 2007.

Figure 5.2. François Tomb, Vulci, 350–330 BC.

Figure 5.3. Sarcophagus of the Priest, Tarquinia, 4th century BC (© Deutsches Archäologisches Institut, Rome, Neg. 80–1827).

Figure 5.4. Amazon Sarcophagus, Tarquinia, 4th century BC (© Deutsches Archäologisches Institut, Rome, Neg. 72–204).

metal parts of linen corselets may provide a tangible way to trace this otherwise perishable armour in archaeological contexts. Surviving metal buttons and shoulder-piece ends may present a concrete evidence for linen corselets, especially in burials.[39]

In some cases, the structure of the garment is clearly depicted in the form of horizontal sections consisting of rectangular, possibly reinforced, plates. These same details are also visible in yet another Etruscan painting, in the Tomba del Orco II at Tarquinia. Here Geryon, as the guardian of the gates to Hades, wears a linen corselet (Fig. 5.7).[40]

In addition to the examples found in monumental painting, white corselets with red decoration also appear on the painted architectural terracottas from various sites in central Italy, including Caere, Civita Castellana, Orvieto, Segni, Satricum etc.[41]

Based on these definitive examples, it seems likely that certain details of appearance, as well as distinctive decorative patterns, allow identification of linen corselets in other representations. The corselet of the so-called Mars of Todi, dated to the late fifth–early fourth century BC,[42] has the same construction and fastening as the painted examples. Same criteria can be applied to the more schematic representations in clay and bronze.

The fact that the linen corselet is so

Figure 5.5. Detail of a warrior showing corselet fastening under the left arm, Amazon Sarcophagus, Tarquinia, 4th century BC (© Deutsches Archäologisches Institut, Rome, Neg. 72–209).

Figure 5.6. Detail of a warrior showing corselet decoration, Amazon Sarcophagus, Tarquinia, 4th century BC (© Deutsches Archäologisches Institut, Rome, Neg. 72–211).

39. Miller (1993, 52 n. 99) reports on finds of metal appliqués from Macedonian tombs, which may have been attached to leather or linen armour.
40. Steingräber 1986, 329, pl. 129.
41. Andrén 1940, 37 and pl. 11B, 107 and pl. 36, 174 and pl. 65, 396 and pl. 120, 461 and pl. 141.
42. Now in the Gregorian Etruscan Museum at Vatican (inv. 693).

Figure 5.9. Drawing of the Revil cist, Praeneste, 325–300 BC (After Bordenache Battaglia 1979, pl. CXXXIX).

(Fig. 5.10), there are corselets with shoulder pieces and *pteryges*, painted white and decorated with red ornaments. Angela Pontrandolfo and Agnes Rouveret call this type of armour Macedonian, and similar examples do, in fact, appear in the painted tombs of Macedonia.[49]

Garments of the deceased on the façades of the 'Great Tomb' at Lefkadia and the 'Tomb with Warrior painting' at Vergina have been both identified as linen.[50] Similar corselets are represented in the Tomb of Lyson and Kallikles and probably reflect the appearance of those employed by its occupant during life.[51] Corselets in paintings of the Tomb of Lyson and Kallikles are also similar to the armour worn by Alexander himself on the Alexander mosaic found in Pompeii.[52]

So it appears that linen corselets were worn in life in both Greece and Etruria but the representational evidence, in addition to being dictated by accidents of preservation and recovery, stems from different traditions of funerary iconography: in Greece and South Italy we have representations of the deceased, while in Etruria we are left with mythological scenes.

CONCLUSIONS

Literary and representational evidence demonstrates that linen corselets were known and worn in both Greece and Etruria from Archaic through at least Hellenistic period. In Greece, their use may go back to the Bronze Age. Literary sources also emphasize their use in the Near East and Egypt. Linen corselets can be identified with high degree of certainty on Etruscan and Greek painted monuments on the basis of their construction, colour and decoration (Figure 5.11). These can be used to identify the type in works of other media and in more schematic representations. Certain details emphasized by the ancient artists, such as bronze buttons, may provide us with a means to identify the presence of linen corselets archaeologically. As far as the association of this armour type with heroic characters in Etruscan art is concerned, the limited amount and nature of the material does not permit definitive conclusions at this point but it seems that both real life warriors and painted mythical heroes were dressed according to the latest military fashion.

---

49. Pontrandolfo and Rouveret 1992.
50. Andronikos 1984, 180 fig. 151 and 176 fig. 147. For other representations, see Miller 1993, 52 n. 98, who also reports on remains of actual corselets in the tombs of Derveni and Vergina.
51. Miller 1993, 52–53.
52. Markle 1982, 87–111, 96; Pfrommer 1998, 19–24. See discussion and image in Grander-Taylor, this volume.

Figure 5.10. Tomb 4, Andriulo, Paestum, 4th century BC (After Pontrandolfo and Rouveret 1992).

Figure 5.11. Drawings of the corselets as they appear in the François Tomb, Vulci (top left and centre); Tomba del Orco II at Tarquinia (top right); Amazon Sarcophagus, Tarquinia (bottom) (Drawings by the author).

6. FRAGMENTS OF LINEN FROM MASADA, ISRAEL – THE REMNANTS OF PTERYGES? – AND RELATED FINDS IN WEFT- AND WARP-TWINING INCLUDING SEVERAL SLINGS

Hero Granger-Taylor

INTRODUCTION

The existence in Antiquity of armour made of linen has always been known from texts. But recent research has concentrated more on military equipment found in excavations, this consisting principally of items of metal and bone.

The study in this volume by Margarita Gleba is a welcome return to the subject of textile armour in literature and art. Gleba is surely correct in interpreting armour represented in white paint as made of linen. Many of her examples are edged in red, a detail we can now understand as a binding of leather.

Actual examples of armour amongst groups of archaeological textiles have been unknown with the exception of one notable find from Dura-Europos in Syria, a linen greave (shin guard) discussed below. The fragments from Masada which form the main subject of this paper are therefore an important additional discovery.

Finally, textile slings of various dates throw light on the twined technique of these surviving examples of linen armour and are themselves a worthy subject of renewed examination.

THE DATING AND CONTEXT OF THE MASADA FRAGMENTS

Masada is a hilltop fortress situated in the Judaean desert, close to the shore of the Dead Sea and within the modern state of Israel. It was there in 73 or 74 AD that the Roman army conquered the remaining elements of the First Jewish Revolt, the *sicarii* and their families who had occupied Masada since 66 and others who had eventually fled there. These events were recorded by the Jewish historian Josephus, whose written account in Greek has in most respects been confirmed by modern archaeology.[1]

The excavation of Masada took place principally from 1963 to 1965, under the direction of Professor Yigael Yadin of the Hebrew University of Jerusalem.[2] Much organic material was discovered, including many textiles, which had been preserved due to the arid and stable desert climate. The

---

1.   Jos. *Jewish War*, especially VII, 275–406; Ben-Tor 2009, 281
2.   Yadin 1965; Yadin 1966.

textile finds have now been thoroughly studied and are the subject of a forthcoming volume in the Masada Final Reports series.[3]

Masada is a relatively simple site in terms of stratigraphy and almost all of the finds uncovered there belong to the main period of occupation, that is, from the point that Herod the Great began to spend longer periods of time there, in c. 28–26 BC, to the last evidence of a Roman garrison, around 115 AD.[4]

Of the textiles discussed here, the find which is least easy to place precisely is the single organic fragment, 1039–764/**13**. Its find spot, locus 1039, known as the Casemate of the Scrolls, is a room within the casemate wall where a great heap of accumulated mixed material had been preserved. Textiles from this room include items which must date from the occupation by the *sicarii* and their families, for example, fragments of women's head veils of local type, as well as finds we can probably associate with Roman legionary soldiers, in particular off-cuts of dark brown cloaks in fine 1:2 twill weave made with Z-spun yarns.[5] We cannot know therefore whether the piece of armour from which this fragment came had belonged to a Roman soldier or to a defeated Jewish fighter.

The context is clearer in the case of the other fragments under discussion, which are all carbonised through burning and come from either locus 9 or locus 16, adjacent spaces on the lowest terrace of the Northern Palace, 9 being one of the rooms in the small bathhouse and 16 being the staircase leading to it.[6] This area was found to be covered with fallen building stone and Professor Amnon Ben-Tor, who was in charge of the original excavation of this part of the site, is certain that the lower levels of this fallen masonry, including the barrel vault of the bathhouse itself, fell during the course of the siege, in 73 or 74 AD.[7] The range of discoveries made beneath this rubble supports this conclusion. It extends from parts of three unburied skeletons, the only human remains found on the site apart from a small number of burials in caves, to useful objects of some value, including many arrow heads and 435 bronze scales with expensive coloured finishes.[8] These objects would certainly have been looted by the incoming Roman soldiers, had they been accessible to them.

For the burnt fragments of twined linen the end of the siege in 73 or 74 therefore provides a *terminus ante quem*. What we cannot say is when they were made. The *sicarii* might have brought these elements of armour with them when they came to Masada from Jerusalem in 66 AD, or they might have pillaged them, or they might have found them amongst the stores which Josephus tells

---

3.   The present author is the principal author of the volume but much of the preliminary curating and cataloguing of the textiles was carried out by Tal Vogel. Granger-Taylor (forthcoming). We are enormously indebted to many people but among those not listed as contributors or editors in the Bibliography below I must mention in particular Tamar Schick, who has helped tirelessly with every stage of the work on the textiles, Olga Negnevitsky and Mimi Lavi, our two conservators, Orit Shamir, curator of the organic collection at the Israel Antiquities Authority, and Avigail Sheffer who was principal author of the Preliminary Report and who has done so much to encourage us since. Please also see Sheffer and Granger-Taylor 1994. In addition to all my colleagues on the Masada textile project, I must thank in particular Margarita Gleba for sharing her research with me and Stephen Quirke for many years' help with Egyptology.
4.   Bar-Nathan 2006, 13–36.
5.   Fragments of veils are 1039–162/188, 1039–162/263, 1039–309/15, fragments of cloaks in 1:2 twill with Z-spun yarns include 1039–49/4, 1039–144/2 and 1039–162/105, 1039–162/31 and 189, 1039–309/28, 1039–309/18 and 42 (Granger-Taylor 2008); the Roman legionary occupation was probably relatively short; after this, auxiliary soldiers would have been left at the site as a garrison.
6.   Netzer 1991, 163–167.
7.   Ben-Tor 2009, 64–65, 303–307 and personal communication (2007).
8.   Yadin 1965, 16–17.

us had been left at the site since the time of Herod (died 4 BC): these stores included "a quantity of weapons of every kind, stored there by the king, (and) enough for 10,000 men".[9]

A catalogue by Guy Stiebel and Jodi Magness of the non-textile military equipment discovered at Masada has recently been published, in volume eight of the *Masada Final Reports* series.[10] Like the corpus of textiles, the military equipment is varied and well distributed across the site, but at the same time is all more or less fragmentary. Stiebel and Magness record only two armour types, laminated (or segmental) armour and scale armour. The laminated armour, which is represented by five fragments from fittings, is interpreted by them as having belonged to Roman legionary soldiers.[11]

The scales recorded by Stiebel and Magness are much larger in number and were found in a total of 50 loci (Fig. 6.9).[12] In addition to the group of 435 from the bath house of the Northern Palace already mentioned, they include a collection of 650 matching scales from locus 162, apparently the remains of single piece of armour which had been deliberately buried, probably to prevent it falling into the hands of the Romans. The impression gained is that, while scale armour was by this period widely used by the Romans, most of the scales found at Masada should be interpreted as coming from the armour of the defenders.[13]

Any elements of armour which came from Herod's store at Masada would have predated the time of direct Roman rule in Judaea (from 6 AD) and would have belonged to a material culture where the Hellenistic influence was still stronger than the Roman.

DESCRIPTION OF THE MASADA FRAGMENTS

All the textiles found at Masada are fragmentary and relatively small in size but they vary very much in texture. The different texture types, when put together with other information, including any decoration, we have found to be a very good pointer to original function. Consequently, for the catalogue, we have been able to organise the majority of the textile fragments into categories according to the different items from which they probably came – cloaks, cushion covers, sacks and so on.[14]

The great majority of the finds are of sheep's wool but some are of goat-hair, some of camel-hair and around 10% of linen. In general the linen textiles show less variety than those of wool and for this reason are harder to categorise. But the small group which is the subject of this paper has a quite distinct appearance: these fragments are particularly thick, are made with composite threads and have an unusual woven structure.

The non-carbonised example found in the Casemate of the Scrolls, 1039–764/**13**, measures approximately 4 × 5 × 0.5 cm and has no obvious front or back (Figs 6.1 and 6.2). Like the great majority of the Masada textiles, it has been extensively damaged by insects; beetle larvae were probably responsible for the drilled holes. But its condition is otherwise good. Where this fragment retains its original surface, it is very flat, as if pressed or polished, and the weave itself is not easy to make out. Any loose fibres or "lint" seem to have been incorporated into this smooth finish and some kind of

---

9.   Jos. *Jewish War* VII, 295–299.
10. Stiebel and Magness 2007.
11. Stiebel and Magness 2007, 32.
12. Stiebel and Magness 2007, 52–66.
13. Stiebel and Magness 2007, 31–32.
14. Granger-Taylor forthcoming.

Cloth

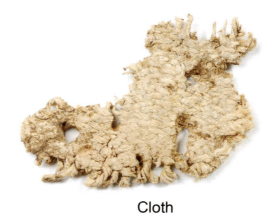

Cloth

*Figure 6.1. Masada 1039–764/**13**, side a), linen, weft-twined, c. 4 × 5 cm. Photograph Inbal Abergil*

*Figure 6.2. Masada 1039–764/**13**, side b). Photograph Inbal Abergil*

Cloth

Cloth

Figure 6.3. Masada 16–1174 and 1181/2, carbonised linen, weft-twined, the longest fragment c. 4.5 × 3 cm. Photograph Inbal Abergil

Figure 6.4. Masada 16–1174 and 1181/2, detail of fragment with two selvedges, width 3.2 cm. Photograph Inbal Abergil

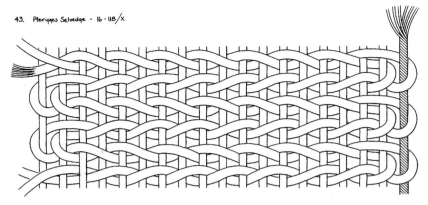

Figure 6.5. Weft-twined technique of Masada 16–1174 and 1181/2. Drawing James Farrant and author

additional material appears to have been rubbed into it, this material now appearing whitish and powdery.

The weave has a superficial similarity to twill but on closer inspection reveals itself to be a variety of "twining", with the threads of one system twining (half-twisting) on themselves in pairs after passing around two threads of the other system.[15] The twined or active threads are worked in staggered reversing rows, hiding the passive threads around which they twist, in principal as in the diagram in Figure 6.5.

The yarns are also distinctive, having been made up from a group of individual threads, and can thus be described as "composite". The yarn of the straight threads, identified here as the warp, is S-plied from a group of S-spun elements, apparently four (ssssS); there are approximately 5 warp threads per cm. The yarn of the twined threads, identified as the weft, is Z-plied from S-spun elements, apparently three (sssZ); there are 6 to 7 pairs of weft thread per cm.

The thick composite threads have been combined with a twined woven structure to produce a fabric which is not only exceptionally thick but which must also have been unusually firm and stable: by definition twined textiles are thicker than most standard weaves because at any point they are three threads thick rather than just two; twining effectively locks in the individual threads and so much reduces the fabric's flexibility. In this variation of twining, the marked widthways or lengthways "ribs" which normally characterise twined structures have been eliminated by the use of staggered "binding points". As a result, the surface here is more or less smooth.

A comparison of all the Masada fragments of this type as laid out in Table 6.1 shows that the yarns of fragment 1039–764/**13** are not the same as the yarns in the carbonised fragments from loci 9 and 16; in the latter, the number of individual elements in each yarn is higher. But Table 6.1 does make clear an overall pattern whereby the warp yarns are all plied in the S-direction and the slightly less thick weft yarns are all plied in the Z-direction.

The carbonised fragments of this type are very fragile and in danger of crumbling to dust. But at the same time, because the burning has apparently destroyed their polished finish and removed loose

---

15. The terminology used here in most respects follows Burnham (1981) and Seiler-Baldinger (1994).

fibres, they are comparatively legible in terms of their structure. The material is still recognisable as having been linen.

As mentioned, these carbonised fragments are from two adjacent loci in the Northern Palace at Masada, 9 and 16. The three fragments from locus 9, all with paired warp threads, are clearly from the same textile and have been numbered 9–286/1. The fifteen or more fragments from locus 16 have been divided on the basis of quality and structure into three different textiles, 16–1174 and 1181/1, 16–1174 and 1181/2, and 16–1174 and 1181/3.[16] It is possible that 16–1174 and 1181 /1, which also has paired warp threads, is the same textile is 9–286/1

Several of the carbonised fragments preserve a selvedge and from this we know for certain that the technique is *weft* twining. The largest fragment of 16–1174 and 1181/2 has a selvedge on both sides giving a complete width of only 3.2 cm (Figs 6.3 and 6.4). The diagram in Figure 5 shows the detailed structure of this fragment. The second largest fragment of 16–1174 and 1181/2 (Fig. 6.3, lower right) is very nearly of complete width; it just lacks the outer warp thread along the right edge as photographed.

On this last fragment (Fig. 6.3, lower right), the warp threads emerging from the bottom of the web turn sideways so as to lie parallel to the lines of weft above them. The lower left corner is also slightly lifted. We may be seeing here the remains of some sort of braided transverse border preceding a warp fringe. There are a number of techniques for finishing off the warp of a textile which cause the warp threads to turn at right angles as they issue from the web. One is a three-strand plaited border with fringe which occurs on tabby weave linen textiles from Masada as well as from the Cave of Letters, Murabba'at and Palmyra.[17] This plaited edge can be worked several times over and in fact all the Masada examples and probably many of the others are double, first worked in one direction and then in the opposite direction.[18] The fragment of 16–1174 and 1181/2 with two surviving selvedges (Fig. 6.3, lower left) is also distorted at the lower edge and perhaps was also finished in the same manner. In any case, these bending warp threads can be contrasted with the very straight warp threads that emerge from the top of the same fragments and from the other Masada finds of this type (Figs 6.1, 6.2, 6.3, 6.6 and 6.7).

On the fragments making up 16–1174 and 1181/3 and 16–1174 and 1181/1 (Figs 6.6 and 6.7), the exposed warp yarn is noticeably shiny, as if it had been treated with some additional material. This material could have had the dual purpose of holding together the separately-spun elements and producing a smoother surface, thus making the compacting of the weft easier to achieve. But once these textiles had lost their original horizontal borders, the smoothness of the warp yarn undoubtedly encouraged the twined weft to slide off, a tendency which is unfortunately still very much present (it is due to this tendency that some of the fragments have also become distorted).

Also visible on all of the carbonised fragments are irregular patches of a light grey deposit. This occurs on the original weft-faced original surface, but on one side only. It is particularly thick on the fragments of 9–286/1 (not illustrated) but is also very evident on 16–1174 and 1181/3 (Fig. 6.6), and on 16–1174 and 1181/1 and /2 (Figs 6.7 and 6.3). This deposit appears to have been more affected by the burning than whatever coats the warp threads. It seems to have run together and

---

16.   The secondary numbers – 1181, 1174 etc. – refer to the individual archaeological 'baskets' into which finds were put during excavation.

17.   Sheffer and Granger-Taylor 1994, nos 9(A), 38(A) and 102 (A); Yadin 1963 b, nos 75–77; Crowfoot and Crowfoot 1961, no. 80; Schmidt-Colinet Stauffer and Al-As'ad 2000, nos 333, 335, 494, see also 25–26 and fig. 27.

18.   No diagram published so far shows this double plait exactly. The closest is Bergman 1975, fig. 51, B8.

Cloth

Figure 6.6. Masada 16–1174 and 1181/3, carbonised linen, weft-twined, the widest fragment c. 6 x 4 cm. Photograph Inbal Abergil

Cloth

Figure 6.7. Masada 16–1174 and 1181/1, carbonised linen, weft-twined, paired warp ends, the largest fragment c. 6 x 6 cm. Photograph Inbal Abergil

become more globular as a result. It is possibly a burnt and congealed version of the surface finish noted on 1039–764/**13**.

In the future, it may well be possible to identify these additional materials, using scientific analysis. The finish on the warp yarn may be some sort of "size"; traditionally it has been common to size the warp with some form of starch when weaving with linen and other bast fibres.[19] On the burnt fragments, the greyish material on the surface of the textiles looks like it was once wax. However, on the still-organic fragment 1039–764/13 the finish now has a powdery rather than a waxy appearance. For the meantime, we must also bear in mind that any deposit on the surface of the textiles could be dirt and grease accumulated during use.

To recapitulate, in all the textiles of this type found at Masada, the warp yarn is S-plied and the weft yarn is thinner and Z-plied. In addition, the carbonised fragments all have yarns with the same structure: the warp is always S-plied from six S-spun elements (ssssssS) and the weft always Z-plied from four S-spun elements (ssssZ).

Table 6.1 makes clearer the similarities and differences between these textiles.

Number	*Warp: ends per cm – paired (pr) or single (s)*	*Warp spin*	*Selvedges*	*Weft: twisted paired picks per cm*	*Weft spin*	*Maximum width (cm)*	*Carbonised (c) or Organic (o)*
9–286/1	3.5 pr	ssssssS	1	16–20	ssssZ	7	c
16–1174 & 1181/1	3.5–4.5 pr	ssssssS	1	16–18	ssssZ	6	c
16–1174 & 1181/2	5–6 s	ssssssS	2	8–8.5	ssssZ	3.2	c
16–1174 & 1181/3	4.5 s	ssssssS	0	10–11.5	ssssZ	4	c
1039–764/13	5 s	ssssS	0	6–7	sss?Z	5	o

Differences in their quality and woven structure have allowed us to divide up the carbonised fragments into different textiles as follows:

- 16–1174 and 1181/2, with single warp threads;
- 16–1174 and 1181/3 also with single warp threads but more weft-faced and with more widely-spaced warp threads than 16–1174 and 1181/2;
- 16–1174 and 1181/1, with paired warp threads;
- 9–286/, also with paired warp threads and perhaps from the same textile as 16–1174 and 1181/1.
- 1039–764/13, the non-carbonised fragment, is the coarsest textile in the group with only 6–7 paired weft picks per cm. Here the yarns are made of fewer elements but the individual threads making up the composite threads are thicker than in the textiles from loci 9 and 16.

It is useful also to consider the widths of the fragments. The widest part of fragment 16–1174 and 1181/3 is 4 cm whereas the widest part of 1174 and 1181/2 – with two selvedges – is only 3.2 cm. Fragments 9–286/1 and 16–1174 and 1181/1, both with paired warp, occur as wider fragments than those with single warp threads, a maximum of 7 cm compared to a maximum of 5 cm preserved on the organic fragment 1039–764/3. We cannot know the original width of the textile where there are no selvedges, or only one selvedge. However, the impression gained is that none of these Masada twined linen textiles was ever very wide.

IDENTIFICATION OF THE FUNCTION OF THE MASADA FRAGMENTS

The greave discovered at Dura-Europos, discussed below, is very valuable in providing confirmation

---

19.   Baines 1989, 106–7; Koh 2007, 85.

of the military application of thick linen textiles. But, while probably also twined, it does not, in its overall form, provide a direct parallel for the Masada fragments, which are much smaller, with a maximum width of only 7 cm. In the case of the narrower Masada fragments, the most obvious interpretation is that these are parts of what were known in Greek as *pteryges*.[20]

Pteryx, plural *pteryges*, has the primary meaning "wing", but its secondary meanings include flaps and flat appendages. In Antiquity the term was used in the plural for the flaps around the bottom of a cuirass or corselet. The clearest instance of this use of the word occurs in a passage in Xenophon's *Anabasis* (4.7.15), where the author writes about the Chalybians or Chalybes, inhabitants of the south-east coast of the Black Sea: it can be translated literally as "having corselets of linen [reaching down] as far as the belly, [with], instead of (the) flaps, a dense [fringe of] twisted cords",[21] i.e. Xenophon is contrasting the pteryges, which would normally have been attached to linen corselets in the Greece of his time (4th century BC), with the fringes of the corselets of the Chalybians. These fringes are perhaps an older form and it is notable that on the vase of the 12th century BC from Mycenae, decorated with a frieze of warriors, their body armour finishes with a fringe.[22] Pteryges could themselves have their own individual fringes and in Hellenistic and Roman art they are almost invariably shown with several comparatively thick coils of thread at the bottom of each individual pteryx, these fringes being usually preceded by a transverse border of some kind.

Corselets of linen had apparently gone out of common use by the Roman period, at least as an outer layer of protection. But pteryges continued to be a very common accessory to body armour. There are many Roman statues where soldiers, mostly apparently officers, wear cuirasses with pteryges at the shoulder and waist.[23] The cuirasses by this time would have been made of bronze rather than the original leather, and it is not clear whether the pteryges were attached directly to the metal or to some sort of linen under-layer.

There are also rarer representations from the Roman period of scale shirts equipped with pteryges. For instance, in a wall-painting of the mid 3rd century AD found in the Synagogue at Dura-Europos, in a scene now known as 'Ezekiel, The Destruction and Restoration of National Life', two soldiers in the background have scale body armour with pteryges attached.[24] There are also a few examples in Roman official art.[25]

On the evidence of works of art, pteryges continued to be used well into the Byzantine period, at least within the diminished boundaries of the Roman empire; in these later representations, pteryges occur most frequently in combination with scale shirts.[26]

Perhaps the most informative coloured work of art showing pteryges is the Alexander Mosaic, where Alexander the Great himself is represented wearing an up-to-date Macedonian corselet of his time (Fig. 6.8).[27] The scene represented is one of the battles fought by Alexander against the Persians, probably at Issus in 333 BC.[28] The mosaic was found in the House of the Faun at Pompeii and is

---

20. It is not here proposed to translate this word into English – 'tabs' perhaps gives the best impression, but historically 'bases' is more correct, with 'lamboys' having been used occasionally.

21. εἶχον δὲ θώρακας λινοῦς μέχρι τοῦ ἤτρου, ἀντὶ δὲ τῶν πτερύγων σπάρτα πυκνὰ ἐστραμμένα.

22. Illustrated for example in Henrik Fich *et al.* 1999, 40.

23. For example, Bianchi Bandinelli 1970, figs. 93, 197, 209, 256, 248.

24. Kraeling 1956, panel NC 1 section C, 194–202, pl. LXXII.

25. See tombstones and reliefs illustrated by Robinson 1975, 156–159, pls 442–444, 446–7, 449.

26. For example at Hosios Loukas, Liapis 2005, 55, 'Saint Merkourios'.

27. Pfrommer 1998, 19–24.

28. Dunbabin 1999, 41–43.

thought to have been made when the house was constructed, in c. 100 BC. But it has long been recognised as a copy of a painting dating to the time of Alexander or shortly after.[29] The depiction of the Greek and Persian armies and their equipment is unusually detailed and generally accepted as accurate.[30]

The precision of this work allows us to deduce many of the materials represented. The principal areas of Alexander's composite corselet are evidently of metal in various forms. The shine on the band around the corselet at diaphragm level suggests it was made of iron. The sections over the chest and the shoulder pieces, in contrast, are duller and have moulded details more characteristic of bronze; the variety of colours used here, for example, a reddish brown for the hair of the Medusa head, point to specialised bronze finishes. The scales in a band below the belt, greyish in colour, were probably in life bronze scales with a silvered surface. Some yellow details, including four circular details on the corselet and the small round brooch holding Alexander's cloak, are no doubt intended to represent gold or at least a gold surface. The gold details on the armour are fixings for the ties which hold down the shoulder pieces to the body of the corselet.

Interpreting the red details as leather, the following were apparently made of leather: the sword belt, the scabbard, the horse's neck strap, the edges of the corselet's shoulder pieces and the ties holding them down.

The metal parts of Alexander's body armour have similarities to the composite corselet of iron found at Vergina, in the tomb thought to be of Philip II of Macedon, Alexander's father.[31] The Vergina corselet, although it has lost its pteryges, does preserve on its inner side the remains of leather and textile.[32] Some of the leather binding of the edges of the shoulder pieces is also still *in situ* and this is exactly similar to the leather binding depicted on Alexander's corselet in the mosaic.

On the mosaic, a knotted belt runs around the corselet just above the band of scales.[33] Obviously a narrow-width textile of some kind, the colour in this case is green, suggesting green wool.

The pteryges, attached to the shoulders and waist of the corselet, are shown as white, as is also the horse's rein. The use of white here can surely once again be interpreted as representing linen. All the pteryges finish in fringes. The darker lines just above the fringes could represent some sort of decoration but more likely are intended to indicate a plaited border of the sort which might once have been present on the Masada fragments 16–1174 and 1181/2 (Fig. 6.3).

On the mosaic, the pteryges on the shoulders are fastened together by two red lines, probably leather laces; these appear to pass right through the linen, through holes presumably made by an awl or large needle. It is not clear whether there are one or two rows of *pteryges* on the shoulder. In contrast, the pteryges of the skirt are clearly in two rows are and are not joined together: one pteryx or flap from the lower row has been able to turn back up on itself; the darker flaps in the middle of this row are presumably intended to be understood as in shadow.

Of the pteryges attached at the waist, those of the lower row appear at first glance to be wider as well longer than those in the upper row. But the greater apparent width could alternatively be explained by the circumstance that the lower flaps are spread out more and overlap less. It is quite

29.   Robertson 1978, 168–170

30.   Pfrommer 2001, 47, fig. 52; Connolly 1981, 72.

31.   Connolly 1981, 72.

32.   Andronicos 1984, 138–144.

33.   Belts in this position, commonly shown over corselets and cuirasses, are usually referred to by modern authorities as 'sashes'. Connolly 1981, 214, fig. 1.

Figure 6.8. Alexander Mosaic, from the House of the Faun, Pompeii, detail showing Alexander the Great; c. 100 BC. Museo Nazionale, Napoli. Photograph Sonia Halliday.

possible therefore that each row was made of the same textile strips folded down on themselves at the top, an impression given by many representations of *pteryges* of Hellenistic and Roman Republican date. The mosaic definitely shows three lines at the end of each of the lower pteryges, just above the fringe, as opposed to only two at the end of the upper waist pteryges. This extra line could represent an extra row of plaiting, perhaps added because the longer flaps would have been subjected to more wear.

Using all this information to interpret the Masada finds, we might consider all the Masada fragments with single warp threads to be from *pteryges*: the fragments numbered 16–1174 and 1181/**2** and 3.2 cm wide where complete could be from pteryges from the shoulders of a piece of body armour; the broader fragments making up 16–1174 and 1181/**3**, with a maximum width of 4 cm as surviving, could be from *pteryges* attached at the waist.

The fragments with paired warp, 16–1174 and 1181/**1** and 9–286/**1**, at least 7 cm wide, have various possible functions within the realm of armour. One possibility is that the fragments with paired warp threads belonged to the body area of a rather antiquated piece of armour entirely of linen, that is, a linen corselet as discussed by Margarita Gleba, or another item, such as a greave. Peter Connolly has suggested that the Vergina composite iron corselet is a translation into metal of a construction type previously made completely of linen.[34] If this is correct, because the Vergina corselet

34.   Connolly 1981, 58.

is divided up very clearly into panels, we could say that that none of the elements of a linen corselet was ever very wide, perhaps not more than 15 cm.[35] Another possibility is that these larger fragments were part of a textile which lay under a layer of metal, perhaps the support textile to which scales were attached.

It is also necessary to consider whether the twined linen fragments belong with any of the other military equipment found at the site. Although much military material was found in locus 1039 it is too mixed to be associated with any certainty with the linen fragment 1039–764/**13**. Of

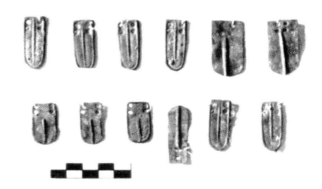

Figure 6.9. Selection of scales found at Masada loci 8, 9 and 16, after Yadin 1965

more significance is the fact that the carbonised fragments, from loci 9 and 16 on the lower terrace of the Northern Palace, were discovered in proximity to one of two larger groups of scales to have been found at Masada. This group consists of approximately 435 scales, all of bronze but of different shapes and colours – they are either silvered or gilded or have a red finish. These scales were spread across four loci within and just outside the bathhouse, 8, 9, 10 and 16, the largest number (214) having been found in locus 8, the *frigidarium*, also the findspot of the three incomplete skeletons.[36]

Almost all of the Masada scales have four holes at the top of the scale and none has holes at the side (Fig. 6.9). The holes at the top would have been used to sew the scales in overlapping rows onto a support textile, possibly with cord reinforcements.[37] At a site where so much organic material has survived it is disappointing for two reasons that no scales survive with any textile or sewing thread still attached: we cannot know exactly what type of thread and textile was used for this purpose; having lost their means of attachment, the scales are no longer joined to each other in any way (the scales at Masada were never linked directly to one another in rows by metal rivets through the sides, as was the case at the later site of Dura-Europos). In the case of the two large groups of scales, this loss of organic elements can probably be put down to fire: the group from locus 162, around 650 matching scales, was discovered within a 'burnt layer';[38] the group from across loci 8, 9, 10 and 16 was also discovered in a context with much evidence of burning, as the carbonised fragments of twined linen themselves show. Judging by finds from other sites, particularly Dura-Europos, both the sewing thread and the support textile would have been made of a bast fibre, probably linen, and, if so, highly flammable.[39] The twined linen fragments from loci 9 and 16 have perhaps survived only because they burned more slowly due to their density, and thus became carbonised rather than burned to ashes.

Stiebel and Magness, drawing attention to the mixed shape and colour of the Northern Palace scales,

35. Where Connolly is not correct, we now know, is in stating, in the same place, that linen corselets were made of layers of linen textile glued together.
36. Yadin 1965, 16–17; Stiebel and Magness 2007, 52–61; Ben-Tor 2009, 243–4
37. Wild 1981; Brown 1936, 440, 442; James 2004, 111–112
38. Stiebel and Magness 2007, 1.
39. Wild 1981; Brown 1936, 440, 442; James 2004, 111–112.

offer one explanation: they may have been "spare scales, perhaps taken from Herod's store rooms".[40] But the alternative they propose is more convincing: that these scales belonged to an item of "parade armour, which was [deliberately] made of two-toned scales of various shapes and sizes".[41]

The twined linen fragments from Masada were identified above as coming from pteryges or from wider textile elements used in some other way in armour. The pteryges could have been part of parade armour envisaged by Stiebel and Magness. The broader fragments, with paired warp, might even be from the support textile to which the scales were sewn: though against this suggestion we have to weigh the fact that none of the support textiles which do survive, the majority from Dura-Europos, have this specialised twined structure.[42]

An alternative explanation might be that there had been several items of armour in the bathhouse, and that among them there may have been, as already suggested above, one or more items principally of linen, perhaps even a linen corselet.

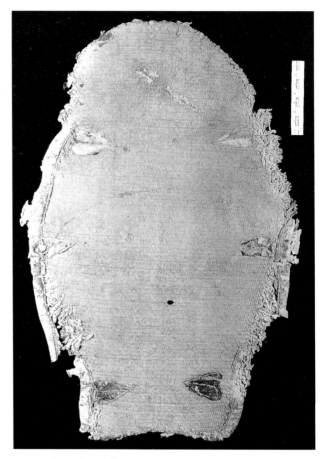

Figure 6.10. Greave from Dura-Europos, Syria, c. 250 BC, linen, probably warp twined, leather additions, c. 44 × 27 cm. Photograph Yale University Art Gallery, New Haven

THE GREAVE AND OTHER MILITARY TEXTILES FROM DURA-EUROPOS

Looking for linen textiles similar in structure to the Masada fragments, the only parallel of the Roman period appears to be the linen greave (shin guard) found at Dura–Europos and now in the collection of Yale University Art Gallery, New Haven (Fig. 6.10).[43] Dura-Europos was a garrison town on the Euphrates, the eastern extremity of the Roman Empire. The greave cannot be later in date than Dura's destruction by the Sasanians, probably in 257 AD, and is likely to have been in use at the time of the siege.[44]

---

40. Stiebel and Magness 2007, 2, 32.
41. Stiebel and Magness 2007, 1–2.
42. See the discussion of the Dura support textiles below.
43. Museum number 1933–481; Pfister and Bellinger 1945, 59, pl. XXX; James 2004, no. 448, 128–9; see also photograph at http://ecatalogue.art.yale.edu/detail.htm?objectId=5960
44. Pfister and Bellinger 1945, 1.

Corroboration for the use of linen greaves occurs in the wall-painting from the Synagogue at Dura, 'Ezekiel, The Destruction and Restoration of National Life'.[45] This painting has already been referred to as one of the places where scale body armour equipped with pteryges is shown. In contrast to the two figures in the background wearing scale armour, the principal soldier in the scene wears a cuirass with pteryges, a plumed helmet and, on his one visible leg, a greave tied at the back of the calf with bows of what appear to be cord. Whereas the cuirass is shown as brownish-yellow, a colour chosen perhaps to represent gilded bronze, both the pteryges and the greave are depicted as white. Once again, following Gleba's observations about the use of white paint, it can be inferred that the artist's intention was to indicate that the greave and the pteryges were made of linen.

The function of the surviving linen greave is confirmed by its characteristic outline, known from greaves of metal and, in one or two cases, of leather, and by the remains of the three pairs of straps.[46]

The straps were of thick leather and were covered at the point of attachment by heart-shaped appliqués of thinner leather, all six of which survive in part. This thinner leather is apparently of the same quality as a leather binding, 1.3 cm wide which is now incomplete but which must originally passed right around the perimeter of the greave. The stain or dye which originally coloured the thinner leather is mostly very faded but where protected, especially below the linen sewing thread, is a purplish dark red. This binding, together with other red leather bindings around items of scale armour from Dura, once again confirms that the red edging often shown on painted representations of linen armour records a binding of leather.[47]

Simon James, in his 2004 catalogue of the military equipment from Dura, has categorised this important object as the lining of a metal greave, rather than as a greave *per se*.[48] The present writer has not yet had the opportunity to examine the greave directly, but James's conclusion does not seem to take sufficient account of the fact that this unusual textile is very carefully and skilfully made. There is also no sign that it ever had any metal attached to it. On the contrary, the greave carries its own evidence of active use in the form of a diagonal cut over the knee area, surely caused by a sharp edge. This cut would not have occurred if the textile had simply been a lining. The cut penetrates the upper layer of the thick woven structure, but does not go right through it.

The greave was included in 1945 report on the Dura textiles, but the authors, Rudolf Pfister and Louisa Bellinger, remained uncertain about its woven structure.[49] They describe the weave as '2–2 / weft twill, irregular' and add that, 'because the surface is "felted", the technique is not easily seen'. But the more precise formation they give confirms the similarity with the Masada fragments: the greave is made of undyed linen, it is very compact and thick (0.5 cm), it is of limited size (44.2 × 27 cm), its yarns are composite (both systems reportedly S-spin, 6 Z-ply, that is sssssZ) and, where intact, the threads of one system completely cover the threads of the other system. (Pfister and Bellinger give 15 by 5 threads per cm; from the photographs, the writer calculates 18 by 7). Comparing photographs, the visual similarity with the non-carbonised fragment from Masada is particularly striking (Figs 6.1, 6.2 and 6.10). The presumption must be that the weave of the greave is also based upon twining,

45.   Kraeling 1956, panel NC 1 section C, 194–202, pl. LXXII.
46.   Connolly 1981, 59, 221, 305; Andronicos 1984, 145–146; Feugère 2002, 106.
47.   James 2004, nos 441, 448, 449, 450 and other examples not illustrated by James but included at http://ecatalogue. art.yale.edu .
48.   James 2004, no. 448, 128–9
49.   Pfister and Bellinger 1945, 59, no. 292, pl. XXX

though confirmation of its detailed structure must wait for a close examination of the object itself.

The most obvious difference between the Dura greave and the Masada fragments is the fact that the greave is quite elaborately shaped. Pfister and Bellinger give no information on an aspect that is key to understanding the technique, the form of the edges. But judging from the photographs, the edges of the textile itself are not cut but were selvedges of some form, though now badly worn. Although a leather binding was added to the edges after weaving, the thinness of the leather perhaps indicates that its function was more to give a smooth finish than to reinforce.

If made with woven selvedges rather than cut from a larger textile, the greave falls into the category of textiles identified by this writer as typifying production in Classical Antiquity, items that were "woven to shape", the best-known examples of this phenomenon being sleeved tunics and semi-circular cloaks.[50] In the case of the greave, approximately oval in shape, the creation of the curved outline would have involved firstly adding warp threads and afterwards casting them off. The very even texture of the greave suggests that this adding and subtracting of warp threads occurred at the perimeter of the web, and not, as in the slings discussed below, at various points across its width.

From other woven-to-shape textiles of the period, we know that weaving would have progressed in a strictly symmetrical manner, with the shaping on the left side of the web mirrored across a central vertical axis by shaping on the right. The greave's own axis of symmetry runs lengthways down the centre of the greave as worn, showing that this is also the direction of the warp. Pfister and Bellinger had interpreted the weave as weft-faced, but the threads lying on the surface of the weave in fact run in this lengthways directions. Looking back again to the Masada fragments, another important difference emerges: the weave of the greave must be warp-faced while the Masada fragments are weft-faced.

The slings discussed below also divide into weft-faced or warp-faced examples, with the earlier examples, those from Egypt, being in warp-faced warp twining. But in detail, the structure of the greave must be rather different from that of the slings, the surface appearance is very distinctive, with deep horizontal grooves reoccurring at a distance of c. 0.8 cm from each other and separated by, on the evidence of the photographs, three picks of weft binding with the warp in tabby.

What follows is hypothetical, being limited to what the writer can see in photographs and deduce from these. The photographs show one side of the greave only. As on the warp-faced slings, the likelihood is that grooves on the greave are formed by pairs of warp threads half-twisting on themselves, i.e. twining. The difference from the slings is that, between the grooves, the warp of the greave appears to bind in simple warp-faced tabby with the weft. It seems unlikely that this relatively fine tabby, a secondary structure, could have made up the full 0.5 cm thickness of the greave. What is probable therefore is that, between the grooves/twists, the structure is divided for a short distance into two layers.

Comparing the greave with the Tutankhamun slings, the difference in the weave seems to be as follows: in the slings, the weft apparently consists of a group of threads which was inserted together into the shed formed between the twists of the twined warp; in the greave, a group of weft threads, apparently six, seems to have been divided up to bind individually with individual warp threads and so forms, for the short distance between the warp twists, a 'doublecloth' structure. In detail, on the side of the greave photographed, this secondary weave appears to be warp faced simple tabby, with three picks of weft between each warp twist.

---

50. Granger-Taylor 2008; Granger-Taylor 1982.

The purpose of this special variation on a twined structure was probably to spread out the thick bundle of weft threads, so producing a smoother surface, less likely to catch the blade of an enemy than the ribbed surface normally associated with twining. The technique of the Masada fragments, a variety of weft twining, achieves a smooth surface by the simple device of staggering the twists, or 'binding points'. With warp twining, staggering the twists may have been a much more awkward procedure; the solution represented by the Dura greave may well have been more straightforward in practice.

Until it has been possible to examine the object itself, it would be misleading the show the presumed structure of the greave in a diagram. A future diagram would ideally show, alongside the ground weave, the form of the selvedges and the manner of adding and casting off the warp threads.

The Dura military equipment, unrivalled in its extent and completeness, also includes a number of examples of scale armour where the metal scales are still attached to their original support textiles.[51] Most of this material is also at Yale though the best known, the first of two remarkably complete horse trappers, described in early publications as 'Housing I', is in the National Museum, Damascus. All these finds date to the mid-3rd century AD.

With one exception, these support textiles were not described by Pfister and Bellinger in their 1945 textile catalogue though they wrote that the "lining of the horse armour will be dealt with in the publication of the armor".[52] It is disappointing, therefore, that in his 2004 volume on the Dura armour, James has not catalogued these textiles either. This then remains a study waiting to be done. For the meantime, using all the available photographs once again, it is possible to gain a good idea of the range of textiles used in this way.[53]

None of the Dura support textiles is apparently twined and the greave remains the only example of twined linen from Dura so far identified. The majority of of the support textiles are clearly of linen, but in terms of structure are in varieties of extended tabby weave, all more or less warp-faced. There are a number of examples of the simplest type of extended tabby, where warp and weft are of paired threads throughout.[54] Others have some sheds with larger groups of weft threads, forming three-dimensional 'self-stripes' or ribs.[55] In two examples, the thicker rib occurs in every other shed. In another, the outer layer of a double-layered support in a fragment thought to belong with Housing 1, there are pairs of ribs, the two ribs separated by two sheds of ground weft and the pairs reoccurring after about twenty sheds of ground.[56]

Some of these linen textiles in extended tabby weave are clearly quite thick, especially those with many ribs, but as structures they would have been much less firm and solid than the twined greave. The ribs may have had the primarily purpose of insulating rather than reinforcing, helping to keep the layer of scales away from the wearer's body, an important consideration in areas with very hot sun. The ribs may also have acted as guides for the attachment of the scales, ensuring that

51. James 2004, nos 437–9, 443–4, 449–450, 452.
52. Pfister and Bellinger 1945, 3.
53. The photographs on the Yale University Art Gallery website are invaluable and include some textile fragments with scales still attached (or *vice versa*) which cannot be identified in James's catalogue. When searching on http://ecatalogue.art. yale.edu, whether for armour or textiles, it is helpful to select 'Ancient Art' for the Department field and to write 'Syrian' for the Culture field, as well as filling in date and other fields as appropriate.
54. James, "accessory to 449" (Yale 1934–465), figs 75–76, lower layer; James 452 (Yale 1929–771), fig. 81; Yale 1933–713, 1938.5999.1156, 1938.5999.1245 and 1938.5999.1254.
55. James 445 (Yale number?), fig. 70; Yale 1938.5999.1289.
56. James, "accessory to 449" (Yale 1934–465), figs 75–76, upper layer.

the previously-prepared rows (at Dura, the scales were joined side to side by metal rivets), were sewn on to the support textile at equal distances from each other.

Two of the Dura support textiles are very different from the linens in extended tabby weave just described. These are in plain 2/2 twill, one with approximately equal numbers of warp and weft thread, and one much more warp-faced.[57] The former can almost certainly be matched with a separated fragment given to the Trocadero Museum in Paris and catalogued by Pfister in an appendix to the 1945 Dura textiles volume.[58] Pfister's entry describes a coarse 2/2 twill weave in "very coarse linen fibre", with six to seven Z-spun threads per cm in each direction. The photographs of the larger fragment of what must be the same textile show a rather fuzzy effect, more so than one would expect with linen, and it seems possible that this is a different plant fibre, perhaps hemp. Linen textiles in 2/2 twill have survived very rarely from the Roman period, especially in the Eastern Empire. Given the continued custom of using multiple threads to create thicker qualities of linen fabric, as seen in the extended tabbies just described, this twill textile, if really of linen, would also be exceptional on account of the thickness of its fibres and yarns.

As mentioned, at Masada, no textile has survived with scales still sewn to it, or indeed any other kind of metal attachment. Fragments of linen in extended tabby weave form a relatively large group at Masada, but examples of the plainest variety, with paired threads in warp and weft throughout, can often be identified as deriving from linen sacks. It is only those with thicker ribs which have a military air about them: fragment 1043–2189/2, for example, where sheds with paired weft threads alternate with sheds with groups of six threads, can be directly compared to two of the Dura support textiles; fragment 1039–206/1, with single threads in the warp and groups of 8 threads in every weft shed, has no direct parallel with Dura in terms of its structure but, in its abraded condition and greyish colour, stands apart from the fragments now identified as from sacks.[59]

The only textile from Masada with an undoubted military context is a "glue-soaked" fabric used as one layer in the shield fragment, 2050–11/4.[60] This textile occurs between the painted leather outer layer of the shield and the plywood board. The weave is warp-faced simple tabby with single threads, c. 15 per cm in the warp and 6.5 in the weft, both yarns S-spun. Although the textile itself is not especially thick, the fibres are noticeably coarse, and once again it seems possible that the material is not linen but some other bast fibre. In the future, it should be possible formally to identify the material.

Stiebel and Magness point out the similarity between the construction of this shield fragment and the description of the Roman *scutum* by Polybius, writing in the 2nd century BC.[61] In this passage, Polybius uses the noun *othonion* for the textile layer, a word usually translated into English in this context as 'canvas'. Unfortunately, the precise meaning of *othonion* remains unclear, and there is no definite connection between it and hemp.

---

57.   James 443 (Yale 1938.4106 and 4111), figs 68–69; James 438–439 (Yale 1934.464 and 1938.5999.1142), figs 63–64.

58.   Pfister and Bellinger 1945, 64, number Tr. 33–28. This fragment should have been with the group of Dura textiles transferred from the Musée de l'Homme to the to the new Musée du Quai Branly. With Sophie Desrosiers, I have there been able to look rapidly through a large group of textile fragments from Dura now at Quai Branly (general number 71.1934.72/1 etc.). Unfortunately, none of the current numbers correspond to '33–28' and there is certainly no linen textile in this group either in twill or in twining. Our thanks to Paz Nunias Regeiro and Marie-Laurence Bouvet of the Musée du Quai Branly for showing us this material.

59.   Sheffer and Granger-Taylor 1994, 175, number 32(A), fig. 34.

60.   Stiebel and Magness 2007, 16 and 21, number 2050–11/4–3, pls 19–20.

61.   Polybius, *Histories*, VI.23.3.

Other shield fragments from Masada, instead of textile, have a layer of fibre between the leather and wood. Stiebel and Magness have described this as "plant fibre (apparently date palm)" but sinew is surely much more likely.[62] The same construction, with fibre rather than textile, occurs as the commonest shield type at Dura-Europos.[63] Shield remains with a layer of textile were found at Vindonissa in Switzerland, a legionary site dating to 1st century AD.[64]

SLINGS IN WEFT OR WARP TWINING

Looking more broadly for parallels for the technique of the Masada fragments of twined linen, we find a number of slings where twining has been used to create the cradle, the structure at the centre of the sling onto which the sling-shot was placed.

One such sling was found in the 1930s at the site of Nessana, in the Negev desert, in the southwest of modern Israel.[65] Finds from Nessana belong mainly to the late Byzantine and early Islamic periods (6th–8th centuries AD), though material recovered in later excavations is noticeably varied in date.[66]

The Nessana sling is missing almost all of one cord and most of the second cord, but is relatively complete in the area of the kite-shaped cradle. This measures c. 12 cm long and just over 7 cm wide and is comparatively thick. It is made of two materials, a warp of unidentified plant fibre, twisted and plied, and a weft of plant material without twist, apparently rush or sedge.

Grace Crowfoot, in her report on the Nessana textiles and basketry, identifies the sling's technique as weft twining; essentially it has the same structure as the Masada linen fragments but with the addition of shaping. Another distinctive detail is that the warp from the twining carries on beyond the pointed ends of the cradle to become the sling's two cords. The shaping of the cradle was brought about by gradually increasing the number of warp elements up to a maximum of ten and then decreasing them again. This would have been achieved most simply by subdividing the two groups of warp threads destined to become the 2-ply cords, but it is also possible that extra warp threads were added during the work. On one face, the cradle has a little rim or up-stand around its perimeter: this effect, a direct result of the way that the weft elements turn around the selvedges, would have helped to prevent the sling-shot from slipping out too early.

Although humble in terms of its materials, this sling was carefully made. The geographer Strabo, writing around the end of the 1st century BC, refers to slings of rush used by the famous specialist sling-wielding soldiers from the Balearic Islands;[67] other materials for slings mentioned by Strabo are animal hair and sinew.

Probably first developed as a hunting and fighting weapon, slings have also had a very long history of use by pastoralists and farmers, who use them to herd their animals and to scare away predators

---

62. Stiebel and Magness 2007, 17–21, numbers IN 1039–139, L92, IN 1276–1785.
63. James (2004, 162) states that the fibre has not been identified: "it is most likely vegetable in nature, but could be shredded tendon" i.e. sinew.
64. Gansser-Burkhardt 1942, 73–89
65. Colt 1962, 59–60, with a technical report on the textiles and basketry by G. M. Crowfoot, and pl. XXV.17. The sling is now in the collection of the Israel Antiquities Authority, number 36–1446.
66. Notably, Baginski and Sheffer 2004, Textile 1, 216–217, with a design of birds within roundels, must date to around 1400 AD and perhaps derives from an intrusive burial; my thanks to Avigail Sheffer for showing me this material, now many years ago.
67. *Geography* III. 5, 1–3.

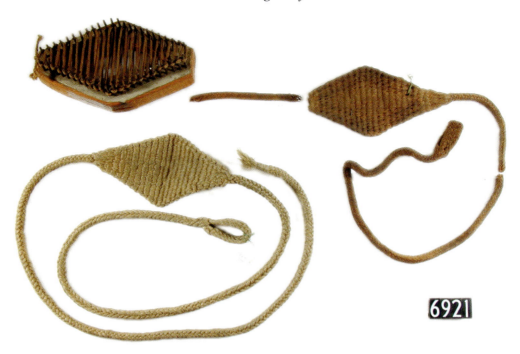

Figure 6.11. Sling from Lahun, Egypt, linen, warp twined, the width of the cradle c. 7 cm. The incomplete ancient sling is shown with a modern reproduction and a frame used to make the reproduction. Photograph Petrie Museum of Egyptian Archaeology, University College London.

and birds from their crops.[68] In Palestine, slings in weft twining were produced until recently and may still be being made. The method of making these modern Palestinian slings was also recorded by Grace Crowfoot.[69] Essentially it is the same as for the Nessana sling but the cords are made independently of the cradle; the threads for the cords are looped through the two ends of the cradle, after the cradle has been constructed.

Two finds of linen slings from Ancient Egypt bring us back to the world of military textiles. The best known Egyptian example was excavated by W. Flinders Petrie at Lahun in the Fayum region (Fig. 6.11). It is now in the Petrie Museum of Egyptian Archaeology, University College London.[70] The Lahun sling has been published several times, in the first place by Petrie himself, in his influential 1917 book, *Tools and Weapons*.[71] It was dated by Petrie on the basis of archaeological context to the Third Intermediate Period, around 800 BC. The dating is backed up firstly by the circumstance of its discovery together with an iron spearhead, placing it firmly in the Iron Age, and secondly by the "spliced-and-twisted" construction of its individual yarns, an early technique for making yarns

68.   Lindblom 1940.
69.   Crowfoot 1943, 85–6.
70.   Number UC 6921, reproduced on the Petrie Museum's own website as well as in the section in *Digital Egypt for Universities*, 'Textile Production and Clothing' by Hero Granger-Taylor and Stephen Quirke (2003), http://www. digitalegypt.ucl.ac.uk/lahun/ucarchivelahun/uc6921.gif
71.   Petrie 1917, 36, pls xliv. 15, li.15.

of linen, prevalent in the Bronze Age, which we believe went out of general use in Egypt in c. 600 BC.[72]

The sling is fragmentary and in relatively poor condition (the complete sling in Fig. 6.11 is a modern reproduction). Its cradle is again kite shaped and measures c. 7 cm across and 0.6 cm in thickness; when complete, its length would have been approximately 15 cm. One cord is missing entirely and, with it, one extremity of the cradle. The remaining cord is now broken into three sections but we know from the photograph in *Tools and Weapons* that it was intact when found and about 57 cm long (the arrangement in Fig. 6.11 is therefore not correct). This is the 'loop cord', which finishes at one end with a flat braided loop. According to estimates by Thom Richardson, the missing 'release cord' would also have been around 57 cm long, giving an overall original complete length of c. 127 cm.[73]

It is worth investigating the principles by which this sling was made, not least because it seems to be the key to understanding the technique of the Dura greave. In the photograph in Figure 6.11 the modern complete sling is a reproduction made by E. Martin Burgess. Burgess's reproduction is very well observed, but he almost certainly misunderstood the method of working. He interpreted the technique of the cradle as weft twining and the little frame also in the photograph is the device on which he laid out his 'warp' in preparation. Burgess's method is not in itself impossible and appears to have been followed by Richardson, though both report that it was "remarkably laborious". In fact, it is not far removed from the technique of a sling from Tibet published by Peter Collingwood: in the Tibetan example, the lengthways threads which sit on the surface of the cradle were added by needle to a series of threads previously stretched between the cords forming the cradle's outline.[74]

Almost certainly the technique of the cradle of the Lahun sling is neither weft twining nor darning but warp twining;[75] In this case, the structure is of the simplest kind, with pairs of warp threads half twisting on themselves after each weft unit. Because the technique is warp twining, it is the warp threads not the weft threads which form the surface of the cradle.

As with the Nessana example, the majority of the warp threads continue into the two cords. In the Lahun sling, the shaping of the cradle is at least partly created by adding warp elements to the basic continuous threads. On the sling as it now survives, the broken end of the cradle, just in from where the second cord should have begun, is the point where the first group of additional warp threads joins the structure; these added warp elements are spaced out between the warp threads which continue as the cords.

The yarns of the Lahun sling are once again composite, as with the Masada fragments and the Dura greave. The warp yarn is Z-plied from a number of S-spliced-and-twisted threads, apparently four (ssssZ). In the cords this composite yarn is additionally S-plied (ssssZZS) and these S-plied threads are used paired to make the square sennit (or senate) of which the cords consist (according to Burgess and Richardson this is a 10-thread sennit).

The yarn used for the weft of the cradle, invisible except at the selvedges, appears also to have the additional S-ply. According to Burgess, these weft threads are also double, with one thread inserted

72. Quirke and Spencer, 1992, 166; Granger-Taylor, 1998a, 106.
73. Richardson 1998, 46. Richardson also discusses slinging techniques. Much additional information is available at www.slinging.org
74. Collingwood, 1998, 52–3, no. 26.
75. Seiler-Baldinger, 1994, 31, in principle the technique is as shown in figure 58c but with the diagram turned on its side.

each shed from either side. Burgess's observations are supported by the low number of sheds per cm. When the second cord was *in situ*, there would have been a total of 25 weft sheds in a complete length of around 15 cm, that is, approximately 1.7 double weft picks per cm. In contrast, there are between 15 and 19 pairs of twisted warp thread per cm. The densely-spaced warp threads combined with the thick double weft threads results in a warp-faced texture with strongly defined weft ribs.

There is potentially much more that could be said about the woven structure of this finely made object. It would be good to record the form of the selvedges as well as the order and manner in which the supplementary warp threads were added and afterwards cast off. Unfortunately, the brittle condition makes this sort of detailed analysis almost impossible.

One feature not included by Burgess in his reproduction is the four rows of small holes or piercings which run parallel to the edges of the cradle (the inner row is approximately 1.8 cm from the selvedges). The holes retain within them the dark residue of a protein-like material, perhaps the remains of a thread made of gut or sinew. The purpose of the stitching may have been, on its own, to reinforce the edges of the sling. More likely, it attached a leather binding similar in principle to the leather binding on the Dura greave and the linen binding on the second pair of Tutankhamun slings.

The other Egyptian find is two pairs of slings from among goods in the tomb of Tutankhamun, the 18th Dynasty pharaoh who died aged perhaps 19 in around 1327 BC. The writer has not examined either of these herself. The first pair is relatively well known and was briefly mentioned in the publication of the discovery tomb of Tutankhamun.[76] The function of the second pair has not previously been recognised: it was interpreted by the excavator, Howard Carter, as possibly a belt. There is apparently no detailed or technical study of either pair, published or unpublished. But Carter's manuscript notes and sketches are available on the website of the Griffith Institute, as are excavation photographs by Harry Burton.[77]

The first pair was found inside the chest numbered 585. Carter's original manuscript catalogue reads: "585 y. Pair of finely plaited (linen) string slings for hurling stones. (Badly perished)".[78] Carter's assessment of the condition of this pair may have been unduly pessimistic and a colour photograph reproduced at www.slinging.org (without attribution but probably comparatively recent), shows these slings in relatively good shape, apparently on display in the Egyptian Museum, Cairo.[79]

The second Tutankhamun pair can be recognized in a photograph of the interior of the very famous War and Hunting chest, numbered 21 by Carter. In two photographs of the interior of the chest by Harry Burton, this pair is lying amongst clothing, shoes and jewellery, a heap we know to have contained very interesting textiles but in tantalizingly poor condition.[80] Figure 6.12 here is a detail of the photograph used for plate XXV.C in the original publication. The following photograph in the publication, plate XXV.D, shows the interior of the chest after further unpacking. In this second photograph, the cords of the slings are more visible, but not for their complete length, and the cradle on the right has already lost the binding from its right side. In his notes, Carter records finding the "belt" or slings "folded in" with a "garment", this being 21x, a textile with sequins and shaped

---

76. Carter, 1933, 120–1 and pl. LXXII.A

77. My thanks to the staff of the Griffith Institute for pointing out the records relating to the second pair of Tutankhamun slings,

78. http://www.griffith.ox.ac.uk/gri/carter/585y.html.

79. Egyptian Antiquities Organization 1982, 320, no. 1084. At the website www.slinging.org, this photograph is image 29 out of 32 (see 4 and 23) in the pre-Roman page of the Image Gallery section.

80. Carter and Wace, 1923, 165–172, pls XXXIV–XXXV.

and embroidered to resemble bird wings which Carter believed to have been a headdress. Gillian Vogelsang-Eastwood is surely correct however in showing such an object as worn by the pharaoh over his shoulders.[81]

Carter does not specifically mention in his notes the condition of the second pair of slings but records that the find was "sprayed with solution of celluloid in acetone", presumably to consolidate it. Poor condition may be the reason this pair has apparently never been exhibited in Cairo and the Griffith Institute has no record of a museum number for it.

Carter's manuscript description of the second pair is principally as follows: "21 kk. Belt? consisting of two and part of a third flat pieces (as per sketch) of very thick tapestry woven cloth, joined by thick cords 4 cm [sic] in diam. Edges bound with plain cloth, 5 mm. wide, overlapping each side. Design of cloth apparently small squares of different coloured threads."[82] Comparing this description with Carter's two sketches and with the photographs it is possible to interpret the two "flat pieces" as the cradles and the " part of a third" as the loop which is broken in this case but which, as on the Lahun sling, must be in the form of a flat braid finishing off the loop cord.

Figure 6.12. Pair of slings among other objects in the War and Hunting Chest from the Tomb of Tutankhamun, probably warp-twined linen, the cradles each c. 14 × 7 cm. Detail of photograph by Harry Burton (no. 0086), Griffith Institute, University of Oxford.

Carter does not give measurements for the first pair, but his smaller annotated sketch of the second informs us that each cradle measures 7 cm across and 14 cm long. The diameter of 4 cm he gives for the cords was surely a mistake for 4 mm. These measurements are very close to the Lahun sling.

In terms of their overall construction, the two pairs of slings differ from each other only in that the cradles of the second pair have a binding, "the plain cloth, 5 mm. wide, overlapping each side". The binding is clearly visible in the photograph (Fig. 6.12) and, on each cradle, is evidently in the form of two lengths of tape, each folded around one edge of the cradle and originally extending to cover the beginning of one cord. The tape is held down with one or perhaps two rows of stitching.

81. Vogelsang-Eastwood, 1999, 28–9 (a second pair of wings) and 103; Vogelsang-Eastwood has not published the slings.
82. http://www.griffith.ox.ac.uk/gri/carter/021kk-c021kkll.html and http://www.griffith.ox.ac.uk/gri/carter/021kk-c021kk.html

The most interesting fact recorded in Carter's sketch of the second pair is that the two cords leading from the top of the two cradles at a distance of about 20 cm join together and become one. In the photographs this join must be hidden by the layers of other textile. In the sketch it is not completely clear which category this united cord belonged to, loop or release. But it is probably safe to deduce that it was the loop cord. The two cords leading from the bottom of the cradles, by deduction, must be release cords. The end of one of the release cords, apparently knotted on itself, is visible in Figure 6.12, lying just above the loose knot of cords towards the bottom of the image.

This is not the place to investigate the feasibility of using two slings joined together; we must presume that this was something that an experienced slinger was able to do, if not necessarily Tutankhamun himself. But the fact that the slings are joined in this way explains why the Tutankhamun examples have been preserved in pairs. In the photographs of the first pair it is not possible to see whether two cords join at any point. The cords are broken in a number of places. But it may be significant that in the original photograph only one loop is present.

We can gain an idea of the technique of the Tutankhamun slings by comparing them to the Lahun sling and to other finds from Tutankhamun's tomb. As with the Lahun sling, the surface of the cradles is marked by strong horizontal ribs with deep groves between and we can be sure that here again the technique is warp-faced. There is no doubt that twining would have created a structure with optimum stability. But it is just possible that the technique is warp-faced tabby. A textile from the same chest in Tutankhaumn's tomb as the second pair of slings, the tunic collar, 21o, a comparatively narrow band shaped during weaving into a flat circle, is also thick with very marked weft ribs. But in the collar the weave is apparently tabby.[83] Whether in tabby or twined, Tutankhamun's slings appear to be made with relatively fine threads in the warp, and from the photographs it is not possible to be certain whether they are composite or single. The weft, clearly much thicker than the warp, must consist of a large group of individual threads which may or may not have been twisted together.

The shaping of the cradles of Tutankhamun's slings seems to have been achieved in principle as with Lahun sling, that is, by taking the threads forming, or due to form, the cords, and adding extra warp elements as required. Evidence of the method actually followed is provided by the decoration of the first pair, where, in the original photograph, the right-hand cradle can be seen to have concentric almond-shaped zones of colour as follows: a dark outer zone; a narrow intermediate zone of alternate light and dark ribs; a dark central zone. Since the structure is warp-faced and these zones were created by warp threads of different colour, we must assume that extra warp threads were added and then subtracted along the centre line itself. In other words, the added threads do not appear to have been introduced at intervals across the width of the fabric, as was the case with the Lahun sling, or at the edge of the web, apparently the method with the Dura greave.

The handling of the threads of the Tutankhamun slings appears to have been especially skilled. In addition to the almond-shaped outline, in contrast to the Lahun sling's kite shape, the cradles have a definite three-dimensional bowl-like form, both these effects surely being intentional. A consequence of the cradles' concave shape is that they have a tendency to fold on themselves: in the photograph of the second pair, the left hand cradle is folded lengthways down the centre line (Fig. 6.12). In the original photograph of the first pair, both cradles are folded horizontally on themselves and the left cradle has folded on itself additionally along the vertical axis.[84]

83. Vogelsang-Eastwood, 1999, 25–26, 31. The shaping of this textile was brought about by returning some of the picks back to the selvedge on the outside of the curve before they had travelled right across the width of the textile to the selvedge on the inside of the curve.

84. Carter 1933, pl. LXXII.A. In the coloured photograph at www.slinging.org they are opened out but do not lie flat.

The photograph at www.slinging.org of the first pair does not reproduce the colours or the patterning of the cradles well; their surface seems to have become rubbed or damaged. However, it does show clearly the colour on the cords, where there are chevrons of undyed, red and black threads: the chevron pattern tells us that the structure of the cords is a sennit, as with the Lahun sling. In the original black and white photos, it is not possible to distinguish the black from the red threads. In the dark zones of the cradles of the first pair the ribs might have been coloured black and red alternately.

In twining, as in 'faced' tabby weaves, by using pairs of thread where one thread is one colour and the other another colour, it is very easy to create lines of colour in the direction of the threads that are hidden, in this case the weft. By staggering the bi-coloured pairs of thread a chequered pattern is also very simply produced. The design on the second pair of Tutankhamun slings is described by Carter as "apparently small squares of different coloured threads", an effect just about possible to make out in the photograph (Fig. 6.12).[85]

Some of the warp-faced bands from high-status Egyptian burials use several colours to create geometric patterns in a variation of tabby which can be called 'compound'. The collar mentioned above is probably one of these, and we know from the structural analysis by Peter Collingwood that the girdle "of Ramses III", now in Liverpool, is definitely of this type.[86] It seems unlikely that the slings' cradles are patterned to this extent; from what is visible in the photographs, no more than two colours were used at once in a single section of warp.

The decoration of small squares on the second pair of slings recalls a detail on a famous Greek vase painting by Sosias, of c. 500 BC, shows a scene from the Trojan War where Achilles is bandaging the arm of the wounded Patroclus.[87] Achilles' body armour is mainly covered by scales. But the *pteryges*, obviously of textile, have a small chequered pattern surely created with contrasting colours of yarn, presumably of linen. Since linen in Antiquity was seldom dyed, and difficult to dye any colour other than blue or brown, the implied use of colour here serves to emphasise the specialness of the object: at Patroculus's request, Achilles later lent this armour to Patroclus who was then killed in battle by Hector, Hector having mistaken the wearer for Achilles himself.

OTHER 'COMPOSITE' THREADS AND ROPES OF LINEN

Before leaving Egypt it is worth considering the ancient references discussed by Margarita Gleba which record the dedication to Greek temples of two linen corselets by King 'Amasis', the Greek name for the Egyptian Pharaoh Ahmose II, reigned 570–526 BC. The first occurs in the *Histories* of Herodotus (III, 47), where, writing in the 5th century BCE, the author describes the corselet given by Amasis to Sparta; it was "of linen, and had a vast number of figures of animals inwoven into its fabric, and was likewise adorned with gold and cotton. What is most worthy of admiration in it is that each of the threads, although fine, contains within it three hundred and sixty threads, all of them clearly visible. The corselet which Amasis gave to the temple of Minerva in Lindus is just such another."[88]

The second reference occurs in Pliny's *Natural History*, where he reports that by his time, the 1st century AD, the corselet given by Amasis to the temple at Lindus on Rhodes survived only as

---

85. Carter's use of the term "tapestry woven cloth" is technically incorrect.
86. Collingwood 1982, 407–411.
87. Illustrated for example in Fich *et al.* 1999, fig. 160; Connolly 1981, 57.
88. Translated by George Rawlinson, *Internet Classics Online*, edited by HG-T.

"small remants"; it had been reduced to this state because of the curiosity of people visiting the temple. But Pliny's correspondent was able to provide confirmation that "each thread consists of 365 threads".[89]

These huge numbers of constituent individual threads, 360 and 365, seem at first incredible. Nevertheless, they might have been achieved if the separate threads were made by the old method of splicing and twisting. This method can result in much finer threads than draft spinning, the technique which replaced it; a team led by Bill Cooke found threads with diameters as low as 35 micrometers among Ancient Egyptian textiles of royal provenance.[90] Because this older method involved processing the fibre stem by stem, and not at any point collecting together unprocessed fibre, the difficulty was not so much making fine threads as thick ones. The method used by the Ancient Egyptians to make ropes out of linen was therefore to group together very many of the separately-produced threads into thick composite yarns.

This is illustrated by a piece of rope from Lahun, again in the Petrie Museum, the date in this case being around 1850 BC.[91] This short length of rope is made of two groups of S-twisted threads, the groups being first Z-twisted on themselves and then S-plied together. Each group consists of around 135 separate threads so that the total number in the plied rope is around 270. This rope fragment has become relatively thick where it has been allowed to untwist. But in the areas where it is still tightly twisted together the total diameter is only c. 1 cm.

The individual threads in the Lahun rope are not noticeably fine. If finer individual threads were used, as no doubt was the case with the armour dedicated by King Amasis, the composite threads in the finished corselets need have been no thicker than the warp threads of the Masada armour fragment 1039–764/**13**, at c. 2–2.2 mm each, and might have been considerably thinner.

The following calculations[92] are based on individual threads with the following diameters:

a) 35 μm – the diameter of the finest threads found by Cooke and team
b) 70 μm – twice as thick as **a**)
c) 105 μm – three times as thick as **a**)

Making three circular bundles of 360 threads from **a**) **b**) and **c**) and compacting them to the extent that there are no gaps between the individual threads would give minimum diameters for the bundles as follows:

a) 664.1 μm
b) 1328.2 μm
c) 1992.2 μm.

If the bundles were not compacted but the individual threads were just allowed to find their way into the most space-saving lattice, the diameters would be

a) 720.3 μm
b) 1440.6 μm
c) 2160.9 μm.

In reality, the group of 360 individual threads would not just have been bundled together but would

89. *Natural History* XIX, II.14.
90. Cooke, El-Gammal and Brennan 1991.
91. Granger-Taylor 1998b; the number is UC 7508 iii; http://www.digitalegypt.ucl.ac.uk/lahun/ucarchivelahun/uc7250_7505IV_7508III.gif .
92. Calculations by Alfie Granger-Howell.

have been twisted to form a composite yarn. If the 360 threads lay in the twisted composite yarn at an angle of 20° from the vertical, by using trigonometry (taking the hypotenuse of a triangle where the adjacent side equals the diameter without twist), we could reasonably expect a wider maximum diameter as follows:

a) 766.5 μm
b) 1533.1 μm
c) 2299.6 μm.

Allowing for the fact that in practice the individual threads would be compacted to a certain extent, estimated diameters could be as follows:

a) 35 μm threads × 360 giving a twisted composite yarn of 0.65–0.765 mm diameter
b) 70 μm threads × 360 giving a twisted composite yarn of 1.315–1.53 mm diameter
c) 105 μm threads × 360 giving a twisted composite yarn of 1.98–2.3 mm diameter

All three of these composite threads would obviously be well within the limits of what could feasibly be used to make twined linen armour.

Although the technique of 'splicing and twisting' seems to have survived for longer in Egypt than elsewhere, on the evidence of textiles which can be independently dated, it appears to have disappeared from ordinary Egyptian textiles in around 600 BC, that is, before the reign of Amasis in the mid-6th century BC.[93] But the technique might well have continued for textiles of special importance or requiring special qualities. The tradition of using composite threads in linen armour, embodied in the Masada fragments and the Dura greave, no doubt predates the application of draft spinning to linen and goes back to the time of spliced and twisted yarn production, when it was evidently common practice to use composite threads when making thicker woven structures.

The corselet donated by Amasis sounds, from Herodotus's description, to have to have been Greek in style, even if probably made from Egyptian linen. A statement elsewhere by Herodotus, implying that the Egyptians themselves were a source of innovation in armour design, need not necessarily be taken as applying to armour made of linen: this is Herodotus's claim that the Persians "wear the Egyptian corselet in war".[94] It is true that, by this period the Egyptians were exporting linen as well as producing it in large quantities. But there is no direct evidence for the use of linen armour within Egypt and the only kind of armour we can specifically associate with the Egyptians is scale armour.[95]

WEFT AND WARP TWINING: PRACTICAL CONSIDERATIONS AND ORIGINS

Twining is usually defined as a form of weaving since it normally uses both a warp and a weft. The warp, although manipulated without heddles and usually open-ended, can also be attached to a loom-like frame.[96] Alternatively, twining can be considered to be a branch of plaiting and has

---

93. Granger-Taylor 1998a, 106.
94. Herodotus *Histories*, I, 135
95. For the limited evidence for amour in Egypt see Yadin 1963 a, 196–197 and 241; see also Spalinger 2005 and Shaw 1991.
96. Burnham 1981, 177, 186–189.

been categorized as such by Annemarie Seiler-Baldinger.[97] In the early history of textiles, twining undoubtedly preceded the development of tabby ('plain') weave. Tabby depends in principle on the use of heddles and one impetus behind the development of heddles must have been the desire to weave thinner cloths than was possible while employing twining.[98]

In Western Asia, tabby weave seems to have first occurred around 7,000 BC.[99] But, as so often the case with older techniques, twining must still have been considered the best structure for certain types of textile, in particular those where thickness and relative rigidity was a positive advantage. Archaeological and ethnographic examples of twining include, for example, rugs or mats made to be used on uneven or stony ground;[100] head bands with which to carry heavy loads;[101] the upper parts of shoes to be worn through dry but thorny scrub.[102] In Western Asia, Egypt and the Mediterranean region, people must have also continued to consider twining the best structure for some armour and slings.

Twining is most easy to carry out when the yarns are comparatively stiff, particularly the yarn used for the passive threads around which the twined threads twist. This is seen for example in traditional Chilkat cloak weaving where a weft of animal fibre is twined around rather stiff warp threads made from vegetable fibre and attached only at the upper end to the frame or 'loom'.[103] Where both 'warp' and 'weft' are stiff, we must define the craft and product as basketry, and indeed weft twining is still used extensively for baskets.

Warp twining as a technique is more baffling than weft twining when viewed from a modern perspective.[104] But this does not mean it was little used. It could have been made more convenient by some arrangement we no longer know about. In particular, it might be worth considering whether the kidney shaped clay weights found in some Late Neolithic contexts were used for warp twining.[105]

Some narrower constructions in warp twining may over time have begun to be made in ply-split braiding, a technique where warp threads made of previously-plied yarn are pierced by 'weft' elements threaded on a needle, and by tablet weaving.[106] When looking at archaeological finds, we should, however, not assume ply-splitting or tablet-weaving was the method used when it is just one possible technique among others. The women's belts with chevron patterning traditional to Palestine have the same structure as diagonal ply-split braiding. But, as recorded by Grace Crowfoot, they are actually made by a diagonal variant of warp twining.[107] These warp twined belts, considered together with a rich variety of weft twining confirm how important twining has been in the traditional textiles of the Palestine/Israel region.

---

97.   Seiler-Baldinger 1994, 31–32.

98.   Albers 1965, 54–56.

99.   Barber 1991, 126–128; Barber correctly documents the first appearance of tabby but without discussing its relationship to twining.

100. Crocker Jones 1989, 49–50 and cover photograph; Collingwood 1998, 72–73, no. 42, believed by Collingwood to be weft-twined but possibly warp-twined.

101. Collingwood 1998, 86–87, believed by Collingwood to be ply-splitting, but perhaps warp-twining with three warp elements, like the Zulu mat Collingwood also publishes, 91–92, no. 53.

102. Zhao 2008, 89. This hemp shoe is in the British Museum, no. MAS.810, and, at the time of writing, photographs and a catalogue description can be found in the Museum's 'Search the Collection' database.

103. Albers 1965, 55, pl. 66; Burnham 1981, 188–9

104. See Collingwood 1982, 402, for a brief account of warp twining by throwing the warp across the weft.

105. Feldtkeller 2003.

106. Collingwood 1998; this technique includes 'ply-split darning', with a straight warp and a separate weft, as well as the better-known 'ply-split braiding', with only one set of threads used diagonally; Collingwood 1982.

107. Crowfoot 1943, 80–82, pl. IV.3–5.

Among the examples of twined linen examined in this article, the Dura greave emerges as an important but late example of warp twining. If warp twining had played a more important role in earlier periods, it is worth thinking how it itself had arisen, and what had influenced the preference for of a warp-faced technique at the very early period when warp twining must first have been used.

The close connection between twining and basketry has already been mentioned. It is worth considering whether warp twining had grown out of another technique almost exclusively associated with basketry, namely 'coiling', the basketry technique which gave rise to coiled pottery.[108] In coiling, as in warp twining, the active elements lie lengthways over the passive elements and in many examples more or less cover them. In some coiling, the active element is made of fibres that have been twisted together, essentially a yarn.

A remarkable instance of coiling using an active element that is twisted and plied is the armour that was made until modern times on the pacific islands of Kiribati.[109] Figure 6.13 shows a set of armour from Kiribati.[110] The material throughout is coconut fibre (coir) and the technique of the yarns is the oldest known type, 'simultaneous twisting and plying'.[111] The limb protection employs such a yarn in a looping technique. The body armour and helmet are in wrapped coiling, the active

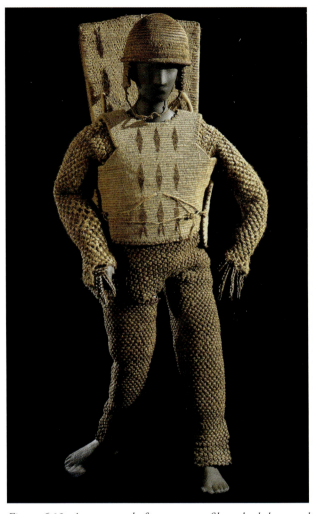

Figure 6.13. Armour made from coconut fibre, the helmet and body armour in coiling. Kiribati, Micronesia, late 19th century AD. Photograph © Trustees of the British Museum.

element a yarn of twisted and plied fibres and the passive element a simple bundle of fibres.[112] The helmet is constructed like a basket, from a continuous coil. In contrast, the body armour is made as a flat piece, shaped around the edges and eventually folded over at the shoulders; a second layer is created for the extension at the back of the neck. In the body amour, the 'passive' element, instead

---

108. Seiler-Baldinger 1994, 32–36.

109. My thanks to Jill Hasell of the British Museum for showing me the Kiribati armour and relevant literature.

110. British Museum AOA 1938.10–1.66; AOA Q72.Oc.100a; AOA 1973; AOA 1914.L.1.22c; AOA +5788.

111. Granger-Taylor 1998a, 105–106; in Egypt and Western Asia, yarns made by simultaneous twisting and plying were used before the development of yarns made by splicing and twisting.

112. As inSeiler-Baldinger 1994, 33, fig. 62b.

of continuously coiling, is turned back at the extremities of the piece, so forming a selvedge in the manner of a textile weft.

In its springy rigidity, with one layer tied down over the other, the Kiribati body armour is reminiscent of representations in ancient art of the corselets almost certainly made of twined linen. For example, a similar springiness is indicated on a red-figure Attic amphora in Munich, where Hector is shown putting on his plain linen corselet.[113] Hector braces his arms to bend the corselet around his body. The corselet's shoulder pieces, not yet fastened down, stand up vertically behind his head.

It is even possible that equipment made by coiling was still in use in military contexts in the Greek and Roman world. A fragment found at Didymoi may be evidence of this. Didymoi is a small fort in the Eastern Desert of Egypt, garrisoned by Roman auxiliaries, where many textiles of a military character have already been identified.[114] The fragment of coiling, with a curved structure and measuring approximately 5 × 7 cm, has not yet been fully studied but has been well photographed.[115] The active element is a composite yarn apparently of linen, S-plied from perhaps four Z-spun individual threads (?zzzzS). The passive element appears to be strips of a bamboo-like material and is obviously rigid.

The Didymoi fragment, very similar in technique and appearance to the Kiribati helmets, might not be part of a helmet as such but perhaps is from a rigid cap worn below a helmet: this could have insulated the wearer's head from metal liable to become very hot and at the same time served to diffuse any blows. In the red-figure vase painting by Sosias mentioned earlier, depicting Achilles tending the wounded Patroclus, Patroclus has taken off his helmet and is shown wearing a plain cap with concentric markings which could well have been made by coiling.[116]

---

113. Reproduced Fich *et al.,* fig. 148.
114. Cardon 2002.
115. D98.2408.1, unpublished.
116. Reproduced Fich *et al.,* fig. 160.

7. A LATE ROMAN PAINTING OF AN EGYPTIAN OFFICER AND THE LAYERS OF ITS PERCEPTION. ON THE RELATION BETWEEN IMAGES AND TEXTILE FINDS

Annette Paetz gen. Schieck

PRELIMINARIES

Thinking of today's military, categorisations of uniforms such as gala and combat dress come to the mind as well as classifications of ranks symbolized by stars and stripes. Thinking of the Roman army the use of occasional dress has to be assumed and the employment of uniforms is widely accepted but the antique sources, and in particular the textile remains of Roman military context, are rare.[1] Those soldiers who died in the battle at Dura Europos in 256 AD and the Late Roman mummy of the so far unexamined *centurion romain* stored in the *Musée de l'Homme* at Paris, also dated to the mid 3rd Century AD, have to be taken as exceptions and still deserve investigation.[2] It is the aim of this paper to correlate a Late Roman Egyptian painting with archaeologically preserved textiles in order to suggest a reconstruction of an officer's uniform and its symbols of rank woven in. Until now classifications of the organic materials such as the textiles, their decoration, and the quality of their material, have never been taken into account when dealing with differentiations among Roman soldiers. A very unique decoration of arrow-shaped clavi and a pyramid-shaped shoulder-ornament will be introduced, appearing to have served as symbols of this kind in the very late 2nd and 3rd Century AD. Deriving from the Near Eastern regions of Egypt and Syria it spread out North quickly (Fig. 7.1).[3]

INTRODUCTION

Images serve as transmitters of sociological information. Especially in Antiquity many of them derive from funerary art, being created to remind of the deceased, and to inform the passer-by about the

---

1. James 1999, 19.
2. Gayet 1904, 4; Calament 2005, 32 fig. 32b; 389 *vitrine 25* (footn. 403: "… La momie de centurion aurait été attribuée au Muséum de Lyon, d'après un projet de préparation, 1902 (Archives nationales) mais elle est aujourd'hui au musée de l'Homme, laboratoire s'anthropologie (MH = 23.714)."); 546. The mummy is dated to the mid 3rd Century AD. It is covered by a shroud and bound with crossing textile bands in a diamond pattern. Two bands carry a Greek inscription, telling the name and title of the deceased. It would be of great interest to examine this mummy, the layers of the garments, shrouds, and the inscription in order to gain a better knowledge about Egyptian burials of Roman soldiers, especially in regard of possible grave goods and *insignia*.
3. See also James 1999, 18–19.

individual. They present him or her in the most positive way: as rich and successful, of high social rank, of free or freed status, of a certain profession and education, within a familial constellation, of an ethnic and regional provenance, and of a religious affiliation. Signs, symbols and codes as well as easily accessible metaphors deriving from common knowledge are employed, decipherable by observers of a certain regional and cultural background.[4] Inscriptions quite often supplement information, but still the main vehicle is the image. It highly depends on the skills of the artist, the material he worked with, the state of preservation, and the local pictorial tradition, of how high the degree of reliance especially concerning information on textiles is to be estimated. Regarding dress, it is the cut and shape of a garment, as well as the look, drapery, and shine of its material that determines the quality of cloth. These aspects are mainly detectable by grip, weaving technique, and the shades of colour, which are barely presentable in pictorial sources.

Due to the special climatic conditions, textiles have not been the only organic materials that survived in the Near East. Numerous paintings like the Egyptian mummy portraits and shrouds, and the frescoes of the Luxor-temple and Dura Europos have been preserved in great quality (Fig. 7.3). These colourful presentations transmit detailed information on dress ensembles, and give an idea of the symbolic function of colour, combined with characteristic and individual features of persons, given in a naturalistic or even realistic manner.[5] Such an image is the painted shroud from Luxor, Egypt, depicting a Roman officer, dating to the first third of the 3rd Century AD (Fig. 7.1).[6] Great care has been taken to give manifold information on the identity and status of the person. The painting was created for funerary purposes, as such being part of the Egyptian tradition of the mummification practise in Roman times and Late Antiquity. This product marks a perfect merge of local traditions and Hellenistic and Roman influences, being an authentic creation of Hellenized Egypt in Roman times.

THE SHROUD OF A ROMAN OFFICER AT LUXOR (EGYPT) *(Fig. 7.1)*

The rectangular piece of textile bears the portrait bust of a young man; the body is given from the head to the pelvis. The canvas consists of a linen weave, which appears to have been made in tabby but has not yet been analysed in terms of the weaving technique. The edges seem to be original and the textile is almost complete, except of the lower left corner that was cut out or ripped off.[7] The

---

4.   For instance: the *kline*, tripod tables, glass-bottles and other vessels, etc. See Petrie 1927, 45–48 pl. XL no. 6, 7, 9, 11, 12, 14, for wooden parts of furniture; see also online database of the Petrie Museum (www.ucl.ac.uk/museums/petrie).

5.   Whether these portraits have been painted during lifetime, or if they have been made of after death and for funerary purposes only, is still being discussed. (See Borg 1996, 191–195; Borg 1998, 34–45; 67–68; Schenke 2001; Walker 1997). The author considers most of the mummy portraits as paintings of living people, having been made for persons of a certain social status and at a certain phase in life. See Paetz gen. Schieck 2010, 81–98.

6.   Inv. no. J. 194/Q 1512 – Parlasca 1981, 186–187, no. 290 fig. 154; 194 pl. XV; Parlasca 1999, 23–48, esp. 39 fig. 31; Parlasca 2003, 63 no. 763 pl. 171,1; Cat. Luxor 1978, 113 no. 290; for colour image see Aubert and Cortopassi 1998/1999, 16 fig. 1; ink drawing see Sumner 2009, 136 no. 65 fig. 98. According to L. H. Corcoran the shroud suffered from water damage (Corcoran 1995, 69–70). – See also Paetz gen. Schieck 2011, 81–98.

7.   Thanks to the mounting of the painted shroud inv. no. I.1 a 5749 of the Pushkin Museum Moscow in the exhibition *Ägypten Griechenland Rom. Abwehr und Berührung*', Städtisches Kunstinstitut und Städtische Gallerie Frankfurt a. M., Nov. 25, 2005–Feb. 26, 2006 (See cat. no. 300 = Borg 1998, 66 no. 80; Parlasca and Seemann 1999, 25 fig. 2), the author had the chance to have a close look at the canvas. It consists of linen, woven as tabby, still has four original selvedges, of which the lower horizontal selvedge is strengthened by insertion of several doubled weft threads. The selvedge itself closes in fringes. Mending can be found at the left hand of the main figure (about 10 cm) and above his right shoulder. Underlying sketches become visible, carried out with black paint.

painted area measures 85.5 cm in height and 70.5 cm in width, an undecorated framing zone of about 5 cm is added to it.

The painting is said to have been found in the Thebaid at Deir el-Medineh opposite to Luxor/Thebes on the West bank of the Nile.[8] No information about the finding context is known, but Klaus Parlasca – who was the first to publish the extraordinary object – assumes that it was found in one of the grave chambers of pharaonic magistrates that have been reused in Roman times.[9] Even though the information is rare, it is obvious, that the painted sheet served as a decorative cover of a mummy, having been one of the outer layers of the humanoid package, the face being positioned right on top of the head.[10] In general, the gender and age of the depicted and that of the deceased is concordant.[11] The mummified body may have been dressed; for sure it has been wrapped in linen bands and covered by linen sheets, being decorated and enclosed by the shroud. Fragments of an undecorated linen tabby cloth are spread about the painting sticking to the forehead, the right part of the neck, his

Figure 7.1. Painted shroud of a Roman officer, Luxor Museum © B. V. Bothmer and K. Parlasca.

right elbow and the body of one of the painted statuettes. They have the brownish colour of aged linen, and show the same structure of the weave having been arranged diagonally to the body.[12] Stains of aged paints and two blackish areas of oval shape seem to derive from substances that secreted from the mummified body and permeated into the shroud, located next to the left cheek and the right shoulder of the depicted, miscolouring the lower part of the cheek, the chin, and the shoulder.

---

8.   Maxfield 2000, 420. The site hosted a Roman garrison from Roman times on.

9.   Parlasca 1981, 186–187, no. 290 fig. 154; 194 pl. XV.

10.   Filer 1999, esp. 83–85. See for instance Walker and Bierbrier 1997, 41–42 no. 15; 108–111 no. 103, 105; 114–115 no. 110; 118–120 no. 114, 116; 149–150 no. 166; 160–161 nos 180–181. General remarks: Borg 1996, 177–178; Parlasca 1966.

11.   *Demetrius* is an exemption to this rule. The portrait depicts a man in his middle ages; the mummy belonged to a man who died in the age of about 90. Filer 1997, esp. 122; Filer 1999, 79–86.

12.   Several portrait mummies are covered by an undecorated linen shroud sparing the face. See for instance Parlasca and Seemann 1999, 230–231 no. 139; 237 no. 144; Parlasca 2003, 39–40 no. 683 pl. J,1; 40 no. 686 pl. K,2, 51 no. 724 pl. 165,2.

THE PAINTING'S COMPOSITION

The artist created a manifold composition in terms of perspectives and arrangements. He evoked the impression of three-dimensionality, a differentiation in deepness and perspective by configuring a foreground, a background, and an open view. The foreground is occupied by the person in the very centre. The focus is drawn onto the face, which is presented in a slight turn, while the body is arranged frontally in upright and standing posture. Below the belt, the body ends in a straight line, and it has to be assumed that the narrow zone below was not meant to be visible. It was rather hidden by a second piece of textile covering the legs, possibly of the same ornamental design. The background is designed as an Egyptian architecture serving as a special frame for the head. The space among the pillars is painted in light blue, evoking the impression of an opening, giving way to the sky behind. Creating open views is a very unique method of composition, which has not been employed in Late Roman Egyptian funerary portraiture other than the painted shrouds.[13]

THE EGYPTIAN ELEMENTS AND THEIR FUNERARY CONTEXT

Egyptian, Greek and Roman elements are combined in this painting, expressing different cultural layers and influences in the Roman Egyptian society. The most influential ciphers are the Egyptian ones, stressed not only by the type of the burial itself, the mummification. Foremost, the depiction of Egyptian Gods associated to death in combination with the quotation of the Egyptian temple architecture, the rhomboid ornament, and gilding is to be named. They were merged with the portrait of a Roman in occupational dress, of Greek name and literacy.

THE EGYPTIAN GODS

Two statuettes flank the portrait, being arranged on different heights. Anubis is placed above the left shoulder of the portrayed. He is given in profile oriented to the cheek of the person, and standing on a rectangular plinth. Above the right shoulder, a statue of Osiris is presented on a circular basis, being shown frontally.[14] Anubis and Osiris signify Egyptian death ritual from early Pharaonic times on. According to Egyptian belief, the deceased turns into Osiris in the moment of death, while Anubis prepares the mummy and leads the dead to the after world.[15] Both gods have been popular symbols of death even in Late Antiquity. The presentation of the gods as statuettes in minor position reduces them to pure ciphers, though.[16]

---

13. The technique has been employed in Pompeian wall-paintings of the 1st Century AD within completely different genres. See for instance Casa dei Labirinto (Pompeii), Stabian baths (Pompeii), house of the Farnesina (Rome). Regarding Egyptian paintings: Doxiadis 1995, 109 no. 78; 116 no. 88; 118 no. 90–94; 166–167 no. 103, 104; Walker and Bierbrier 1997, 102 no. 95; 107–108 no. 101; 110–111 no. 105; 114–115 no. 110; 118–119 no. 114; 160–161 no. 181.
14. Walker and Bierbrier 1997, 107–109 no. 101.
15. Few variations are Horus, the four canopies as the sons of Horus, Maat, winged demons, a griffin, a horse and birds. See for instance Doxiadis 1995, frontispiece; Parlasca 1969, 31 no. 18 pl. 5; 72 no. 166 pl. 40; 84 nos 215–216 pl. 53; Parlasca 1977, 29 no. 248 pl. 61; 117 no. 89; Parlasca 1980, 49 no. 601–602 pl. 143; Parlasca 2003, 130 no. 35 pl. I; 177 no. 588 pl. XV,1; 39 no. 682 pl. I, 4; Walker and Bierbrier 1997, 39–40 no. 12; 111–112 no. 105; 114–115 no. 110; 118–119 no. 114.
16. Parlasca and Seemann 1999, 25 fig. 2; 246–247 no. 153; 260–261 no. 165.

WREATHS AND BRANCHES

Flowers and garlands have always been employed in funerary rites. Large numbers of plant remains have been found in pharaonic graves as well as in burials of later date, and many images show their use.[17] Within the Luxor painting, three types of flower bouquets have been depicted: a pinkish garland with bands is held in the person's right hand, referring to a braid of flowers, called the 'wreath of immortality', an accessory that has been employed throughout Egyptian times and that is still in use in Late Roman times.[18] Shown on mummy portraits and painted shrouds this garland is held as a sling, while mummy masks present it as a wreath worn on the head.[19]

A green leaved object is held in the other hand of the person. The lower part simply shows the pedicel, while the upper part consists of a bunch of pointed green leaves. It depicts a branch of laurel, the *persea*, not a whip, as Michael P. Speidel interprets it.[20] Laurel has often been proven as a grave good especially in Late Antique Egyptian graves such as the female burial of Myrithis at Antinoopolis, which was completely covered by *persea*.[21] In general, it has been considered a symbol of triumph, granted as an award, held not only by the victorious sportsmen but also by Emperors and military men. Mummy decorations exclusively picture laurel related to males,[22] as well as the combination of laurel and pinkish garland which is then always held in the right hand while the branch of laurel is held in the left.[23]

A third garland stretches out above the architrave and is fastened by loop bands. White flowers form the centre and tiny wreaths of pinkish and dark green plants are wound around it diagonally. The motive refers to very popular decorative arrangements that have been preserved in funerary contexts in original but also have been pictured in various ways in mosaics and wall-paintings.[24]

THE ARCHITECTURE

A dominant part of the painting's composition is occupied by the background of the painting: the Egyptian architecture. Two slim columns built of drums of varying colours, are crowned by capitals

---

17.   Inv. no. UC28262, online database of the Petrie Museum (www.ucl.ac.uk/museum/petrie); Walker and Bierbrier 1997, 207 no. 295.

18.   Turcan 1971, 94, 99–100, 126–133. Garlands held in the hand on painted shrouds: Walker and Bierbrier 1997, 41 no. 15; 114 no. 110; on mummy portraits: Walker and Bierbrier 1997, 102 no. 95; on a triptychon: Walker and Bierbrier 1997, 123–124 no. 119; on plane cartonages: Walker and Bierbrier 1997, 156–159 nos 175–178.

19.   Seipel 1998, 68–71 nos 7, 8a; 78–79 no. 11; Walker and Bierbrier 1997, 80–81 nos 57–59; 136–138 nos 141–143.

20.   Speidel 1999, 87.

21.   Calament 2005, 311–316, esp. 312.

22.   The painted shroud of a boy, a branch of laurel is held in his left hand in front of his chest (Walker and Bierbrier 1997, 118–120 no. 116 (= Borg 1998, 50 fig. 62; Seipel 1998, 49 fig. 5)).

23.   Parlasca 1969, 75 no. 175 pl. 42,2; 84 no. 215 pl. 53,1; Parlasca 1977, 38–39 no. 286 pl. 69,1; 63 no. 383 pl. 93,1; 69–71 no. 405 pl. 100,2, no. 411 pl. 102,1; 71 no. 413 pl. 102,3; 74 nos 421–422 pl. 105,2; 75 no. 425 pl. 106,1; Parlasca 2003, 38 no. 678 pl. H,2; 41 no. 688 pl. L,2; 42–43 no. 693 pl. N,1 pl. 159,1 (two laurel branches frame the head of a man); Seipel 1998, 170–171 no. 55; Walker and Bierbrier 1997, 118–120 no. 116. Compare also the central and square panel of a triptych depicting a bearded man in a white tunic and cloak, holding the pinkish wreath in his left and the branch of laurel in his right hand. The side panels depict the busts of Isis and Serapis (Walker and Bierbrier 1997, 124–124 no. 119). The laurel is held in his right hand and the wreath in his left hand (Parlasca 2003, 63 no. 772 pl. 172,4; 61–62 no. 765 pl. 171, 3).

24.   See for instance the temple of the Palmyrene Gods at Dura Europos, Cumont 1926, pl. XXXII.

of lotus shape, of which details are lost. They carry an architrave decorated with uraeus-snakes.[25] These architectonic features are of genuine Egyptian origin and can be found throughout Egyptian architecture such as kiosks and sanctuaries. They have also been adapted on wooden cupboards that furnished the *atrium* of Roman houses in Egypt, storing the mummies of the ancestors before burial.[26] The decoration of the Luxor painting may refer to such a cupboard or a religious shrine.

THE RHOMBOID ORNAMENT

The purely ornamental element of Egyptian origin, the decoration of the outer zone, embraces the architecture, serves as a frame and background for the depicted torso. It consists of a regularly arranged ornament and it is structured in a perpetual rhombus pattern on dark red ground. Dark lines of slightly oval shape form rhomboids, while the intersections are given in white dots; rosettes of seven dots fill the fields. The ornamental arrangement turns out to be a typical trait of Egyptian funerary setting, which can be found on other painted shrouds and various pieces of artwork such as paperboard masks in Egyptian style, or the moulded lower part of a Gods' body, being carried out in *mille fiori* glass.[27] The endless pattern refers to decorative nets made of beads and pearls that have been used to cover mummies in burials and that have been in fashion in Pharaonic times already.[28]

BEATEN GOLD

Attention is to be drawn onto a section of the person's neck. Beaten gold of rectangular sheets can be traced just below the line of the chin, sparing the face. Gold has long been used in funerary rites in Egypt, covering only the skin of bodies. The famous and most precious mask of king Tut-Anch-Amun, buried in Thebes-West, serves as the best known example.[29] It was considered as a divine symbol of eternity and as a vehicle of preservation for afterlife. Since the gold leaf application of Roamn times often overlaps from the portrait to the textile covering of the mummy, it is to be assumed that gilding was done when the portraits were (re-)used for the funerary preparations of the mummy.[30] Late Antique Egyptian human bodies such as that of Leukyôné and the singular head of a woman prove this chronological order since they bear beaten gold applied directly onto the skin.[31]

---

25.   Parlasca 1977, 75 no. 425 pl. 106,1; Parlasca 2003, 42–43 no. 693 pl. N,1 pl. 159,1.

26.   Sanctuary of Alexander the Great, Luxor temple, north wall: Abd el-Raziq 1984, pl. 11. Painted shrouds: Parlasca and Seemann 1999, 25 fig. 2; 299–301 no. 199. Wooden closets: Parlasca and Seemann 1999, 25 fig. 3; Seipel 1998, 88–91, no. 15.

27.   Parlasca and Seemann 1999, 307 no. 203; Parlasca 2003, 55 no. 740 pl. 168,2; 109 nos 1002–1003 pl. 199, 1–2; Willems and Clarysse 1999, 226–227 no. 138. *Mille Fiori* glass: Loeben and Wiese 2008, 82 no. 33 c.

28.   Seipel 1998, 58–59 no. 1; 60 no. 2 (net of beads, 7th Century BC); 61 no. 3; Strecker and Heinrich 2007, 216–227 esp. 218, 224; 83 no. 78. Compare the shroud depicting the mummy as Osiris: Parlasca and Seemann 1999, 33 fig. 19; 248–249 no. 154; Seipel 1998, 58–86. Plastered anthropoid sarcophagi dating from 50 BC to 50 AD: Walker and Bierbrier 1997, 30–31 no. 2; 34–35 nos 7, 8.

29.   Parlasca and Seemann 1999, 15; 58–59; 104–108 nos 3–6; 110–111 no. 11; 306–308 nos 202–204; 334–337 nos 228–230. Gilded mummy portraits: Parlasca and Seemann 1999, 124 no. 27; 158–159 no. 57; 182–183 no. 83; 276–277 no. 180; 277, 279–280 no. 181; 339, 341 no. 233. Golden wreaths added at a later date: Parlasca 1999, 162–163 no. 60; 174 no. 74; 210–211 nos 117–118; 214–215 no. 122; 223 no. 131 (wreath, jewellery and golden lips); 236 no. 143; 258–259 no. 164.

30.   See for instance Parlasca 2003, 169–170 no. 480, pl. XIV,2 (gold on the lips, background and as a wreath), 37–38 no. 677 pl. H,1 (application of a golden wreath, jewellery, golden frames of the *clavi*, and golden squares onto the pinkish garland).

31.   Leukyôné: Calament 2005, 38 fig. 38a–b. The head: Aubert and Cortopassi 1998/1999, 46–47 no. 9.

THE GREEK INSCRIPTION

The Egyptian elements of the painting prove that death rites and beliefs regarding afterlife still continue with Egyptian traditions even in Roman times. The portrait itself and its inscription, though, refer to contemporary customs and even relate the image to an individual person. Mummy portraits and painted shrouds seldom bear inscriptions. Few known exceptions are Hermione Grammatike, Didyme, Eirene, Isa/rous, Klaudiane, Artemidoros, Eutyches, Sarapon son of Haresas and Titos Flavios Demetrios.[32] This might be due to the practice of tying separate wooden labels to the mummy in case of shipping.[33] The shroud at Luxor bears Greek letters in black paint or ink that have been arranged in the space among the right side of the person's neck and one of the statuettes. Two horizontal lines can be determined as 'ΤΥΡΑ_ _ _ Ο ΚΑ_ ...', traces of a third line are visible but not identifiable. Klaus Parlasca first interpreted the inscription as 'ΤΥΡΑΣ', while Georges Nachtergael read 'ΤΥΡΑΝΝΟΣ Ο ΚΑΙ ...', and Gesa Schenke reads 'ΤΥΡΑΝΟΣ Ο ΚΑΙ ...' and translates "Tyranos (as proper name), alias ...", the alias name is lost.[34] Even though the name *Tyranos* is of Greek origin, it does not necessarily imply that the depicted was of Greek ethnic provenance.[35] Numerous combinations of Greek, Roman and Egyptian names can be traced and Roger S. Bagnall records variations even within one family.[36]

THE ROMAN PORTRAIT AND ITS DATING

The main element of the painting, the portrait, presents a male; his self-awareness and pride in being a Roman officer is demonstrated by his occupational dress.[37] Tyranos' face has an oval shape of rather young features, perfectly shaven, and stressed by the very short cut of his almost black hair. Especially his eyes attract the attention, looking straight at the observer. The eyeballs are painted in bright white; the iris is partly covered by the upper lid. The dark eyelashes, the bushy black eyebrows, which are drawn together, and a crease above the nose, stress this facial area. The forehead is slightly wrinkled; the nose is moulded by strong colour contrasts, and the lips are narrow, closed,

32. Hermione: Walker and Bierbrier 1997, 37–38 no. 11 (= Borg 1998, 53 fig. 67); Didyme: Walker and Bierbrier 1997, 108–109 no. 102; Eirene: Borg 1996, pl. 1 fig. 2 (= Borg 1998, 77 fig. 92; Walker and Bierbrier 1997, 115–116 no. 111); Isa/rous: Walker and Bierbrier 1997, 45 no. 19; Klaudiane: Doxiadis 1995, 152 no. 94; Artemidoros: Walker and Bierbrier 1997, frontispiz, 56–57 no. 32 (= Borg 1998, 64 fig. 78); Eutyches: Borg 1996, pl. 86 fig. 3 (= Borg 1998, 48 fig. 60; Walker and Bierbrier 1997, 116–117 no. 112); Sarapon son of Haresas: Parlasca 2003, 65 no. 780 pl. 173,5; plaster mask of Titos Flavios Demetrios: Walker and Bierbrier 1997, 84–85 no. 74. Other notes such as '*Farewell! Be happy*' (Walker and Bierbrier 1997, 106–107 no. 99), '*Sarapi*' (Walker and Bierbrier 1997, 111–112 no. 106). On the evaluation of the handwriting in regard of dating, see Montserrat 1996.
33. Seipel 1998, 180–187 nos 60–64; Walker and Bierbrier 1997, 180–183 nos 235–241.
34. Parlasca 1981, 186–187; Parlasca 2003, 63. – My special thanks go to Gesa Schenke for her reading and translation. The name seems to have been quite common in Egypt. It has been attested in various papyri and graffiti found in the region of Thebes dating to late Antiquity. Both dictions are known. See Łajtar 2006, 252–254 nos 167–168, 261–264 nos 172–173; Preisigke 1922, 449.
35. At Karanis (Fayum), though, veterans received the Roman citizenship after serving the Roman army. Their children were given Roman names (Alston 1995, 117–126, esp. 123–126).
36. Bagnall 1993, 232–235; compare Borg 1998, 33–45. Concerning their ethnicity, people of Egypt were not classified as 'Egyptian' or 'Greek' after the beginning of the 1st century AD. Romans differentiated among citizens of Greek cities (such as Alexandria, Ptolemais, Naukratis, and Antinoopolis), and the rest, which included everybody who did not live in a Greek city. Compare Bagnall 1997, 7–15.
37. Roman military was part of Egyptian society, and recruitment was done locally. Bagnall 1993, 172–180.

Fig. 7.2 Portrait of Gordianus III, Capitoline Museums Rome inv. no. 479, detail of © www.arachne.uni-koeln. de<http://www.arachne.uni-koeln.de> FittCap73-15-11_36146,16.tif.

and compressed. The very pale tan enhances the harsh contrast of the skin, eyes, and hair.[38] Face and posture express tenseness, underlined by the position of the bent arms in front of the body. The portrait transmits the impression of a serious young man, expressing leadership abilities, and strong impulse to act.

The characteristics of Tyranos' portrait are most remarkable; they refer to innovative features of a new type of portraiture that was created in the beginning of the 3rd Century and that dominated throughout the Century.[39] These traits and changes were initiated by Caracalla and his brother Geta about 208 AD, when Caracalla chose to break the tradition of imperial self-representation started by Hadrian.[40] While earlier Emperors related themselves to Greek philosophers expressed by full beards, long hair, and little decisive facial expressions, Caracalla was the first to present himself with a short haircut, well shaven, and with a concentrated and somewhat brutal facial expression.[41] Later, the rather square shape of his face and his rough incarnate was reduced again, changing the physiognomy to a slender boyish type, but keeping up the hairstyle and the look.[42] It is this pictorial tradition that is mirrored in the portrayal of Tyranos. The shape of his face, the very short hair with drawn-in temples, the realistic depiction of the inner corner of the eye, the heavy eyelids, the eyelid crease, the voluminous brows, and the short but rolling lips of almost equal width, resemble the features of Severus Alexander or Marcus Antonius Gordianus (Fig. 7.2).[43] It has to be assumed that the Luxor painter has been inspired by the new imperial style and that the shroud has to be dated to the first third of the 3rd Century AD, tending to the first quarter.[44]

Roman imperial fashion, not only of the Emperor but also of the empress and the royal family in general, was transferred to the provinces by the Emperor's portraits. Official portraits have been

38.   Male depictions on mummy portraits show a rather dark tan: Walker and Bierbrier 1997, 46–53 nos 20–27.
39.   Fittschen and Zanker 1994, 102–104 no. 88 pl. 107; 122–123 nos 102–103 pl. 125–126.
40.   Rößler 1993, 334–343.
41.   Rößler 1993, 337.
42.   Rößler 1993, 340–343. Fittschen and Zanker 1994, 127–128 no. 107 pl. 131–132 (Gordianus Pius, 238–242 AD); 110–112 no. 94 Beil. 80a (Caracalla, 215–217 AD); 114–115 no. 81a Beil. 81 (Geta, 218–219 AD); Beil. 85a–d, 87a–d, 88, 89a–d (Pupienus), 90a–f.
43.   Fittschen and Zanker 1994, 117–121 no. 99 Beil. 86a–d pl. 86–87 (222–224 AD); 105 no. 90e–f; 127–128 no. 107 (238–242 AD).
44.   When first publishing the painting, Klaus Parlasca dated it to the 2nd and 3rd century AD. Later a likeness to Severan portraits of the first half of the 3rd century AD was suggested (Parlasca 2003, 61). On dating mummy portraits through stylistic comparisons with imperial portraiture, see Borg 1993, 19–80.

designed in order to spread the knowledge of the new Emperor's look, personality, and attitude. They enhanced vogues, transferred fashion models not only regarding the hairstyles but also modelling the looks, the incarnate, facial outline, the proportions, the view and the overall look, to the farthest regions of the Empire. Ciphers of political strength and power were transmitted through them.[45]

Imperial fashion was transferred quickly, especially to the army in Late Roman times when the Emperors were closely related and highly dependant to the army. From the beginning of the 3rd century AD, several Emperors became such by the votum of the military. Heirs changed quickly, and the army became a powerful body, the *corpus militare*.[46] Thus the Princeps spent most of his time with his troops, travelling the provinces, and spending *donativa* on the army. The impact of the ruler on the army and the other way around was great and immediate, also comprising fashion of dress and hairstyle, and a very fast spreading has to be assumed especially in case of the military.

2ND AND 3RD CENTURY AD DEPICTIONS OF SOLDIERS. ATTRIBUTES DETERMINING THE ROMAN OFFICER *(Fig. 7.3)*

According to Simon James – who basically focuses on the Julius Terentius wall-painting from Dura Europos – the following elements determine the Roman officer: the cloak, the tunic, undergarment, breeches, footwear (the *calceus*), the purse, but most of all, the sword on a baldric, the military belt, the golden finger-ring (the *annulus aureus*), and the military staff.[47] The most decisive element is the weapon, though, since civilians were not allowed to carry a sword or a dagger. The painting of Tyranos envisages the handle of a weapon appearing from beneath the cloak, worn on a *balteus* which is covered by the cloak.[48] This detail very closely relates to a unique presentation in the bust of Caracalla or Geta in the 2nd predecessor type, dating to about 208 AD, at the *Museo Capitolino*.[49] In a much reduced presentation this detail can also be observed on mummy portraits depicting soldiers from the Fayum (Fig. 7.4). Regarding Tyranos it is astonishing that his weapon is not being presented in a realistic manner and dimension and it appears to have been added after finishing the painting simply as a determination of the soldier. The colour of the handle is white with yellowish shades, referring to the materials bone or ivory which quite often have been employed for handles.[50]

The Luxor portrait is highly detailed in these terms, but due to artistic reasons and the original purpose of the painting, the image presents an individual person known even by name.[51] The context is personal but official, meant to be perceived only by a small group of visitors, mostly family members and comrades. It derives from a rather private and to some extent even religious context. Concerning the elements of dress, items such as underwear, breeches and footwear, are not displayed and the length

---

45. Rößler 1993, 321–322.
46. Alföldy 2000, 44, 45, 52; according to Alston 1995, 110, the political situation of the 3rd century AD became dangerous and the Emperor greatly depended to the sympathy of the soldiers. Therefore "… the donatives were paid annually or even more regularly and were an important part of a soldier's annual income by AD 300." Alston 1995, 144, "Emperors remain close to the army at all times and gradually, during the 3rd century, we see the emergence of a central force, stationed with the emperor, which would form the nucleus of any major expeditionary force."
47. James 2004, 58; Bishop and Coulston 2006, 110–111, 144; Sander 1963, esp. 148–149, 162–163.
48. James 2004, 61 "… the right to bear arms in public was a fundamental attribute of status of a soldier, and so swords were routinely worn as a mark of this status …".
49. Fittschen and Zanker 1994, 102–104 no. 88 pl. 107. "Die Skulptur ist ein charakteristisches Beispiel für die in mittelseverischer Zeit einsetzenden Versuche, die überkommenen Büstenmodelle durch neue Formen zu ersetzen oder durch Attribute zu beleben… ."
50. Miks 2007, see for instance pl. 160–164.
51. Parlasca 1981, simply describes the elements of dress.

Figure 7.3. Wall-painting of Julius Terentius from Dura Europos, after Cumont 1926, pl. L.

of the tunic cannot be determined. Those elements that are visible, such as the white tunic, its purple *manicae* and the arrow-shaped *clavi*, the ochreous cloak, the belt, and the handle of the dagger, the golden gem-stone-ring worn on the small finger of the left hand but also the pure golden ring on his forefinger of the same hand[52] are of characteristic nature, thus determine the officer of high rank, a high centurion or even commander.[53] According to Erich Sander, the most striking symbol of military

---

52.   According to Géza Alföldy, the military gained prestige which can best be seen in the fact that Septimius Severus granted the right to wear the golden ring to the centurions and the *principales* in order to state that they were potentially considered as *equites*. Alföldi 1952, 26–35 (with further quotations); Alföldi 2000, 45.

53.   It is noteworthy that the weapon is carried almost above the waist, and that the cloak is draped behind the hilt, in order to show it. The presentation of the sword refers to a unique Emperors portrait, kept at the *Museo Capitolino* at Rome. The identity of the portrayed cannot definitely be determined; the Roman Emperors Caracalla and Geta have been suggested, thus the bust is to be dated at about 208 AD. Just like the painting, the hilt appears from beneath the cloak, being modelled in a much more elaborate and naturalistic way, though. According to Klaus Fittschen and Paul Zanker, this bust is an innovation, marking a new style in Emperors' portraiture, formative for the whole 3rd century AD. See Fittschen and Zanker 1994, 102–104 no. 88 pl. 107. "Panzer-Paludamentumbüste des Caracalla oder Geta im 2. Thronfolgertypus (Consulartypus). Gegen 208 n.Chr., Museo Capitolino, Stanza degli Imperatori 41. Inv. 468. ... : die beiden Prinzen folgen nicht mehr dem höfisch-urbanen Ideal des 2. Jhs., sondern orientieren sich an dem äußeren Habitus, der schon vorher an Bildnissen von Offizieren und Athleten zu beobachten ist. Mit Caracalla und Geta tritt ein neues Herrscherbild in Erscheinung, das das ganze 3. Jh. geprägt hat. Symptomatisch ist dafür auch die Panzer-Paludamentumbüste der capitolinischen Replik: ihre Form, vor allem die Wiedergabe des Schwertgriffes unter dem Mantel, ist ganz ungewöhnlich." Plinius the Elder, *naturalis historia* VII, 29.

rank is transmitted through the type of cloak:[54] a white cloak with red or purple fringes determined the tribune, just as it is being shown in the wall-painting of Julius Terentius at Dura Europos (Fig. 7.3); a brown or rather ochreous cloak without fringes determined the *centurion*. The mantle is of the *sagum* type, being a rectangular sheet. It became the dominant military cloak from the first quarter of the 2nd century on.[55] The Tyranos painting well demonstrates the drapery: it completely covers the left shoulder and arm up to his wrist, falls down in the back, stretches about the chest, forms a slight bow accompanied by two main folds, and runs to the shoulder and to the middle of the upper arm. On the neck, one major fold runs parallel to the upper fold, then turns in direction and returns to the back. The inner part of the neck opening shows a double layer of cloth. The area where the *fibula* has been depicted in the portrait is deeply stained, partly covered and mostly destroyed. According to marble portraits of Roman Emperors, the shape type of *fibula* is to be reconstructed as a circular element.[56] A certain group of mummy portraits painted on wooden boards suggests the *fibula* to have been of oval shape, made of gold and a large oval gemstone in the centre, being surrounded by a row of small gems. The tunic worn beneath will later be the subject of discussion.

According to Simon James and Stefanie Hoss the belt also became an essential symbol of military.[57] Tyranos' belt consists of a simple band of red leather, framed by golden bands, being bound on the right side of the waist ending in a loop and cut in two loose straps. In the centre of the body, a tiny golden ring buckle becomes visible, being a typical military buckle of the 3rd century AD.[58] It is accompanied by two silver buttons, domed studs, that served the fastening of the leather strap which has been pulled straight. This depiction of this type of belt is unique because it is very narrow and the buckle appears to be very small, while grave reliefs of the same period tend to depict this belt in a rather oversized version. Just like the handle of the dagger, it seems to have been of importance to show it but there was no need to depict it in realistic dimension.

EGYPTIAN PAINTINGS: MUMMY PORTRAITS DEPICTING ROMAN SOLDIERS OF THE 2ND CENTURY AD *(Fig. 7.4)*

Depictions of soldiers of the 2nd and 3rd centuries seem to present traditions in regard of the combination of elements of dress and their specific colours. Especially the combination of Tyranos' garments seems to have been defined in the 2nd century already. Details such as the type of *clavi* though, represent changes in garment decoration in the late 2nd and early 3rd Century. Among the Egyptian portrait presentations, the members of the Roman army form a small but distinctive group.[59] Within this category of images, soldiers are characterised through their uniform dress, two groups can be determined, possibly referring to ranks of two types of higher ranking officers.[60] Nine portraits show men in white tunics with dark and narrow clavi, carrying a dark blue mantle as a bunched

---

54. It has been common practise to wear the tunic and the *sagum* in private situations as well. See Sander 1963, 149–150; Sueton Caligula 45.
55. Sander 1963, 152–153; compare also Mac Mullen 1963, 179–180.
56. See for instance Fittschen and Zanker 1994, nos 1, 28, 59, 61–62, 69, 73–74, 81, 88, 94, 96, 103, 106, 109–110, 113, Beil. 17, 28, 32, 39–41, 49c, 50–53, 60 a, 72a. c, 79–81, 95–96.
57. James 2004, 60–61 fig. 31.
58. I thank Graham Sumner for pointing me to the buckle, and Stefanie Hoss for the personal communication on the function and interpretation of this type of belt. See Sumner and Hoss in this volume.
59. Compare painted shrouds depicting the person and dress in full size: Walker and Bierbrier 1997, 107–108 no. 101; 110–111 no. 105; 118–120 no. 114, 116. Parlasca 1999, 39–40 (Parlasca dates them from the early to the late 2nd Century AD).
60. Paetz gen. Schieck 2010, 92–93 fig. 11, 12.

piece of textile with a silver coloured bowed *fibula* on one of the shoulders, wearing a red leather *balteus* with golden buttons, *bullae*, across the chest (there seems to have been no preference regarding the left or right direction), serving as a carrying device for the sword, which is hinted at through a white globular knob positioned at the very corner of the painting.[61] As mentioned earlier, this detail serves as a symbol for the military man. The second group consists of ten portraits depicting men dressed in white tunics with a dark blue linear decoration of the neck-opening, forming a band with gabled ends running along the shoulders.[62] They also wear an ochreous *sagum*-type cloak, sometimes with fringed edges, being fastened on their right shoulder with a golden brooch with gemstone and a row of round gemstones. This type of brooch varies in design, but all of the depictions show it in oval shape. Since it is being carried out with great care, other than the silver bow *fibula* of the other group of portraits, it seems to represent not only a costly piece of jewellery but also an object of symbolic meaning. Since the portraits of all men show them with long curly hair and full beards, they are to be dated to pre-Severan times. Parlasca calls these men *centurios* and interprets them to have been chiefs of a company of the Roman military, even though he mentions that Roman troops have not been stationed in the Fayum during the 2nd century.[63] Thus he concludes that they served as commanders of the local police.

THE JULIUS TERENTIUS PAINTING AT DURA EUROPOS (*Fig. 7.3*)

The tradition of military garments has also been followed in the wall-painting of Julius Terentius found at Dura Europos shows a convention of Roman soldiers.[64] It was found in the ruins of the city that has been abandoned in 256 AD, after the Roman defeat by Sasanian troops in a spectacular siege. It measures 107 × 165 cm, and it is dated to 239 AD.[65] Its

Figure 7.4. Mummy Portrait of a Roman Soldier found in the Fayum (Egypt), Antikensammlung, Staatliche Museen zu Berlin inv. no. 31161/2 © Ingrid Geske-Heiden, Antikensammlung, SMB.

---

61.   Borg 1996, colour plates 14,1; 32; 157: in Trajanic and early Hadrianic times, the cloak was arranged voluminously on one shoulder. In hadrian times, it was closed in front of the chest. From Antonine times on, the cloaks show fringed edges. Borg 1998, 54 no. 68; Doxiadis 1995, 22–24 no. 15–19, 34 no. 2; Parlasca and Seemann 1999, 149–150 no. 49; 149; 151 no. 50; 184–185 no. 86; Stamm 2007, 22 no. 10, 28 no. 22, 28 Nr. 22; 55 no. 20.

62.   Borg 1996, pl. 50.1; Parlasca 1977, N. 326 pl. 78.3, N. 354 pl. 85.7, N. 364 pl. 88.2, N. 372 pl. 90.2, N. 389 pl. 94.4, N. 409 pl. 101.1; Parlasca 1980, N. 546 pl. 132.3; etc.

63.   Parlasca 1966, 84–85; Parlasca and Seemann 1999, 52, 87–88.

64.   It was found by British soldiers in 1920 in the southern chamber (K) of the temple of the Palmyrene gods – see Cumont 1926.

65.   Baur and Rostovzeff 1931, 67–69; Breasted 1922, 199–206; Cumont 1926, 89–100; James 2004, xxiii–xxv. It has been cut out and transferred to the Yale University Art Gallery at New Haven (inv. no. 1931.386). See Weitzmann 1977, 197–198 no. 177.

composition presents two sections: the left side is occupied by three statues of male and armed gods being interpreted as the statues of the Palmyrene gods of war. In the lower left corner, the *Tychai* of Dura and of Palmyra are depicted. Below their feet, swimming figures signify Ephka, the Palmyrene spring Goddess, and the river God Euphrates. The very centre of the painting is occupied by *Julius Terentius trib (unus)* being the chief of a group of men belonging to the *cohors XX Palmyrenorum*. He is shown offering incense, his name and military rank is given by an inscription next to his head. Opposite to him a young man is holding a *vexillum*, a red flag on a golden standard.[66] In his back, four men line up in the front, four in the second row, further appear in the upper part of the panel. Their order is stressed through the decreasing age and size, which at the same time seems to illustrate the ranks within this group. All of them bend their left arms to the waist and hold up their right hands as a sign of adoration. The figures are depicted with individual features in regard of their headdress and beard. Some of them are presented with nicely cut short full beards, others, especially the smaller ones, are plainly shaven, possibly too young for a beard at all. The hairstyles vary to a great extent: Julius Terentius seems to have a short cut hairdo with his hairline far above the forehead; others have more voluminous cap-like hairstyles, straight lines of fringes on the forehead, and some show receding hairlines. Their dress, though, is partly presented in a homogenous manner without individual traits. All of them wear white tunics covering half of the upper thigh, dark and long pants, darkish shoes (no sandals), and long cloaks being tied on the right shoulder, covering the chest and the left shoulder, reaching to the knees in the back. A red *balteus* is worn diagonally across the chest, bearing the dagger/sword on the left side. The circular knob and the handle are visible especially at the side of Terentius. Furthermore, all men wear belts, and one man seems to have a writing tablet held by it. Three types of cloaks are employed: Terentius wears a white cloak with long and purple fringes; one of the officers wears a whitish cloak without fringes; three men wear ochreous cloaks with plain selvedges. The soldier's dress implies a standardised uniform that matches the painted shroud at Luxor: all tunics of the Dura painting are of a short and narrow cut, have long sleeves of tight fit. The so called *tunica manicata* was taken over from civil dress into the military dress in the 3rd century AD being used by all parts of the army.[67] The adornments in the Terentius painting are decorated in two shades of red. Two narrow bands (the *manicae*) of dark red are positioned in the middle of the lower arm leaving respectable space in between and being arranged within a distinct distance to the wrist. Of rather pinkish red, two broad bands run along the neck opening and the hem of the tunic. It is impossible to tell if the broader bands are meant to be decorations of the same tunic, or if they rather depict an undergarment of pinkish-red colour. No further decorative ornaments such as *clavi* can be traced. Dealing with the Dura painting, Simon James calls the ensembles the 'camp dress' and defines them as garments worn on special occasions, in a more private atmosphere like a religious offering, not in campaigns or combat situations.[68] The author thus prefers to speak of a sort of 'gala uniform', worn only at official occasions such as festivities, or offerings to the Gods.

ON THE RELATION OF TEXTILE REALIA AND DEPICTIONS.

---

66. An original *vexillum* is kept in the Hermitage, St. Petersburg, see Parlasca and Seemann 1999, 186–187 no. 89.
67. Pausch 2003, 197.
68. James 2004, 59–61; Bishop and Coulston 2006, 110.

DRESS DECORATIONS OF PURPLE COLOUR

It is quite difficult to determine Roman military symbols of rank. Erich Sander claims that civil symbols of social ranks also served as symbols within the military system.[69] Such were the *clavi* of shellfish purple, decorating the tunics. According to written sources a distinction was achieved by the width of these purple bands.[70] Narrow bands were symbols of the *ordo equestris*, the knights (*equites*), and authors like Plinius the Elder called them *tunica angusti clavi*. A tunic with wide bands was called *tunica lati clavi*, worn by officers of senatorial status, the senators and the legates, being named the *tribunus laticlavus*.[71] Thus, no information on the real widths has been handed down to us but some archaeological evidence may lead to the suggestion that the narrow bands have been of about 1 cm in width. Further symbols of distinction among officers and soldiers have been the cloaks, the *fibulae*, and the golden ring.

Dealing with the painted shroud at Luxor, the high quality of the detailed pictorial information on the elements of dress and military equipment need to be stressed as well as artistic freedom in treatment and positioning of the elements. In general, paintings of the same period show little evidence of the material of the dress they depict. Tyranos' tunic is of narrow cut, with long and tight-fitting sleeves. The visible edge of this sleeve shows a twined cord, which is to be interpreted as the warp threads, that finished the weave, kept it from dissolving, and gave it a strong edge (Figs 7.1, 7.5a, 7.8, 7.13). When investigating Late Roman textile finds it becomes evident that these twines are typical traits of purely woollen textiles, both warp and weft are made of wool, while the edges of linen weaves have been bundled to fringes also being depicted in mummy portraits such as the portrait of a young and beardless male.[72] Thus the cord hints at the basic material to be wool, which matches the off-white ground colour of Tyranos' tunic which's folds are given in bright white. The depiction intentionally refers to a material that is not of a bright-white shade, just like non-pigmented woollen textiles. The intentional use of different shades of white becomes evident when looking at the bright white eyeballs.

The decoration of the Tyranos' garment consists of purple elements, two narrow bands on the selvedge of the sleeve, the *manicae*, and two parallel arranged arrow-shaped *clavi* to which a pyramid-shaped motif with a stepped contour is attached, decorating the shoulders. Differing from originally preserved textiles and the Terentius-painting at Dura, the *manicae* are always positioned in the centre of the lower arm, never moved to the selvedge. Thus their position in the Luxor painting may be due to the stylistic or artistic reason and the urge of presentation (Figs 7.1, 7.6). Still, the degree of realism fascinates the observer especially when comparing original textile remains from Egypt and Syria. Until now the comparison of these textile *realia* and the depictions has not been undertaken, even though the results are intriguing, and allow suggestions of what officers' tunics may have looked like.

TEXTILE FRAGMENTS FROM DURA EUROPOS

Numerous textile fragments of the late 2nd and early 3rd Century AD have been found in the ruins

---

69.   Sander 1963, 152–153; see also Alföldy 2000, 38, 43.

70.   Alföldi 1952, 69–72.

71.   Plinius the Elder, *naturalis historia* VII, 29; Quintilianus, *Institutio oratoria* XI, 3, 138; Sueton, *Augustus*, 73. See also Pausch 2003, 104–114; Sander 1963, 152–153.

72.   Parlasca 2003, 43 no. 694 pl. N,2; 43 no. 695 pl. XIV,1 and 159,2. For woollen cords see for instance Paetz gen. Schieck 2003, 49 no. 77, 51 no. 81, 56 no. 93, 63 no. 113, 64 no. 114, 65 no. 118; Paetz gen. Schieck 2005, 54–58 no. 14 (3), 82–92 no. 29; for linen finishing see Paetz gen. Schieck 2003, 40, 50, 47 nos 71–72, 80 no. 159; Paetz gen. Schieck 2005, 30–35, no. 5.

of Dura Europos, some of them are closely related to the tunic of Tyranos. The debris of a tower, for instance, contained two fragments of a tunic showing the same features:[73] an off-white woollen ground weave, purple *manicae*, an arrow-shaped *clavus*, and a pyramidal ornament attached to it, pointing to the sleeve (Fig. 7.6).[74] When being puzzled together, the object measures 16.5 × 29.7 cm and 21.4 × 54.6 cm, in completion of the garment, a second arrow-shaped *clavus* has to be reconstructed as well as a second set of *manicae* woven into the other sleeve. The same decorative concept, going along with the colour-combination and material, can also be found in other textile fragments of adults' garments (Fig. 7.7).[75] Rudolphe Pfister and Louisa Bellinger determine it to have been worn by a small person.

Figure 7.5a. Sleeve, DTM Krefeld inv. no. 00024 © DTM, D. Gasse.

PURPLE MANICAE: TWO SLEEVES. DISJOINED AND VIRTUALLY REUNITED

Keeping the purple *manicae* of the Luxor painting, the wall-painting of Julius Terentius, and the textile fragments from Dura in mind, a unique textile fragment stored at the *Deutsches Textilmuseum* at *Krefeld*, Germany, sticks out of the mass of the Late Roman textiles from Egypt (Fig. 7.5a, b).[76] It measures 31.7 cm in warp- and 28.5 cm in weft-direction, being the cut-off sleeve of an off-white woollen tunic of highest textile quality.[77] Unfortunately no information

Figure 7.5b. Detail of DTM Krefeld inv. no. 00024 © A. P. g. Schieck.

of the find context, or even the general provenance within Egypt, is available. The only accessible information is contained within the object.

---

73. Inv. no. 1929.489; Wilson 1931, 179 pl. XIX no. 1; Pfister and Bellinger 1945, 17 no. 3, 5 fig. 1.3 (reconstruction of the motif), pl. VII, 3; the decoration is carried out in tapestry weave.

74. Tapestry weave, undyed woollen warp, single yarns, s-spun, 7–11 threads per cm; purple weft, single yarns, s-spun, 44 threads per cm, and undyed wool, single yarns, z-spun, 36 threads per cm.

75. Pfister and Bellinger 1945, 18–19 nos 11–14, 5 fig. 1.11–1.14 (reconstruction of the motive), pl. IX, 3.

76. DTM inv. no. 00024. The object was one of the very first textiles to be inventoried. It has been given to the collection by Ernst von Scheven on April 8, 1908 (Paetz gen. Schieck 2002, 21; Paetz gen. Schieck 2003, 49 no. 77).

77. The textile underwent several conservations. Nowadays it is spread out horizontally. Either when being cut off the garment or in the course of conservatory work, the stitching has been unseamed, and the threads removed, that formed a hose out of the piece of textile. Slight discolouring, though, indicates that the former joints started at the corded selvedge and ran parallel to the original turning edges, passing-by close to the narrow ends of the *manicae*.

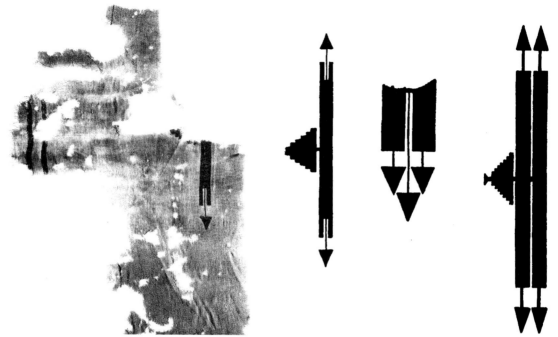

Figure 7.6. Tunic found at Dura Europos, terminus ante quem 256 AD, after Pfister and Bellinger 1945, pl. VII.3.

Figure 7.7. Sketches of textile decorations found at Dura Europos, terminus ante quem 256 AD, after Pfister and Bellinger 1945, fig. 1.

Modern technology helped to get an insight into some aspects kept within the textile: warp and weft are carried out in very fine s-spun yarns of whitish non-pigmented wool. The ground weave consists of a plain weave showing rep-structure. It was executed with great care, regularity and density, having about 17 warp-threads and about 38 weft-threads per cm. The textile still contains the two original turning edges of the wefts, and one finishing border that has been stabilized by twined warp-threads forming a thick, S-plied cord ending in a knot, about 3.5 cm from the corner of the cloth. The decoration is inserted by tapestry weave with open slits at the turning edges of the decorative band wefts. The decorative bands measure 22.7 cm width and 0.8 cm in height, which is very narrow compared to other doubled bands forming the *manicae* of a tunic. The separating zone measures 2.8 cm and the first band has been inserted into the ground weave within a distance of 11.3 cm from the corded edge. Additional decoration consists of ornaments repeating the same motive carried out in flying shuttle technique and very fine white woollen threads. Each strip contains three endless bands, subdivided in three zones, twisted and forming four loops. A second motif of four heart-shaped ivy-leaves forming a square of 0.9 cm has been inserted twice per band.

According to these technological data the garment's production process is reconstructable (Figs 7.12, 7.13). The wefts run parallel to the corded finishing border and the tunic was woven to shape, including the decorative elements and the neck opening. The loom must have been of the two-beam loom type and had an estimated width of at least 2.80 m. After finishing the textile, it was cut out of the warp, folded in half along the shoulder, and sewn along the sides and the bottom of the sleeves.

Since the colour of the two bands is very bright, intensive, and differs greatly from the usual more brownish and much less bright purple colours, it urged for an analysis of the textile dyes. The investigation was carried out by Robert Fuchs with the non-destructive method of colour-spectrometry.[78] Three analyses of the purple bands documented shellfish purple that has been dyed over with cochineal – possibly of Armenian origin – in order to achieve a much brighter shade.[79] The off-white ground-weave revealed no dyes, thus the yarns are of non-pigmented wool of whitish colour. According to Plinius the Elder, non-pigmented wool was considered as the most expensive type of wool, since it provided the greatest possibilities of use and the largest spectrum of dyeing colours and shades.[80]

In order to achieve a scientific dating, the Krefeld sleeve was sampled for radiocarbon dating and the ^{14}C-analysis has been carried out by Wolfgang Kretschmer and his team at the *Kernphysikalisches Institut Universität Erlangen*. The analysis revealed a large dating margin of 261 and 538 AD with a 2 sigma 95.4% confidence range.[81] The diagram thus shows several individual peaks. The earliest peak suggests a dating period just after 260 AD, which is about the period that has to be taken for the time when Tyranos' painting has been created.

Figure 7.8. Sleeve, Metropolitan Museum New York, inv. no. 90.5.442 © The Metropolitan Museum of Art.

As research continued, Maya Naunton, curator of the textile collection of the Metropolitan Museum, New York, introduced a sleeve which turned out to be the exact copy of the Krefeld object (Fig. 7.8).[82] It shows about the same size of 35.4 cm in warp direction and 29.4 cm in weft direction, similar technical traits, such as the two turning edges of the wefts, a finishing border which has been twined to a cord and one cut off edge, it bears the same colour-codes, and ornaments. The bands are

---

78. Paetz gen. Schieck 2002, 27. On shellfish purple dye: Schweppe 1976, 30–31; Schweppe 1993, 304–307. The shade is very rare among the Late Roman textiles from Egypt. Prof. Dr. Robert Fuchs of the University of Applied Sciences at Cologne determines dyes with an SPM 100 colour spectrometer. I am grateful for his kind and spontaneous help in determining the dyes of the sleeve. This object was the start of a series of investigations that was presented at the Purpureae Vestes III conference at Naples in November 2008, Paetz gen. Schieck and Fuchs 2011, 109–118.

79. The species of the insects cannot be determined by the colour-spectrometry method.

80. Plinius the Elder, *nat. hist.* VIII, 190–193.

81. The radiocarbon dating was carried out in 2003 by Prof. Dr. Wolfgang Kretschmer and his team using their AMS-machine. Special thanks go to the Fritz Thyssen Stiftung Cologne, Germany, for generously financing the project. See Paetz gen. Schieck 2002, 80, appendix table 4 no. 9.

82. Metropolitan Museum, inv. no. MMA 90.5.442. The sleeve was acquired in Egypt in 1890 for the collection of "Coptic" textiles by George F. Baker. My special thanks go to Maya Naunton, textile conservator of the Metropolitan Museum New York, whom I met at the Purpureae Vestes III conference at Naples in November 2008. She shared the technical data and took care of the photographs and the publishing permission. I also thank Navina Haider, curator of the textile collection.

made in tapestry weave with added ornaments carried out in flying shuttle technique, measuring 23 cm in width and 0.8 cm in height. The warps of the ground weave number 14–16 threads per cm, those of the weft count 26 per cm, and 32 within the tapestry weave. All yarns are simple s-spun woollen and the purple dyestuff has been tested positive on Bromine and revealed shellfish purple as well.

Many arguments such as the style and design, information on weaving technology contained in both sleeves, the quality of the textiles, the information on the dyes, especially on the shellfish purple, which has been determined by different methods in both cases, and the cutting edges, prove that these two sleeves derive from the same workshop and they even suggest that they belonged to the same tunic, also testified by the pattern of the folds and creases of the same features, running parallel in the upper part, near the shoulder. The textile has been crinkled in this area, centrally folded in warp direction, starting at the cord. These details imply that both sleeves have not been worn when being deposited but have been folded up and positioned on top or next to the mummy if it was a grave-good at all.[83] When being found in modern times, they have been cut off and sold to different collectors; still the hope remains that fragments of the body of the tunic are stored in collections anywhere in the world.[84]

A third sleeve of this kind but of slightly different decoration is hosted by the Louvre.[85] According to the description, the material is wool, but no details are listed concerning the technique or spinning direction. Lose threads appear to be fringes but are the warp threads that originally have been twined to a cord similar to the Krefeld and New York objects. Again, two purple bands decorate the sleeve; the additional ornaments being carried out in flying-shuttle, differing from the other sleeves. Three endless and twisted bands form five loops organised in the same system and placement. The two intermediate motives are designed as vine-leaves in rhombus-shape.

The close parallels in material and decoration prove the fragments to belong to a distinctive type of garment of a common design. Their technical data and appearance demonstrate that this type of garment – if it was serially produced – has been of extraordinary quality in regard of the regularity and the density of the weave. The material and dye, and the workshop where it originates from must have been specialized on high-quality textile products. It is quite sure that this tunic was an expensive product in antiquity.

Comparing the textiles with the painted shroud from Luxor, many parallels can be determined: the ground weave of off-white colour and a purple decoration; the long and tight fitting sleeves with a finishing by a plied cord; the purple band decoration of narrow width. The only difference is the position of the bands. This may be due to artistic reasons since the bands were of great importance, and had to be visible in the painting. They were in danger of not being recognised when moved to an upper position on the arm. The stylistic evidence evokes the impression that the textile has been produced in the Roman military spirit of the mid 3rd century AD, just as the Julius Terentius painting at Dura Europos (Fig. 7.3). Thus the close relationship suggests an interpretation of the textile fragments as tunics of the *equites* possibly in military service, as parts of officers' tunics especially of a higher rank of a centurion, dating to the first half of the 3rd century AD. The depictions and

---

83.   Compare consideration Paetz gen. Schieck 2005, 82–92 no. 29.

84.   It is most likely that the Krefeld object was bought by the private collector in the same period. After keeping it for a while has been handed over to the museum.

85.   Louvre, Paris, inv. no. X 4408 (du Bourguet 1964, 68 B 11) The fragment measures 22 cm in warp direction and 20 cm in weft direction, being cut in modern times, leaving only one original edge.

original textile finds also suggest these *manicae* to have been combined with a distinctive type of *clavi*, of the arrow-shaped type.

ARROW-SHAPED *CLAVI* AND THEIR ORIGIN

Just as the textile fragments from Dura Europos, Tyranos' tunic is decorated by a doubled purple *clavus* showing up on his right shoulder: purple bands arranged vertically, end up gabled, lead to an arrow-shaped ornament pointing downwards (Figs 7.1, 7.6–7.7, 7.12–7.13). A second set of *clavi* is to be reconstructed on the other shoulder, being covered by the cloak. Such ornaments carried out in tapestry weave have been found in the ruins of Dura Europos, but also in the waste dumps of the small Roman fort (*praesidium*) of Didymoi, Egypt, located in the Arabian Desert, on the road from Koptos to Berenike.[86] The fortress was abandoned in the middle of the 3rd century AD. The inhabitants have exclusively been Roman soldiers, thus the population has basically been male. According to Dominique Cardon, director of research at the CNRS, nine textile fragments resemble an arrow-shaped *clavus* of the Dura type, being concordant to Tyranos' dress.[87] The fragments of Didymoi consist of an undyed whitish ground weave and purple tapestry weaves. They prove the use of these arrow-shaped ornaments in military contexts in Egypt and Syria, during the period of the fourth quarter of the 2nd century up to the middle of the 3rd century AD. In concordance with the painted shroud from Luxor, the arrow-shaped, purple decorations may thus be considered as symbols of rank within the Roman army, being rarely depicted in Egyptian art. Only one mummy portrait,

Figure 7.9. Mummy Portrait of a Young Man found in the Fayum (Egypt), Antikensammlung, Staatliche Museen zu Berlin inv. no. 31161/23 © J. Laurentius, Antikensammlung, SMB.

which is kept by the *Staatliche Museen Preußischer Kulturbesitz Berlin*, shows a beardless man with a slender face, long, dark brown hair tied together in his neck (Fig. 7.9).[88] He is dressed in two tunics; his upper tunic shows the purple arrow-shaped *clavi*. Whether this portrait depicts a soldier,

86. Maxfield 2000, 424–428; Bender Jørgensen 2004, 87–91. Some of the arrow-shaped ornaments have been presented by Hero Granger-Taylor at the Purpureae Vestes III conference in November 2008.
87. My special thanks go to Dominique Cardon, who was so kind to share the information on her finds from Didymoi with me. Her results will be published in D. Cardon and H. Granger-Taylor, What did they look like? Clothing textiles from Didymoi: case studies. In H. Cuvigny (ed.), *Didymoi – Une garrison romaine dans le desert Oriental d'Égypte I, Les fouilles et le matériel*, Cairo, IFAO, in preparation. The finds from Didymoi: D99.3306.1. A and B (two fragments, phase 11 of the rubbish dump, discarded between 176 and 210 AD, the purple shade was dyed with indigo and madder), D98.10204.2 (filling of cistern 2, discarded between 200 and 225 AD), D99.13103.1. A, B and C (fort, discarded between 220 and 250 AD), D99.13501.2 (fort, discarded between 220 and 250 AD), D99.13705.1 (fort, discarded between 220 and 250 AD), D2000.12207.3 (fort, discarded after 220 AD), D2000.12015.2 (fort, discarded after 230 AD).
88. Staatliche Museen Preußischer Kulturbesitz Berlin inv. no. 31161/23. Borg 1998, 69 no. 82. Differing from Annemarie Stauffer and Andreas Schmidt-Colinet, the author observed only male depictions among the Egyptian mummy portraits. Compare: Schmidt-Colinet and Stauffer 2000, 42 footn. 153.

still has to be discussed since his long hair is bound to a 'Horus-curl', which is a typical trait of the Isis-cult in Roman Egypt.[89]

Textile finds of the described features and arrow-motives, but of earlier date derive from Palmyra, Syria. Completely woollen tapestry weave, whitish ground-weave, and purple arrow-shaped decoration have been found in the elevated ground floors of the grave towers of Palmyra, located in the western necropolis, dating to the 1st and 2nd century AD (Fig. 7.10).[90] Two larger pieces of textiles derive from the tomb of Jamblicho being fragments of the chest and shoulder of an upper garment of local type. One of the fragments is decorated with the pyramid-shaped shoulder element, the other comprises four *clavi* with gabled ends out of which rather heart-shaped arrows evolve.[91] To one of them a pyramid shaped shoulder decoration is still attached. From the tower tomb no. 46 derives a tapestry woven piece of textile, which Annemarie Stauffer and Andreas Schmidt-Colinet were able to determine the fragment a shirt's hem, being worn with trousers.[92] They related it to the limestone relief found in the hypogeum called *tombeau dit de l'aviation* in the south-eastern nocropolis at Palmyra, dating to the 3rd century AD. The deceased is presented in an almost lying position, comforted by cushions and being dressed in local costume. He wears a pair of trousers and a shirt, the selvedge of which is supplemented by arrow-shaped *clavi*, and the sleeves carry *manicae* (Fig. 7.11).[93] Schmidt-Colinet and Stauffer suggest the derivation of the motives from stylized arrows or merlons, and imply a religious or cultic connotation.[94] The Palmyrene depictions imply that the arrow-shaped decorations traditionally have been used by males only, even in Palmyrene context. It is quite likely that Palmyrene dress-codes had an impact on the Roman military garment, since Palmyrene auxiliary units served in the Roman army especially in the desert posts along the trading routes of Egypt.

RECONSTRUCTION OF TYRANOS'S DRESS

Since the painted shroud of Tyranos only shows the upper part of the body, questions arise of what the dress looked like below the waist. As described before, the men pictured in the wall-paintings of Dura Europos resemble several features with the Tyranos-painting the date of production, and the elements of dress that are visible. Most of all, though, the military context is of importance, which is especially expressed through the belt and the setting. In analogy to the Dura depictions, Tyranos' tunic was worn with brownish trousers and boot like shoes, the reaching half way down the upper

89.   Borg 1996, 112–121.
90.   A second fragment of this type originally contained seven arrows and decorated either the hem or the shoulder of a shirt. My special thanks go to Annemarie Stauffer and Andreas Schmidt-Colinet for the provision of the images of the relief depiction and the textile find, and for the permission to publish the images in this context. Schmidt-Colinet 1995, 46 fig. 70, 51; Schmidt-Colinet and Stauffer 2000, 15 pl. 3, 91 (on the dating); 187 no. 514 pl. 49 a; pl. 26 c and 49 b.
91.   Pfister 1934, 17 T 11 pl. IIIb, 17 T 13 pl. IIIa.
92.   Schmidt-Colinet 1995, 31, 46 fig. 69. On the dating of the grave-types: Schmidt-Colinet 1985, 677–678. – Schmidt-Colinet and Stauffer 2000, 187 cat. no. 514 pl. 49a, nos 150–153 (13.2 × 66 cm, tabby, tapestry weave, wool, z-spun, 30 threads per cm, dye analyses: weft: Indigo (*Indigofera tinctoria*) + Kermes (*Kermes vermilio*); Schmidt-Colinet 1995, 46, colour pl. 70. Further arrow-shaped ornaments at Palmyra: Schmidt-Colinet and Stauffer 2000, 11 pl. 2; 42; no. 272 pl. 47d (arrow-shape in combination with pyramid motive; z-spun yarns, tyrian purple). See also Pfister 1940, 22 fig. 8, 31 fig. 16, pl. IVc no. L 95; Pfister and Bellinger 1945, 17–19 nos 3, 8, 11–14 fig. 1; 6 pl. 7. 9; 42 footn. 151; Seyrig 1937, 21 fig. 12.
93.   Images of this area are not available.
94.   Schmidt-Colinet and Stauffer 2000, 42.

Figure 7.10. Textile fragment from Palmyra, Damascus National Museum, Palmyra-Archiv. © A. Schmidt-Colinet.

Figure 7.11. Funerary banquet scene from Palmyra, limestone relief, Palmyra-Archiv. © A. Schmidt-Colinet.

thigh, when belted. Other paintings of the same period show men dressed in tunics with arrow-shaped *clavi* depicting the dress in two different lengths, according to the context, which are both rather private but still connected to the military, showing only single *clavi*, and being worn without a belt. A long version reaching the ankles seems to have been common within the symposium-context, while the short version without a belt can be traced as costume for riding hunters.[95] Concerning the decoration of the lower selvedge of the tunic, it is quite sure that it was accompanied by purple coloured *paragaudae*, which bending upwards on both ends, running upwards the tunic and ending in arrow-shaped ends, just like the *clavi* (Figs 7.12 and 7.13). *Paragaudae* can be traced in every depiction of tunics of this kind; they are evident in the Dura-paintings as well as the Brigetio-paintings,

---

95.   For the long tunic version in wall-painting see Borhy 2005, 51–55; Paetz gen. Schieck and Pásztókai-Szeőke, 2010, 106–109. For the long tunic version in mosaic see Doppelfeld 1964, 37–38 no. 19 pl. 31–33. For the short version as gold-glass plate see Cleveland Museum of Art (inv. no. 69.68); diameter: 25.7 cm; it was found at about 1900. The object was first published by Rostovzeff and dated to about 200 AD. Cooney dates it to the period 300–350 AD (Cooney 1969, 255) and the author R. B. (Weitzmann 1977, 89–90) dates it to the mid 3rd century AD. The inscription says: *ALEXANDER HOMO FELIX PIE ZESES CUM TUIS.* For the short version as mosaic see Di Vita and Bacchielli 1999, 43.

mosaics, and gold-glass plate. They appear to have been a major detail even in the pre-composition of the Palmyrene local depictions. (Fig. 7.11)

RÉSUMÉ

Wherever Roman soldiers appeared, they represented the power of the Emperor and the Empire transmitting a distinctive self-awareness, and self-confidence. Religious sacraments consolidated the corporate feeling of unity of a genuine masculine world. Considering themselves as elite evoked a sense of pride among the members of this group, and inspired the invention of distinctive markers determining the soldiers from the rest of society.[96] These signs may have become evident in the *habitus*, the body language, the tongue, the smell, and the dress-codes, and were also stressed by certain sounds such as that of *caligae* and the belts' metal applications.[97] Regarding the outfit, so far, the weapon, the *balteus*, and the ring-buckle belt were taken for distinctive markers of soldiers, and the golden gemstone ring and the ochreous cloak determined centurions of higher rank – all of these markers determine Tyranos to have been a high ranking centurion just below the tribune. Starting from this point, his special dress-decoration proved to have been of symbolic meaning in the military system as well.

Regarding the period of the 3rd century AD, the social affiliation of an individual to the military community can best be traced in the painted shroud of Tyranos. No other funerary painting from Egypt gives such detailed information about individual self-awareness and various identities. Either Tyranos himself, or those who took care of the burial, which might have been his comrades or his family, chose to stress the military context in his commemoration. But they also decided not to leave out the genuine Egyptian aspects and the Greek literacy and naming, proving Tyranos' familial tradition. Thus the painting documents an amalgam of various social and cultural traditions. It perfectly demonstrates that, due to context and occasion, an individual may have implied different markers, symbols, and uniforms in order to indicate his belonging – in this case they are even merged .

Despite these aspects, the quality of this image has to be stressed, especially regarding the textile details such as the ornaments, the cloth, and the twined warp-threads forming the sleeves edge. It even permits the comparison with textile remains. The correlation of different archaeological categories of material, the images and the textile remains, finally leads to the suggestion of uniforms and dress-codes within the Roman military that seem to have become custom in the early 3rd century AD, initiated by the Severan dynasty and coming from the East, particularly Syria.

Syrian textile production had a great impact on the Late Roman textile ornaments, colours, and techniques. Palmyrene textile finds suggest the use of tapestry woven decorations in the 1st to the 2nd century already. It was not before the late 2nd–early 3rd century at all, that decorative element on tunics and cloaks such as *tabulae* and *orbiculi* can be proven beyond Syria.[98] Earliest *clavus*-motifs of arrow shape carried out in tapestry weave and being designed in purple and off-white appear to have been forestalled in limestone sculptures and in weaves.[99] They originate from local dress, ornamenting the neck opening and the selvedge of shirts worn with trousers. Whether they had

---

96. James 1999.
97. See Stefanie Hoss in this volume.
98. Schmidt-Colinet 1995, 47 fig. 72, 49 fig. 77; Schmidt-Colinet and Stauffer 2000, 162–163, pl. 3a–c, 15a, 54–55 no. 355, pl. 15a no. 355.
99. Schmidt-Colinet 1995, 46 fig. 69–70; Schmidt-Colinet and Stauffer 2000, pl. 49a–b.

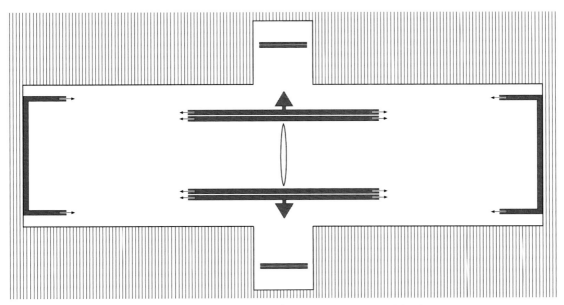

Figure 7.12. Tunic woven to shape © cesrem, A. P. g. Schieck.

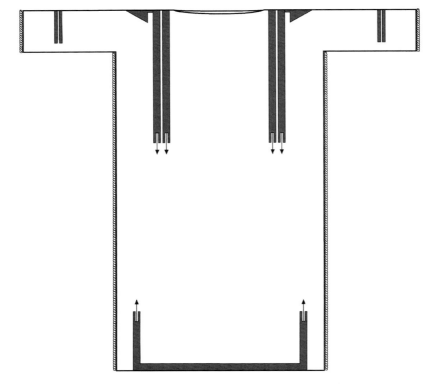

Figure 7.13. Reconstructed Tunic © cesrem, A. P. g. Schieck

a certain meaning in regard of social ranks or professions in Palmyra, is not determinable at the moment. Their spreading started within the region, reaching Dura Europos, influencing the Roman tunic decoration, when the Roman military began to incorporate regional 'barbarian' elements of dress into military dress, due to recruitment of local and foreign people.[100] The spreading to Egypt may have occurred through Syrian soldiers whose units have been transferred to Egypt. Such a unit is the *Palmyreni sagittarii* that have been employed in order to guard the trade route from the most important marketplace in the region, Koptos, to Berenike, at the coast of the Red Sea, during the reign of Caracalla.[101] At Koptos military units and caravans received their supplies, and Palmyrene tradesmen were major participants in the trading system. Along this road, Didymoi is located, which is the tiny fort that existed up to the mid 3rd century, where several of these arrow-shaped ornaments have been found.

Concluding from the investigation of the images depicting Roman military and textile fragments, it becomes evident that they date to the same period which is the first half of the 3rd century AD. It appears that the adaptation of decorative markers as symbols of distinction within the Roman military may have been initiated in Severan times. Possibly in the course of Caracalla's military reforms, the impact of the military on the Emperor and vice versa has to be considered greatly. It is the spirit of the Severan dynasty, which makes the establishment of military uniforms and signs of distinctions quite probable, and there seem to have been further distinctions of ranks that were emphasised by the number of *clavi*. Some tunics simply show one band on each shoulder, others show two. Still it needs to be stressed that the dress described is to be considered as the 'gala-dress', not being worn in combat situations. What the latter clothes looked like still deserves further investigation.

ACKNOWLEDGEMENTS

I am grateful for the personal exchange with numerous colleagues, and the permission to publish various images and information within this article. My special thanks go to Klaus Parlasca (Frankfurt) who has sent me his original slide of the painted shroud and gave permission to publish it; Brigitte Tietzel, director of the *Deutsches Textilmuseum* (Krefeld), who granted the permission to investigate and publish object no. 00024; Maya Naunton and Navina Haider of the *Metropolitan Museum of Art* (New York) kindly exchanged information on an object of their collection, provided the image, and gave permission to publish it; Annemarie Stauffer and Andreas Schmidt-Colinet, who provided the images of a textile fragment and a limestone sculpture from Palmyra, and granted their publication; Gesa Schenke (Oxford) who read the inscription anew; Dominique Cardon (LaSalle) who kindly provided the information on the textile finds from Didymoi; and Robert Fuchs (Cologne), who employed his non-destructive colour-spectrometry technology on the Krefeld textile. My thanks also go to Graham Sumner, who has been dealing with the reconstruction of the painted shroud from the graphic illustrator's point of view with re-enactor background. The discussion on the details depicted has been fruitful; the results can be found in this volume as well. Finally, my thanks go to Michael Tellenbach, coordinator of the DressID-project, which is funded with the support of

---

100. James 1999, 21–23; Bagnall 1993, 177. Flavius Abinnaeus, commander of Dionysias, was first stationed in Upper Egypt in charge of a Syrian unit. Recruitment was done locally, thus the army has not been an "alien body" as Roger S. Bagnall calls it, but part of local society. Bagnall 1993, 179, 177: "… should have made them fit fairly easy into the society they guarded."; Lesquier 1918, 159, 203–205; Mitthof 2000, 378–379, 381–382. Most of these men have been born as free persons within the garrisons, being members of dynasties of soldiers.

101. Drexhage 1982, esp. 20, 32; Maxfield 2000, 426; Ruffing 1995, 33. A stelae found at Koptos presents two Palmyrene soldiers, see Aubert and Cortopassi 1998, 163 no. 112.

8. WARRIOR COSTUMES IN IRON AGE WEAPON DEPOSITS

Susan Möller-Wiering

INTRODUCTION

1700 years ago, hundreds of warriors made their way to South Scandinavia, seeking fame and booty. Elegantly shaped boats brought them to the Danish coast. The leader on his adorned horse holds up a red shield decorated in silver and gold while his officers loosen their swords from beautiful baldrics. The men's bright lances and spears are shining. An impressive army ... unless one notices the leader's hairy chest and sun burnt knees because he wears neither tunic nor trousers... unless one hears the warriors coughing because they are lacking cloaks to keep away the cold at night... and unless one realizes that their ships are half drowned because they did not caulk them properly. Simply leaving out the textiles, the picture of this army is not only incomplete but even bizarre.

Recalling military aspects of that time and region – i.e. the Roman Iron Age north of the Empire – the textiles are only one of many still open questions. Some answers may be found in the weapon deposits, which seemingly contain the equipment of defeated foreign warriors.[1] But is that true for the accompanying textiles as well – i.e. did they belong to the foreigners? If so, are they the remnants of the warriors' clothing or are they textiles of any other function? And if they were clothes, what did they look like? What is known about materials, types of weave and colours?

THE WEAPON DEPOSITS

Weapon deposits from Roman Iron Age are wide-spread. They concentrate along the east coast of Jutland and its hinterland as well as on the island of Fyn but are also well known from further east, e.g. from the Baltic islands.[2] While the oldest ones belong to a quite early period, possibly already around the birth of Christ,[3] the majority of deposits were laid down from about 200 AD onwards.[4] The most recent sites noteworthy in this context date to the 5th century. They are interpreted as sacrifices given by the local or regional population to their gods after a successful battle. For the deposit of their offers, the people chose lakes and bogs.

Some deposits contained only few pieces, e.g. half a dozen in Gremersdorf-Techelwitz in north Germany.[5] Others consist of many thousand items: weapons like shields, swords, lances, spears and

---

1. For the discussion of this point, see Ilkjær 2003,59f; Lund Hansen 2003, 85f.
2. Ilkjær 2003, 45, fig. 1.
3. Pauli Jensen 2008,138.
4. Ilkjær 2003, 46, fig. 2, plus table on the cover of the same book.
5. The material is kept at Archäologisches Landesmuseum, Schleswig.

axes, horse equipment and personal belongings like knives, combs, fishing hooks etc. The following results are based on the investigation of four of the largest sites, i.e. – from north to south –

- Illerup Ådal, situated southwest of Aarhus in Jutland,
- Vimose on Fyn, in the vicinity of Odense,
- Nydam in the region of Sønderborg, a little north of the Danish-German border,
- and Thorsberg which is south of this border, not far from Schleswig.[6]

Three of these sites – Thorsberg, Nydam and Vimose – were already excavated in the 1850s and 1860s by the Danish archaeologist Conrad Engelhardt.[7] In Nydam, the excavations were resumed mainly in the 1990s.[8] And already somewhat earlier, the deposit of Illerup Ådal was investigated.[9]

One result of the analysis of the non-textile materials was the identification of regions where the foreign warriors may have come from. Although this is still under discussion[10] the main idea may be described as follows:

- During the first attacks the aggressors came from the south, i.e. Germany mainly north of the Empire. Vimose and Thorsberg are concerned here, both characterized by a strong Roman impact.
- During the second phase additional attacks occurred also from the north, in particular from south, west and middle Norway. This is the time when the enormous deposit of Illerup Ådal was created.
- Finally, during the third phase, the foreigners seem to have come from other regions in Scandinavia than before, i.e. from further north and east. The deposit of Nydam belongs to this group.

Thus, the textiles presented here may well be regarded as a homogeneous group because they all belong to the same type of archaeological sites. For their interpretation, however, it must be kept in mind that they are of a similar but not of the same age and that they may be connected to different regions within a very large geographical area.

PRESERVATION

Chemically, the bogs of Illerup Ådal, Vimose and Nydam are more or less alike. Because of their basic character, textile fibres were usually destroyed. Some did survive nevertheless, mainly when they were in contact with metals, particularly with iron. On the other hand, the acid in the bog of Thorsberg helped to preserve textiles as flexible tissues while the iron often has deteriorated.

When Conrad Engelhardt worked in Nydam in 1864, he was interrupted by the German-Danish war. This conflict had great impact not only on the region and the people, on politics and history, but also on the finds from the weapon deposits, which – to some extent – were then shared between the two countries. In case of e.g. lance heads with dozens or rather hundreds of items, sharing was rather easy. In case of the textiles of which only few had survived, a crude solution was chosen: some of them were simply cut for this purpose.

---

6.   The research project was connected to Danish National Research Foundation's Centre for Textile Research in co-operation with Archäologisches Landesmuseum Schleswig, and was financed by the Danish Forskningsrådet for Kultur og Kommunikation. The complete report will be published soon.
7.   Lived 1825–1881. For excavation reports please see Engelhardt 1863; 1865; 1869.
8.   Jørgensen and Vang Petersen 2003, 258f.
9.   Ilkjær 2003, 47.
10.   Lund Hansen 2003, 87ff.

THE TEXTILES: MATERIALS, WEAVES AND COLOURS[11]

As far as it was examined, all preserved material is sheep's wool.[12] This does not mean that only wool was in use – but textiles made of vegetal fibres were either not laid down in the bog or they have deteriorated. In general, the wool fibres were well prepared before spinning in order to achieve a homogeneous yarn material. The weaving was similarly carefully carried out, resulting in generally few weaving faults.

Figure 8.1. Thorsberg, chequered cloak (3686), not to scale. Copyright and courtesy Susan Möller-Wiering and The Danish National Research Foundation's Centre for Textile Research.

An important aspect characterizing textiles are their patterns. One can distinguish between those on the basis of colours and those connected to variations in spinning and weaving. Regarding the types of weave, the whole material of more than 200 items consists of only few tabbies, but many 2/2 diamond twills, often in z/s. Although the differences may not be obvious to the naked eye, they are visible. I.e., even if one perhaps doesn't perceive the pattern as such, the various weaves create clearly different impressions of the fabrics as a whole. It is the author's hypothesis that the quality in the sense of spinning and weaving patterns is related to a textile's function on the one hand and to prestige or the owner's status on the other hand.

Like most other archaeological textiles in the north, the colours nowadays mainly consist of various shades of brown. During the stay in the bog – and possibly during conservation as well – the colours changed and formerly existent shades are lost. However, much of the wool seems to be unpigmented and thus suitable for dying. A few unconserved items from Illerup Ådal have indeed preserved some red and blue dyestuff. At least red is very probable for Nydam as well. In Thorsberg, evidence for dyed textiles is very well preserved. There is, for example, a chequered tissue (no. 3686) with two different shades of blue (Fig. 8.1) and an additional reddish material in the weaving border. Another example is a reddish fabric with blue sewing threads (no. 24824a). Most interesting in this respect is item no. 3683, a red dyed piece on which the colour is well preserved on the inside while the outside has become pale. The microscopic study showed that much of the colour had faded already before the textile was brought to the bog. To the same piece belongs a tablet woven band, which looks purple. The dye, however, was not real purple but a mix of red and blue.[13] More tests will be carried out in the near future. Coloured patterns in the sense of stripes or checkers also occurred such as item no. 3686 already mentioned. Since the colours are usually so much alike to the eye nowadays, it is difficult, however, to estimate how representative dyed textiles were, and it may well be that in the Iron Age, not everybody could afford colourful textiles.

---

11. For further details see Möller-Wiering 2008 as well as Möller-Wiering 2010.
12. E.g. Schlabow 1976, 61–66, 70, 76f, 80–83; Hald 1980, 70ff.
13. Fischer 1997, 108.

PRIMARY FUNCTIONS

One of the central questions of the investigation focuses on the textiles' primary function: are they the warriors' clothes or did they fulfil any other purpose? Amongst the Thorsberg material, there are a few pieces of unquestionable function. So it is nothing new to claim that shirt or tunic, trousers and cloak constituted the main male dress elements of that time – as also known from numerous Roman depictions. Still, some details can be added or corrected in comparison to former descriptions.[14]

One of the complete pieces of clothing from Thorsberg is a tunic, no. 3683 mentioned above because of its red inner and pale outer side plus the purple tablet woven band. The band was sewn onto both cuffs, as a decoration. Furthermore, the tunic contains at least two other peculiarities, firstly the seams on the right and left side of the body. Nowadays they are open, and fragments of blue plied yarns stick out from the tissue (Fig. 8.2). Some details like stitching holes and the lack of signs of pulling on the thin blue cords or rather on the tissue indicate that the cords were not used for closing the seam but probably had some decorative function. The second amazing detail is a small hole, which was neatly trimmed. The diameter of the hole is about 0.4–0.5 cm, the trimming c. 0.3 cm wide. The sleeves as well as the neck opening demonstrate that the position of the hole was on the back, on the left shoulder. Unfortunately, its function remains unclear. All in all, this tunic must be seen as a high quality piece of clothing.

Besides the tunic, tight fitting trousers were found. The good quality of the piece no. 3684 is similar to that of the tunic. Generally, trousers may be seen as typical garments for the peoples of the Eurasian steppes, particularly the Scythians, whose way of life was connected to riding.[15] From there, they seem to have come westwards. In a Germanic or provincial Roman context, riding is associated with high status – the horse equipments found in the deposits were already mentioned. In the case of the Thorsberg trousers, their integrated stockings are remarkable. Unambiguous parallels for this type are rare and chronologically as well as regionally very diverse. The most ancient example to be mentioned here comes from the King's Palace in Persepolis in Iran and is dated to the 5th century BC.[16] The relief depicts a Skyth delegation presenting their tribute. A chronologically close parallel is a painting from a Roman grave in Silistra in Bulgaria, dated to around 300 AD.[17] The trousers there do not only have attached feet but also roughly made loops for a narrow belt as the Thorsberg trousers have (Fig. 8.3). On the fresco, it is a servant who carries the trousers and shoes for his master. Both these well-known parallels are thus connected to persons of more or less high status. A third parallel may be added, although much younger. It was excavated in Alpirsbach in south Germany and dated to the early 16th century.[18] The material is linen and the integrated stockings were fashionable at that time. Although they were not any more a specific part of a riding costume, fashion was certainly connected to prestige.

The best parallel to these trousers, however, comes from Thorsberg itself, i.e. a second pair of trousers was excavated there (no. 3685; Fig. 8.4), and stockings were also sewn to this piece. In this case, the uppermost edge of the trousers was cut off. But still, they reach quite far up the body. Therefore, loops – like on the other trousers – still further up do not seem probable. So a different way

---

14. E.g. Schlabow 1976.
15. Widengren 1956, 229; Nockert 1991, 116.
16. E.g. Widengren 1956, 238.
17. E.g. Croom 2002, 58, fig. 17–1.
18. Sturm 2003, 17f.

Figure 8.2. Thorsberg, side seam of the tunic (3683), warp horizontally, scale in cm. Copyright and courtesy Susan Möller-Wiering and The Danish National Research Foundation's Centre for Textile Research.

of keeping the piece in place should be assumed and that is rolling it down over a simple belt. Some details on Roman reliefs may be interpreted in this way.[19]

When Conrad Engelhardt excavated the remains of rather large, non-tailored textiles, he called them "kapper" in his diary (1860), meaning 'cloaks'. It seems that he never used another word for them, e.g. 'blanket' or any other neutral expression. Evidently, he was very sure of their function. This may be due to the many Roman depictions of soldiers and barbarians with cloaks. Another reason may be that Engelhardt knew sleeveless cloaks still from his own time. In this context, Prinz von Arenberg from Belgium may be mentioned briefly. The prince was an officer in the Austrian army and was involved in the German-Danish War.[20] In the summer of 1864 he spent a day in Nydam – after Engelhardt had left the site. His digging – for treasures? – ended in a mess and his finds are today lost. Illustrating this anecdote, Bemmann and Bemmann reproduce a painting of the prince. Prinz von Arenberg wears a long,

Figure 8.3. Thorsberg, belt loop on trousers (3684), warp horizontally, scale in cm. Copyright and courtesy Susan Möller-Wiering and The Danish National Research Foundation's Centre for Textile Research.

19. See Schlabow 1976, Abb. 61; Hald 1980, 331, fig. 394.
20. Bemmann and Bemmann 1998, Bd. 1, 79f.

Figure 8.5. Nydam, clasp with textile (7093), scale in mm. Copyright and courtesy Susan Möller-Wiering and The Danish National Research Foundation's Centre for Textile Research.

sleeveless cloak, rather tight fitting trousers, a helmet, a weapon – one may detect more than one similarity with the Iron Age finds. Another interesting reproduction, given by Stine Wiell[21], is an early reconstruction based on the Thorsberg finds, published shortly after the German-Danish war. It shows an armed Iron Age chieftain wearing pale trousers, a red long-sleeved tunic reaching almost down to the knees and worn under another tunic – blue, less long and with short sleeves – plus a dark greenish blue cloak. The second tunic is pure fiction in shape and colour. Yet, the combination of white, red and blue in one costume may be interpreted as a signal against Denmark – as was the case with a later depiction using similar colours.[22] Blue, red and white are the colours of the country of Schleswig-Holstein the status of which was the reason for that war. In any case, the picture of that chieftain does give the impression of wealth and high status.

Figure 8.4. Thorsberg, trousers (3685). Copyright and courtesy Roberto Fortuna, National Museum of Denmark.

Due to their state of preservation, the material from the three other sites Nydam, Vimose and Illerup Ådal cannot contribute very much to the question of what ancient warrior clothing looked like. At first sight, the textiles do not reveal their primary function at all. There are, however, solid arguments for interpreting them as clothing. In

---

21. Wiell 2003, 73, fig. 7.
22. Wiell 2003, 81, fig. 16.

Figure 8.6. Illerup Ådal, textile with cuts on shield boss (RGZ), scale in cm. Copyright and courtesy Susan Möller-Wiering and The Danish National Research Foundation's Centre for Textile Research.

Nydam, many small silver clasps were found in different variations (Fig. 8.5). Clasps are well known in Scandinavia from around 300 AD onwards.[23] Such hooks and eyes had the same function as cuff links or simple buttons nowadays and were often placed in rows. Yet, sleeves are not the only possibility of where to put clasps. There are examples where they closed the bottommost part of a tunic along the seams on the right and left side – again a decoration of the seams – as well as on trousers down on the ankles. In any case, they are valuable decorations of clothing. Some of the tiny fragments of textiles connected to clasps found in Nydam are reddish in colour, thus resembling Thorsberg.

Regarding the textile quality in terms of fibre preparation and number of threads per cm the range of qualities is practically identical at all four sites. As indicated by the Thorsberg textiles, these are qualities suitable for good clothing. No trace of coarse or carelessly made textiles was found. Simpler, contemporary textiles are known, for example, from the settlement of Feddersen Wierde in Lower Saxony.[24] While they may be interpreted as every day textiles, the difference in regard to the high standard of the fabrics from the weapon deposits is remarkable. Finally, there are parallels between the sites which are connected to the textiles' secondary or final function and to the question whether they belonged to the defeated foreigners or perhaps to the victorious local people.

23.   Nockert 1991, 108.
24.   Ullemeyer and Tidow 1981.

THE SACRIFICE

This latter question refers to the ritual meaning the period from the end of the battle and until the textiles reached the bottom of the bogs or lakes. The investigation of the weapons has shown that many of them were damaged.[25] One can distinguish between damages due to the battle and damages inflicted afterwards. On the shield bosses from Illerup Ådal in particular, there are sometimes conspicuous straight cuts in the textiles (Fig. 8.6). A simple and plausible explanation for these cuts is that they are an equivalent to the strokes on the weapons. The same is observable in the material from Vimose, although there are only four shield bosses with textiles preserved. Furthermore, the phenomenon is not restricted to the fragments connected to iron but occurs also on the large pieces of clothing from Thorsberg, on the tunic as well as on cloaks. This means that all these textiles were treated in the same way as the weapons were. As a consequence, one could say that the textiles belonged to the foreigners, that it was their clothing.

CONCLUSION

Four of the largest Roman Iron Age weapon deposits – Illerup Ådal, Vimose and Nydam in Denmark as well as Thorsberg in Germany – contained not only huge amounts of weapons and personal belongings but also textiles. This paper focuses on the primary function of these textiles, i.e. clothing. The picture still relies to a great extent on the well-known and well-preserved Thorsberg finds, with tunic, trousers and cloak as the main elements of the male dress. Yet, this knowledge is partly corrected and supplemented with new details about how the clothes were worn. The state of preservation is much worse at Illerup Ådal, Vimose and Nydam but the comparison between Thorsberg and the other places shows that at all four sites, the quality of the textiles is practically identical. Clasps typical for tunics were found in large amounts in Nydam. Finds from Illerup Ådal, Vimose as well as Thorsberg – textile and non-textile – possess remarkable cuts which point to a common custom, i.e. of selecting the same kinds of materials and of treating them in the same way as a preparation for the sacrifice and thus for the creation of the deposits.

---

25.   Petersen 1995, 24; Bemmann and Bemman 1998, Bd. 1, 318.

9. PAINTING A RECONSTRUCTION OF THE DEIR EL-MEDINEH PORTRAIT ON A PAINTED SHROUD AND OTHER SOLDIERS FROM ROMAN EGYPT

Graham Sumner

INTRODUCTION, BACKGROUND AND RESEARCH[1]

This paper deals specifically with the background behind two painted reconstructions of one Roman soldier illustrated in a surviving portrait believed to have been found at Deir el-Medineh near Luxor in Egypt dating to the third century AD. (This portrait is discussed in further detail by Annette Paetz gen. Schieck elsewhere in this publication.)

For over thirty years the author has worked as an archaeological illustrator specializing in reconstruction paintings relating to the Roman period and he is a member of *The Association of Archaeological Illustrators and Surveyors (AAI&S)*. Principally his work has involved reconstructions of Roman military life and latterly learning more and more about the clothing of the individual Roman soldier. Ideally the author is commissioned directly by and works together, with the archaeologists who are involved with the subject being reconstructed. As a freelance illustrator however many other projects by necessity have to rely on published reports to supply the source material. An example of this process is illustrated in Figure 9.1.

As a former re-enactor for almost twenty years with the highly respected British Roman military re-enactment society, *The Ermine Street Guard*, the author is well aware of the unquenchable thirst for knowledge with regards to clothing that exists amongst the re-enactment community but also how difficult it is for non academics to find this information even in the age of the Internet. Many finds remain unpublished often decades after discovery or for various reasons are published in works too expensive or inaccessible for the general reader. The terminology too can often be confusing to the novice and during the course of ten years research into Roman military clothing the author rarely found material in publications with 'Roman' in the title! The author believes the present publication is a massive step in the right direction.[2]

---

1. It was a great privilege to be invited by Marie Louise Nosch of CTR Copenhagen to provide a contribution.
2. The first attempt at reconstructing the portrait was made using only the published material the author was able to find. The second revised portrait was produced after consultation with Ms. Schieck herself. The author himself is not a specialized textile historian and therefore some of the problems relating to clothing encountered during the first reconstruction may seem trivial to someone well versed in that subject. However other difficulties also arose as a result of how information relating to this subject is published, in some cases not published, or is interpreted.

Figure 9.1. Reconstruction of two early Principate soldiers based in Egypt. The figure on the left represents one of the most well known characters from Roman Egypt, Claudius Terentianus after a series of letters written to his father Claudius Tiberianus. Terentianus is at first a recruit into the navy based with the fleet at Alexandra. In his letters he sends requests for various items of clothing and perhaps more illuminating other pieces of military equipment such as swords and spears which he wishes to be sent from home. Blue clothing is associated with the navy from the days of the Roman Republic, (Sumner 2009) while the footwear is based on finds from Mons Claudianus. This illustration was prepared for the popular 'Ancient Warfare' magazine for an article by the magazine's editor Jasper Oorthyus. The man on the right is the Decurion, Marcus Caninius, a soldier mentioned on an ostraca from Mons Claudianus in Egypt and who is depicted wearing clothing and footwear which is all based on the published finds from the site itself (Bender Jørgensen 2000; Mannering 2000). The author always feels it adds more of a personal touch if an authentic Roman name can be given to the character being illustrated, even though in this case no portrait or graffito sketch of Caninus exists from which to base a portrait. Illustrations © Graham Sumner.

Although the Roman army was probably amongst the largest institutions in the ancient world using and purchasing textiles the standard general works on the Roman army available in English make few references to clothing in comparison with the armour and equipment and yet there is little evidence that Roman soldiers fought naked. There are also few references in these works to the specialist textile volumes and the works of the historians whose names have become so familiar to the author over the last few years. The issue of gender bias was raised by Gillian Eastwood (1983) who implied that only women were interested in textiles. There may be a grain of truth in this because as any casual observer will notice the majority of Roman military armour and equipment experts and enthusiasts are male while the majority of textile experts and published authors are female.

Two landmark works by Graham Webster (1979) and Yann Le Bohec (1989, English translation 2000) will serve to illustrate the almost cheerful indifference to Roman military clothing in popular publications. Webster (1979, 123) briefly mentions that soldiers wore a linen undergarment with a short sleeved wool tunic over it. He himself did not understand how that tunic was arranged and suggested it might have been fastened by brooches. Webster does not cover third century tunics or later and, in fact until recently, it was rare for books on the Roman army to cover anything other than the early Principate in any great detail, even those that include something on the Late Roman army still tend to neglect the third century.

Le Bohec also has little to say about clothing and even states that the answer to soldiers dress is "not obvious" (Le Bohec, 125) and only gives a very brief description of clothing in the chapter on tactics! Problems in translation also arise and the text does not mention cloaks by name but refers to them as 'cassocks' or 'coats'. No illustrations of clothing are provided nor any references to archaeological finds are included in either books. Neither works includes any reference to the changes in clothing fashions which occurred throughout the Roman period which were equally comparable to the changes in equipment, weapons and tactics employed by the Romans.

Apart from these general works the study of military clothing has only really been touched upon elsewhere by two articles. The first by Erich Sander (1963), was perhaps influenced by recent and contemporary military practices because he tried to categorise Roman military clothing shown on military tombstones into the various categories that would have been familiar in nineteenth and early twentieth century armies. Therefore he identified various uniforms worn during different activities including an exercise uniform, a field or battle dress and a parade dress. He also tried to identify rank with cloak colour and suggested that tribunes wore white cloaks and centurions wore dark brown cloaks.

The second example, an article by Nicholas Fuentes (1987), concluded that the military tunic was of wool and made from two sheets of material sewn together which in shape was long and narrow. Although principally about tunic design his article took the issue of clothing colour much further than anyone else had done to that date. He argued that white tunics were the standard colour for all soldiers tunics apart from centurions who were distinguished by a red tunic. This certainly caused a lot of controversy and division amongst the re-enactment community which lasts to this day. Many publications since have followed this theory even though Fuentes only supported his theory by discussing eighteen pieces of evidence from frescoes to mosaics roughly covering the first to the fourth centuries AD.

Two immediate points should be obvious to those studying roman clothing. Firstly there is certainly far more evidence for clothing colour than the eighteen examples that Fuentes selected. For example he does not include any of the Egyptian funeral portraits which ironically he could have used in support of his argument that military tunics were white. Secondly his conclusion and subsequent reconstruction of the early imperial tunic as being long and narrow was in fact based on a misinterpretation of the evidence from Nahal Hever where surviving tunics both from here and elsewhere are broad and wide (Yadin 1963).

Neither of these two articles discussed in any great detail the later style of clothing or the transition from short sleeved tunics to the combination of long sleeved tunics with trousers that were a feature of third century clothing.

More recent publications have added little more. For instance the large 600 page *A Companion to the Roman Army* edited by Paul Erdkamp (2007), devotes little more than a single paragraph to soldiers' clothing! In the words of one contributor, James Thorne, "... the evidence for military clothing is problematic". Adrian Goldsworthy (2003, 118–121.) goes much further than most but supplies no patterns or examples of textile finds and once again it is really the imperial army of the Principate that is being described.

Most illustrators or re-enactors therefore wishing to recreate Roman military clothing would probably turn first to the works of the author and illustrator, Peter Connolly (1975). Or the popular series of illustrated books on military subjects published by Osprey of Oxford, Great Britain, which include several titles on the Roman army, for example Michael Simkins (1984). Unfortunately many of these titles go into little detail of the clothing, provide few examples of original sources and again rarely describe anything outside the popular early imperial period. In Britain at least they are also often rather unfairly categorised as children's books because of their illustrative nature and perhaps are seen as little value to academics.

This lack of any readily available information for the general public has led to an ongoing debate and division amongst the worldwide re-enactment community over what colour the Roman military tunic was. Humorously labelled 'the Tunic wars' this consequently led the present author to begin to study the subject himself and this resulted in two books for Osprey (Sumner 2002, Sumner 2003) and more recently a much larger volume on Roman Military Dress (2009), in which almost one hundred and fifty sources for the colour of clothing were cited. Otherwise the best introduction into the topic of military clothing are the sections in the chapters which deal chronologically with all the equipment of the Roman soldier in the revised edition of Mike Bishop and Jon Coulstons' *Roman Military Equipment* (2006). Although other than sculpture they show no textile finds or any of the painted portraits. Fortunately for the proposed reconstruction of the Deir el-Medineh soldier an excellent discussion of third century Roman military uniforms is also available, from Simon James (2004).

PAINTED PORTRAITS OF SOLDIERS

The painting of the Deir el-Medineh soldier does not of course exist in isolation. Hundreds of painted portraits have been discovered in Egypt and some of them have now been identified by various authors as being soldiers. Previously according to Euphrosyne Doxiadis (1995) they had been seen as members of the Ptolemaic dynasty – or even modern fakes – however these theories have now been discounted. The present author (2009, 130–136) has suggested that at least 23 of the portraits that he has seen illustrated, could represent military personnel. This identification rests on the simple observation that males are generally depicted in the paintings wearing a white tunic with *clavi* and a white mantle draped over the man's left shoulder (see also Schieck 2010, fig. 11–12, 92–93).

Anything which deviated from this pattern was therefore deemed worthy of further scrutiny. This process included a number of characters that had already been long regarded as soldiers, mostly the men with bright blue or red cloaks worn over their left shoulder who also wore a studded red belt crossing over the body. Sometimes associated with this belt was what appeared to be the pommel of a sword, which further enhanced the identification of the individuals as soldiers.

To this list the author added a number of other possible candidates, normally classified elsewhere simply as males that might require further investigation. If the latter are included then it would seem that the soldiers are wearing in most cases a white tunic decorated with either red or black *clavi*, with either a red, blue or yellow ochre cloak. One cloak in this series is white while another is black. A couple of examples may show red tunics and while most cloaks appear to be of *paludamentum* type, the classic cloak worn by senior officers, others appear to show the rectangular *sagum* or even the hooded cape known as a *paenula* (Sumner 2009, 131–136). This 'uniform' may be seen as an undress or parade uniform comparable to what soldiers wore in the Victorian staged studio portraits. However once again that may be too modern a viewpoint.

It is difficult to determine what rank any of these soldiers might have had. It is common to assume that these portraits show the wealthier members of Romano-Egyptian society and therefore any portraits that might depict soldiers must show officers. However, a papyrus letter from a certain *Apion* records how a new recruit into the fleet stationed at Alexandria commissioned a portrait before he left so his family would remember what he looked like [BGU 423] (see Campbell 1994, 13). Therefore it is possible that some of the surviving portraits show quite humble soldiers. To further complicate matters the range of cloak colours does not really tie in with either of the theories proposed by Sander and Fuentes. The direction the belt crosses over the shoulder might provide a clue but one which may only apply to the early Principate. At that time according to Bishop and Coulston (2006) only centurions and some standard bearers wore their swords on their left and some soldiers in the portraits are wearing swords on their right (Fig. 9.2).

By the third century judging from sculptural evidence, chiefly tombstones, all soldiers whatever their rank up to and including the emperor, wore their sword on their left side. The consensus of opinion is that left handed recruits would be trained to use their right hand, as otherwise military formations might be compromised. Furthermore as James (2004) notes by the early third century a clear military identity has been adopted. This even extends to the soldiers physical appearance where soldiers in general had effected a short cropped haircut and short trimmed beard. Soldiers wear a long sleeved belted tunic with tight fitting cuffs, a *sagum* style cloak pinned over the left shoulder, tight fitting trousers and enclosed boots. In sculpture, from common soldier to emperor, this 'uniform' appears almost identical (James 1999). Of course this might be somewhat misleading as the sculptures now lack colour and give few clues as to what the original clothing might have been made from or their quality and these elements may have been very important factors in determining rank.

Based on both the stylistic grounds and analysis of the fashion elements and hairstyles depicted the majority of the portraits appear to date well before the example from Deir el-Medineh. The latter therefore is unique in several ways. Not only is it later in date than most of the other examples but it incorporates details not illustrated elsewhere, it shows more of the individual than usual and is the only painted portrait of a soldier which shows a waist belt and even the persons arms, although one is largely covered by the folds of his cloak. This is why the painting of the Deir el-Medineh soldier is so fascinating and important as it also provides the missing colour factor.

One aspect of this is the two dark purple bands visible around the cuffs. The emperor Aurelian is credited with presenting soldiers tunics with one band and others with two or more bands up to five (SHA *Aur* XLVI.6.) While it is clear from artistic sources that the practice of soldiers wearing bands of cuffs predates Aurelian, it is also clear that every tunic from this period found in Egypt, many clearly not belonging to soldiers at all, had two bands on the cuffs. The red brown ochre colour of the cloak worn by the Deir el-Medineh soldier would suggest that it had been made from un-dyed wool retaining the natural lanolin helping to make the cloak water resistant. Sander had suggested that this colour of cloak might indicate centurion rank. Nevertheless the author himself found few other examples of red ochre brown cloaks worn by soldiers depicted in Roman art. (This point would have consequences later when the first re-construction painting was commenced.) One notable example was from the Via Latina catacomb. (Sumner 2009, 147). Instead many soldiers, like the officers in the Luxor fresco, have yellow ochre cloaks which is quite a common cloak colour (Sumner 2009, figs 75–7, 88–89). Cloaks of this colour also appear in the *Terentius* Fresco from Dura Europos, where apart from the white cloaks worn by two men they are the only other coloured cloaks depicted. (Sumner 2009, 137 and pl. 19).

The beardless appearance in the Deir el-Medineh portrait suggests youth. Perhaps the man was a new recruit like *Apion* who commissioned a portrait for his family upon enlistment. However it is equally possible that he might have been a young man of equestrian rank perhaps indicated by the finger ring in the portrait and had obtained a commission purchased by a wealthy patron and been some sort of junior officer.

DEIR EL-MEDINEH SOLDIER, RE-CONSTRUCTION: THE FIRST VERSION
(Fig. 9.3)

With the impending release of his publication on Roman Military Dress, the author wanted to promote the work in as many ways as possible. As it would be generally agreed that the more spectacular textile finds from the Roman period actually come from Egypt the author therefore approached the editor of Ancient Egypt magazine with the idea of an article on the Roman military in Egypt which would be illustrated with re-constructions of various Roman characters based on archaeological finds from Egypt.

The proposed illustrations for the article would include, a soldier wearing clothing discovered at Mons Claudianus (Fig. 9.1), an officer based on the Tetrarchic period fresco from Luxor, a late Roman period officer with one of the Sassanid Persian style riding coats (Fig. 9.5) and two re-constructions based on two of the famous encaustic portraits (Figs 9.2 and 9.3). The latter would include the painting on linen said to have been discovered at Deir el-Medineh dated to the late second or early third century AD and now in the collection of the Luxor Museum. Overall within the constraints of a magazine article it was hoped that the paintings would cover a broad time frame and illustrate some of the changes in clothing styles.

All the paintings would be painted on watercolour board in Gouache. While this medium is diluted with water it is less opaque than watercolour and it is possible to repaint over certain areas of paint, which is often a useful tool in archaeological illustration as archaeologists rarely agree when it comes to re-construction and a painting can expect to go through many revisions! However the medium has its limitations and it would be very difficult to re-paint over large areas of red with white for instance.

With the publication date of the military dress book imminent, time as always was also limited and work began in the summer of 2009. The author was confident that enough easily sourced background material for the chosen subjects existed and was readily available for the project to be achieved. The only subject where there appeared to be very little published information available was the Deir el-Medineh portrait.[3]

The *Luxor Museum Guidebook* (1979) stated that the soldiers clothing consisted of a white *chiton* (tunic). The sleeves of the tunic appeared to be fringed and it looked like there were two decorative bands on the visible arm and further decoration in the form of two bands *clavi*, each with a notched end. Furthermore the text in the guidebook also said that the cloak which appeared to be of *sagum* type was red. This did seem at odds with the colour image from the French site which appeared to be brown ochre. However most of that picture had an overall brownish tinge and red was at least consistent with what the author knew about other mummy portraits and the surviving colour of Roman cloaks elsewhere in Roman art and literature. A previous work of re-construction by the author, an earlier Antonine period painting, also had a red cloak but of *paludamentum* type (Fig. 9.2). Together the two re-constructed portraits would show important clothing changes even within a short space of time.

---

3.   The author only possessed a single black and white image from the *Luxor Museum Guidebook* (1979). Subsequent research only produced one other image which nonetheless was in colour, from the French website 'Portraits Du Fayoum' (portraits.fayoum.free.fr). The author even attempted to contact the Luxor Museum itself but without any success.

Figure 9.2. Reconstruction of an unknown soldier based on a portrait now in the Manchester museum, England. The portrait dating from the mid second century AD, shows a man wearing a bleached white tunic with a single visible red clavus. Over his left shoulder he has a red cloak. In the original painting the white pommel of a sword can just be seen together with a red belt decorated with alternate bronze and silvered discs. It is possible that the belt is not a baldric as is usually interpreted but a type of belt illustrated in the Chatsworth relief, (Sumner 2009). This is how it is depicted in this reconstruction showing how the belt prevents the tunic from interfering with the sword and a further example can be seen worn in the reconstruction of Terentianus in figure 1. Illustration © Graham Sumner.

Some other problems of interpretation however were immediately obvious. The sword appeared small and indistinct and of unusual type. It appeared to have been added as an afterthought perhaps even by another artist, there was no baldric visible and no other means of attaching it to the waist belt. The waist belt itself was narrow and appeared to have no obvious method of fastening. A small single white disc was visible although the guide book stated that two white, possibly silver, buckles were present. There was no obvious sign of a ring buckle a common means of fastening the belt in the third century, however a loop did seem to be visible on the man's right side which was another feature of belts at this period. Also missing because of damage to the linen around the man's right shoulder was any type of cloak brooch or *fibula*.

Figure 9.3. Reconstruction of the Deir el-Medineh soldier, version 1. Illustration © Graham Sumner.

Some decisions then had to be made and the reconstruction would try to fill out the missing elements in the original such as the brooch and perhaps to recreate the man as he might have appeared in life rather than in a contrived funeral setting. The reconstruction would also highlight some of the less obvious elements in the original and try to interpret them for the viewer. In effect the reconstruction would be a reconstruction of what the ancient artist might have seen before him and to compare this with what he actually recorded.

To help fill out the apparent missing details the author drew heavily on the work of James (2004). Normally the aim would be to include as much evidence from as near to the location of the subject as possible. Unfortunately published finds of military equipment from Roman Egypt appear to be almost non-existent by comparison with those in the west. Another Eastern site that was well published, like Dura Europos in Syria would therefore provide suitable replacements. Fortunately in the third century military equipment was beginning to achieve a measure of standardisation. For example a boot found at Dura Europos is practically identical to one found in Usk in South Wales, while helmet fragments from Dura Europos were similar to other examples found in Germany. It hence felt reasonable to include a brooch or other equipment found at Dura Europos into the reconstruction.

The sword in the Deir el-Medineh portrait did not appear to be a regular standard of this particular date. The third century sword, now called a *spatha*, was a much bigger weapon than the famous *gladius* worn by early imperial troops. Overall the weapon in the painting was very small and as mentioned earlier did not appear to be attached to either the waist belt that was visible in the original or to a baldric that was not visible. Swords from Dura Europos and elsewhere appeared to be by comparison much larger with very prominent pommels (James 2004, Bishop and Coulston 2006). The missing baldric was not too much of a problem as tombstones too do not always show them, presumably hidden by the folds of the cloak. The baldric was chosen to be included in the reconstruction, otherwise the sword would apparently float in the air.

The main concern therefore was what type of weapon to actually show. The small size might suggest either a dagger or another type of weapon called nowadays a *semi-spatha* which was closer in size to the earlier *gladius*. None of the latter type of weapon illustrated in Bishop and Coulston (2006) had surviving hand guards, grips or pommels. Furthermore the weapon in the painting did not look like any surviving dagger either. Therefore a decision was made to incorporate a standard sword based on an example from Dura Europos. The various elements of the sword handle were painted white to match what was shown in the original, which presumably indicated that the handle was made from either ivory or bone, both common materials used for making sword handles.

With all the problems concerning the waist belt and no obvious source of local references to supply any clues as to what was indicated in the original, the author thought it wise not to attempt a reconstruction which might prove to be either misleading at best or at worst totally inaccurate. With the same concerns in mind the man is depicted holding a papyrus scroll rather than make any interpretation of the two objects the man was holding in the original, one of which looked like corn on the cob. As it transpired more than one scholar had been confused over these objects; classical military historian Michael Speidel believed the right hand object to be a whip (Schieck 2010).[4]

DEIR EL MEDINEH SOLDIER, RE-CONSTRUCTION: THE SECOND VERSION *(Fig. 9.4)*

Some additional observations however may be included here which occurred during the painting of both re-constructions of the Deir el-Medineh soldier.[5] The original reconstruction had also been shown to a textile historian, Hero Granger-Taylor, who first drew the authors attention to the dark

---

4.   Soon after classical archaeologist Annette Paetz gen. Schieck was consulted on the topic, and she was happy to comment on the work and offer suggestions for improvements regarding the colour of the cloak, the edges of the sleeves, some details on the *clavi,* and whether to leave out the belt or not.

5.   The author was invited to provide an article and illustrations for this publication and hence Annette Paetz gen Schieck was consulted as she was working on the very same soldier's portrait from Deir el-Medineh. The author is extremely grateful for her assistance and the mutual collaboration at every stage on the reconstruction.

band on the mantle over the soldiers left arm which she interpreted as maybe a stripe or an early example of a popular cloak decoration from the later Roman period called a *tablion* (pers. comm.). This was incorporated into the final version as something possibly worthy of debate by other textile scholars.

Initial fears that the sword drawn by the ancient artist was too small were somewhat allayed by using a modern full size reconstruction of a *spatha* worn by a model. However while it was clear that the pommel and hand guard were drawn at approximately the correct scale in the original it was obvious the ancient artist had illustrated the hand grip itself at a much smaller size. This would even apply if a dagger rather than a sword was what was intended. Unless the ancient artist had based his painting on a weapon as yet undiscovered this was possibly so he could clearly show the entire weapon to the viewer. The modern reconstruction painting shows that otherwise the hand grip and hand guard are mostly obscured by the soldiers left arm.

The sword used in the second reconstruction was based on an example from the book on Roman swords by Christian Miks (2007 pl. 32. A90) because it showed a straight sided hand guard like the one illustrated in the original. The sword would in all probability have been attached to a leather baldric passing over the right shoulder. If this was not the case it would still have to be attached to the waist belt by some other form of fastener. The original source showed neither method but from the position of the pose one version or another would have to be included in the modern reconstruction. Again it is possible the ancient artist left this detail out as it might have been confusing to the viewer, or perhaps because he had already made a compromise with the scale of the sword grip then this additional detail was not thought important enough to include. It was decided, however, to include the lower part of a baldric in the reconstruction because the modern replica worn by a model indicated that it would be visible. As it can be seen in the reconstruction it could indeed be confused for being part of the cloak because of the similar colour.

The two objects held in the hands were based on the descriptions in the article by Ms. Schieck (2010). The wreath of immortelles was based on an actual example found in an Egyptian tomb (Walker and Bierbrier 1997, 207 pl. 295). Another missing detail from the original was a *fibula*, perhaps as mentioned earlier due to damage to the original linen painting rather than by a mistake of the artist. One of the more general types of brooch in widespread use in the Eastern empire and therefore suitable for use in Egypt was therefore included in the reconstruction.

One final point can now be made. As a result of seeing a hi-resolution image of the original painting it was possible to discern what may well be the faint outline of a bronze ring buckle on the soldier's belt. This was a vital component of soldier's belts and it was surprising that at first something like this did not appear to be shown in the original. This missing element could now be included in the revised reconstruction.[6]

CONCLUSION

It is always fascinating how people can look at a subject and arrive at totally opposite conclusions. This is especially apparent with regards to archaeology and in particular Roman military subjects. Do we see what we want to see, what we are conditioned to expect to see or see what is actually there? Any attempt at reconstruction for whatever reason usually involves the process of trying to marry

---

6.   A final personal touch was that as a result of working with Ms. Schieck a name could be given to the soldier which is just visible on the original portrait: *Tyranos.*

Figure 9.4. Reconstruction of the Deir el-Medineh soldier, version 2. Illustration © Graham Sumner.

Figure 9.5. A late Roman officer from Egypt c. AD 550–600. This illustration is based on another painting of the same character prepared by the author from interpretations and information supplied by the Italian author Dr Raffaele D'Amato for the publication Roman Military Clothing 3 *Oxford (2005). In marked contrast to the much plainer costume of the early Principate this officer wears clothing inspired by Persian costume in particular the riding costume, numerous examples of which were discovered in Egypt at the end of the nineteenth century. He wears a linen hooded dalmatica over a linen under-tunic both decorated with Coptic period motifs. Over his trousers is a pair of silk leggings, now on display at the Textile museum in Lyon and he holds one of the very long sleeved Persian style riding coats (Fluck and Vogelsang-Eastwood 2004). Illustration © Graham Sumner.*

the pictorial sources, ancient literature and archaeological finds together. In re-construction the latter will always take precedence over the first two. However if a reconstruction is to be attempted, what happens when the archaeological evidence is not clear or simply missing all together?

With regards to the reconstruction of the Deir el-Medineh soldier in this paper the process involved two people who, because they came from very different backgrounds and expertise, saw and understood things very differently when studying a single source which to all intents and purposes would have been regarded at first by both parties as fairly straightforward. Even with the benefit of a better source photograph the author would never have included or been aware of some of the textile details that were so obvious to A. Schieck, while the years of experience of wearing and carrying recreated clothing, equipment and weapons made the author more aware of how the sword should be attached. Nevertheless while more familiar with the clothing and the drapery of early Principate military costume and how it may hang and function, this experience was not always of relevance to a re-construction of the fashion of a later period and the clothing in the first reconstruction was not as tailored as it should have been. Therefore the experience was mutually of benefit to both and both learnt something from the other. The difference between the two painted re-constructions is visually striking.

Nevertheless it is rare that the evidence from the Roman period for any particular subject is so irrefutable that any form of reconstruction can be regarded as 100% accurate. When there are still so many gaps in our available knowledge it is clear that collaborations from as many disciplines as possible must inevitably be required in order to achieve something that can be presented as being as accurate as possible. At least through the medium of paint a simple but effective method of re-construction and public presentation is available and where, if things do go wrong it is relatively easy to correct.

Carlisle

NORTH SEA

Mogontiacum

Vicani Marosallenses

Augusta Vindelicorum
Ovilavis
B

ATLANTIC
OCEAN

Flavia So
Poetovio

Lugudunum

Mediolanum

Aquileia

Ravenna

Burum
Salon
Nov

Orvieto
Caere
Tarquinia
Rome

Vulci
Civita Castellana
Veii
Segni
Satricum

Paestum

Caesarea

Syracuse

Carthago

MED

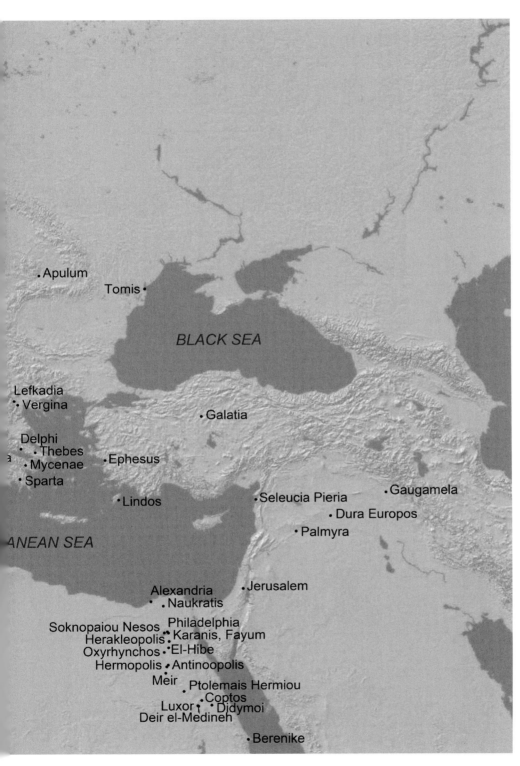

Apulum

Tomis

BLACK SEA

Lefkadia
Vergina

Galatia

Delphi
Thebes
Mycenae
Sparta

Ephesus

Gaugamela

Lindos

Seleucia Pieria

Dura Europos

Palmyra

ANEAN SEA

Alexandria
Naukratis

Jerusalem

Soknopaiou Nesos
Herakleopolis
Oxyrhynchos
Hermopolis
Meir

Philadelphia
Karanis, Fayum
El-Hibe
Antinoopolis

Ptolemais Hermiou
Coptos
Luxor
Deir el-Medineh
Djdymoi

Berenike

BIBLIOGRAPHY

ABBREVIATIONS

AJA	*American Journal of Archaeology*
AJAH	*American Journal of Ancient History*
Ant.Afr.	*Antiquities Africaines*
ATN	*Archaeological Textile Newsletter*
Cd'É	*Chronique d'Égypte*
DNP	*Der Neue Pauly. Enzyklopädie der Antike*
IEJ	*Israel Exploration Journal*
JAAS	*Journal of the Arms and Armour Society*
JRMES	*Journal of Roman Military Equipment Studies*
JRS	*Journal of Roman Studies*
MBAH	*Münstersche Beiträge zur Archäologi und Handelsgeschichte*
MKDAIAA	*Mitteilungen des Keiserlich Deutschen Archaeologischen Instituts, Atenische Abteilung*
PCPS	*Proceedings of the Cambridge philological Society*
ZPE	*Zeitschrift für Papyrologie und Epigraphik*

Abd el-Raziq, M. (1984) *Die Darstellungen und Texte des Sanktuars Alexanders des Großen im Tempel von Luxor.* Mainz.

Adams, C. E. P. (1995) Supplying the Roman Army: *O.Petr.* 245. *ZPE* 109, 119–124.

Adams, C. E. P. (2007) War and Society. In Ph. Sabin, H. van Wees and M. Whitby (eds), *The Cambridge History of Greek and Roman Warfare. Vol. 1, Greece, the Hellenistic world and the rise of Rome. Vol. 2, Rome from the late Republic to the late Empire* Vol. II. Part I, 198–135.

Albers, A. (1965) *On Weaving.* London.

Aldrete, G. S., and Bartell, S. (forthcoming) *Unraveling the Linothorax Mystery: Reconstructing and Testing Ancient Laminated Linen Armor.*

Alföldi, A. (1952) *Der frührömische Reiteradel und seine Ehrenabzeichen.* Baden-Baden.

Alföldy, G. (2000) Das Heer in der Sozialstruktur des Römischen Kaiserreiches. In G. Alföldy, D. Dobson, W. Eck (eds), *Kaiser, Heer und Gesellschaft in der Römischen Kaiserzeit. Gedenkschrift für Eric Birley.* Stuttgart, 33–57.

Alston, R. (1994) Roman Military Pay from Caesar to Diocletian. *JRS* 84, 113–123.

Alston, R. (1995) *Soldier and Civilian in Roman Egypt. A Social History.* London/New York.

Alston, R. (2002) *The City in Roman and Byzantine Egypt.* London/New York.

Anderson, J. K. (1970) *Military Theory and Practice in the Age of Xenophon.* Berkeley.

Andrén, A. (1940) *Architectural Terracottas in Etrusco-Italic Temples.* Lund/Leipzig.

Andronikos, M. (1984) *Vergina The Royal Tombs and The Ancient City.* Athens.

Aubert, M. F. and Cortopassi, R. (1998/1999) *Portraits de l'Egypte romaine.* Paris.

Baginski, A. and Avigail S. (2004) Textiles from Nessana. In D. Urman (ed.), *Nessana*. Beer-Sheva, 216–221.

Bagnall, R. S. (1993) *Egypt in Late Antiquity*. Princeton.

Bagnall, R. S. (1997) The People of the Roman Fayum. In M. L. Bierbrier (ed.), *Portraits and Masks. Burial Customs in Roman Egypt*. London, 7–15.

Baines, P. (1989) *Linen: Hand Spinning and Weaving*. London.

Bar-Nathan, R. (2006) *The Pottery of Masada* in *Masada VII – The Yigael Yadin Excavations 1963–1965 Final Report*. Jerusalem.

Barber, E. W. (1991) *Prehistoric Textiles*. Princeton.

Bauchhenss, G. (1978) Germania Inferior. Bonn und Umgebung, *CSIR Deutschland* III:1. Bonn.

Baur, P. V. C. and Rostovzeff, M. I. (eds) (1931) *The Excavations at Dura-Europos conducted by the Yale University and the French Academy of Inscriptions and Letters. Preliminary Report of the Second Season of Work, October 1928–April 1929*. Yale, New Haven.

Beck, F. and Chew H. (1992) *Masques de fer. Un officier romain du temps de Caligula. Exhibition St.-Germain-en-Laye 1991–1992*. St.-Germain-en-Laye.

Bemmann, G. and Bemmann, J. (1998) *Der Opferplatz von Nydam. – Bd 1: Text, Bd 2: Katalog und Tafeln*. Neumünster.

Ben-Tor, A. (2009) *Back to Masada*. Jerusalem.

Bender Jørgensen, L. (2000) The Mons Claudianus Textile Project. In D. Cardon and M. Feugère (eds), *Archéologie des Textiles des Origines au Ve Siècle*, Actes du Colloque de Lattes, *Octobre 1999*. Motagnac, 253–263.

Bender Jørgensen, L. (2004) A matter of material: Changes in textiles from Roman sites in Egypt's Eastern Desert. *Tissus et vêtements dans l'Antiquité tardive. Antiquité tardive*, Revue internationale d'histoire et d'archéologie (Ive–VIIIe s.) 12, 87–99.

Bergman, I. (1975) *Late Nubian Textiles*. Copenhagen.

Bianchi Bandinelli, R. (1970) *Rome the Centre of Power: Roman Art to AD 200*. London.

Birley, A. R. (1997) Supplying the Batavians at Vindolanda. In W. Groenman-van Waateringe *et al.* (eds), *Roman Frontier Studies*. Oxford, 273–280.

Birley, A. R. (2002) *Garrison life at Vindolanda*. Stroud, Gloucestershire.

Birley, A. R. (2007) Two Types of Administration attested by the Vindolanda-Tablets. In R. Haensch and J. Heinrichs (eds), *Herrschen und Verwalten. Der Alltag der römischen Administration in der Hohen Kaiserzeit*. Köln/Wien, 306–324.

Bishop, M. C. (1989) Naming the parts – did the Roman army use technical terminology? *Exercitus* 2, 102–103.

Bishop, M. C. (1992) The early imperial 'apron'. *JRMES* Vol. 3, 81–104.

Bishop, M. C. and Coulston, J. C. N. (1993) *Roman Military Equipment from the Punic Wars to the Fall of Rome*. London.

Bishop, M. C. and Coulston, J. C. (2006) *Roman Military Equipment from the Punic Wars to the Fall of Rome*. 2nd ed. Oxford.

Blanck, H. (1982) Die Malereien des sogenannten Priester-Sarkophages in Tarquinia. In *Miscellanea Archaeologica Tobias Dohrn Dedicata*, 11–28. Rome.

Blanck, H. (1983). Le pitture del "Sarcofago del Sacerdote" nel Museo Nazionale di Tarquinia. *Dialoghi d'Archeologia*, Terza Serie 1, no. 2, 79–84.

Bocci, P. (1960) Il sarcofago tarquiniese delle Amazzoni al Museo Archeologico di Firenze. *Studi Etruschi* 28, 109–125.

Bonfante, L. (1978a) The Language of Dress: Etruscan Influences. *Archaeology* 31 no. 1.

Bonfante, L. (1978b) Historical Art: Etruscan and Early Roman. *AJAH* 3, 136–162.

Bonfante, L. (1989) Nudity as a Costume in Classical Art. *AJA* 93, 543–570.

Bonfante, L. (2003) *Etruscan Dress*. 2nd edition. Baltimore and London.

Bordenache Battaglia, G. (1979) *Le Ciste Prenestine I. Corpus*. Rome.

Borg, B. (1996) *Mumienporträts. Chronologie und kultureller Kontext*. Mainz.

Borg, B. (1998) Der zierlichste Anblick der Welt … In *Ägyptische Porträtmumien*. Mainz.

Borhy, L. (2005) Ganz nach römischem Geschmack. Neu entdeckte Wandmalereien aus der einst blühenden Legionsstadt Brigetio am nordöstlichen Limes (Komárom/Szőny, Ungarn). *Antike Welt* 4, 51–55.

Boppert, W (1992) Militärische Grabdenkmäler aus Mainz und Umgebung. *CSIR Deutschland* II:5.

Bottini, A. and Stari, E. (2007) *Il Sarcofago delle Amazzoni*. Milano

Bourdieu, P. (1984) *Distinction: a Social Critique of the Judgment of Taste* (transl. by R. Nice). Cambridge, MA.

Breasted, J. H. (1922) Peintures d'Epoque Romaine dans le désert de Syrie. In *Syria. Revue d'Art Oriental et d'Archéologie* III. Paris, 177–206.

Breeze, D. J., Close-Brooks, J. and Ritchie, G. (1976) Appedix: The Ownership of Arms in the Roman Army. In Soldiers' Burials at Camelon, Stirlingshire, 1922 and 1975. *Britannia* 7, 73–95.

Brélaz, C. (2005) *La sécurité publique en Asie Mineure sous le Principat*. Basel.

Brown, D. (1976) Bronze and Pewter. In D. Strong and D. Brown (eds), *Roman Crafts*. London, 25–42.

Brown, F. E. (1936) Arms and Armor. In A. R. Bellinger, M. I. Rostovtzeff, C. Hopkins and C. B. Welles (eds), *The Excavations at Dura-Europos: Preliminary Report of Sixth Season of Work, October 1932–March 1933* , 439–466. New Haven.

Brunt, P. A. (1976) Did Rome disarm her citizens? *Phoenix* 29, 260–270.

Buranelli, F. (ed.) (1987) *La Tomba François di Vulci*. Rome.

Burgess, E. M. (1958) An Ancient Egyptian Sling Reconstructed. *JAAS* II, 10, 226–231.

Burnham, D. K. (1981) *A Textile Terminology: Warp and Weft*. London.

Busch, A. W. (2003) Von der Provinz ins Zentrum – Bilder auf den Grabdenkmälern einer Elite-Einheit. In P. Noelke. (ed.), *Romanisation und Resistenz in Plastik, Architektur und Inschriften der Provinzen des Imperium Romanum. Neue Funde und Forschungen. Akten des VII. Internationalen Colloquiums über Probleme des Provinzialrömischen Kunstschaffens Köln, 2. bis 6. Mai 2001*. Mainz, 679–694.

Busch, A. W. (2007) Militia In Urbe. In L. de Blois and E. Lo Cascio (eds), *The Military Presence in Rome*, 315–343.

Busch, A. W. and Schalles, H.-J. (2010) *Waffen in Aktion*. In *Akten des 16. Internationalen Roman Military Equiptment Conference (ROMEC) Xanten 13.–16. Juni 2007*, Xantener Berichte 16.

Cagiano de Azevedo, M. (1970) L'autenticità del sarcofago di Orvieto da Torre San Severo. *Römische Mitteilungen*, 10–18.

Cahn, E.-M, Fischer, Th., Hanel, N., Höpken, C. and Rose, H. (2003) Ausgewählte Kleinfundgattungen der Ausgrabungen des Jahres 1998 im Flottenlager an der Alteburg in Köln, *Kölner Jahrbuch* 36, 683–702.

Calament, F. (2005) *La révélation d'Antinoé par Albert Gayet*. Histoire, archéologie, muséographie, Institut Français d'Archéologie Orientale Bibliothèque d'Études Coptes 18, 1/2.

Campbell, B. (1994) *The Roman Army, 31 BC–AD 337: A sourcebook,* London/New York.

Campell, J. B. (1999) Legio. *DNP* 7, 7–22.

Carandini, A., Ricci, A. and de Vos, M. (1982) *Filosofiana: the villa of Piazza Armerina : the image of a Roman aristocrat at the time of Constantine*. Palermo.

Cardon, D. (2002) Chiffons dans le désert: textiles des *praesidia* de Maximianon, Krokodilô et Didymoi (fin du Ier – fin du IIIe siècle ap. J.-C.). In M. Durand and F. Saragoza (eds), *Égypte, la trame de l'histoire: Textiles pharaoniques, coptes et islamiques*. Paris, 40–43.

Cardon, D. and Feugère, M. (eds) (2000) *Archéologie des Textiles des Origines au Ve Siècle, Actes du Colloque des Lattes, Octobre 1999*. Motagnac.

Carter, H. (1933) *The Tomb of Tut-Ankh-Amen Discovered by the Late Earl of Carnarvon and Howard Carter. III.* London.

Carter, H. and A. C. Mace (1923) *The Tomb of Tut-Ankh-Amen Discovered by the Late Earl of Carnarvon and Howard Carter. I.* London.

Cat. Luxor (1978) Egyptian Antiquities Organization (ed.) *The Luxor Museum of Ancient Egyptian Art*. Cairo.

Coase, R. H. (1937) The Nature of the Firm. *N.S.* 4/16, 386–405.

Collingwood, P. (1982) *The Techniques of Tablet Weaving*. London.

Collingwood, P. (1998a) *The Maker's Hand*. Revised edition. London.

Collingwood, P. (1998b) *The Techniques of Ply-Split Braiding*. London.

Colt, Dunscombe H. (ed.) (1962) *Excavations at Nessana*. Jerusalem.

Connolly, P. (1975) *The Roman Army*. Oxford.

Connolly, P. (1981) *Greece and Rome at War*. London.

Connolly, P. (1998) *Greece and Rome at War*. London.

Cooke, W. D., El-Gamal, M. and Brennan, A. (1991) The Hand-Spinning of Ultrafine Yarns, Part 2. The Spinning of Flax. *Bulletin du CIETA* 69, 17–23.

Cooney, J. D. (1969) *The Gold-glass Alexander Plate*. Bulletin of the Cleveland Museum of Art for September, 253–261.

Corcoran, L. H. (1995) *Portrait Mummies from Roman Egypt (I–IV Centuries AD) with a Catalogue of Portrait Mummies in Egyptian Museums*. Chicago.

Coulston, J. C. N. (1983) Arms and Armour in Sculpture. In M. C. Bishop (ed.), *Roman Military Equipment. Proceedings of a Seminar held in the Department of Archaeology and Ancient History at the University of Sheffield, 21st March 1983*. Sheffield, 24–26.

Coulston, J. C. N. (1987) Roman Military Equipment on Third century tombstones. In M. Dawson (ed.), *Roman Military Equipment. The accoutrements of war. Proceedings of the 3rd Roman Military Equipment Research Seminar*. BAR International Series 336. Oxford, 141–156.

Coulston, J. C. N. (2005) Military Identity and personal Self-Identity in the Roman Army. In L. de Ligt, E. A. Hemelrijk and H. W. Singor (eds), *Roman Rule and Civic Life: Local and Regional Perspectives*, Impact of Empire 4. Amsterdam, 133–152.

Coulston, J. C. N (2007) Art, Culture and Service: The Depiction of Soldiers on Furnerary Monuments of the 3rd Century AD. In L. de Blois, E. Lo Cascio (eds), *The Impact of the Roman Army (200 BC–AD 476). Econimic, Social, Political, Religious and Cultural Aspects*, Impact of Empire 6. Leiden, 529–561.

Crocker Jones, G. (1989) *Traditional Spinning and Weaving in the Sultanate of Oman*. Ruwi.

Crowfoot, G. M. (1943) Handicrafts in Palestine, Primitive Weaving, I. Plaiting and Finger-Weaving. *Palestine Exploration Quarterly* 75, 75–88.

Crowfoot, G. M. and E. Crowfoot (1961) The Textiles and Basketry. In P. Benoit, J. T. Milik and R. de Vaux (eds), *Les Grottes De Murabba'at (Discoveries in the Judaean Desert II)*, 52–63 + pls. Oxford.

Cumont, F. (1926) *Fouilles de Doura-Europos (1922–1923)*, Atlas. Paris.

Davies, J. L. (2002) Soldiers, Peasants, Industry and Towns. In P. Erdkamp (ed.), *The Roman Army and the Economy*, 169–203. Amsterdam.

Davies, R. (1989) *Service in the Roman Army*. New York.

de Blois, L. and Lo Cascio, E. (eds) (2007) *The Impact of the Roman Army (200 BC–AD 476): Economic, Social, Political, Religious and Cultural Aspects*. Impact of Empire 6. Leiden and Boston.

Devijver, H. (1989) *The Equestrian Officers of the Roman Imperial Army*, vol. I. Amsterdam.

Devijver, H. (1992) *The Equestrian Officers of the Roman Imperial Army*, vol. II., Amsterdam.

Di Vita, A., Di Vita-Evrard, G., and Bacchielli, L. (eds) (1999) *Das antike Libyen. Vergessene Städte des römischen Imperiums*. Köln.

Doppelfeld, O. (ed.) (1964) *Rom und Karthago, Mosaiken aus Tunesien. Exhibition*. Cologne.

Doxiadis, E. (1995) *The Mysterious Fayum Portraits. Faces from Ancient Egypt*. London.

Drexhage, R. (1982) Der Handel Palmyras in Römischer Zeit. *MBAH* 1,1, 17–34.

Drexhage, H.-J., Konen, H. and Ruffing, K. (2002) *Die Wirtschaft des Römischen Reiches (1.–3-Jahrhundert). Eine Einfürung* (Studienbücher Geschichte und Kultur der Alten Welt). Berlin.

du Bourguet, P. (1964) *Musée National du Louvre. Catalogue des Étoffes Coptes I*. Paris.

Dunbabin, K. M. D. (1999) *Mosaics of the Greek and Roman World*. Cambridge.

Eastwood, G. (1983) A Dirty Piece of Rag. *Popular Archaeology* Jan. 1983, 45–46.

Edmonson, J. (2008) Public Dress and Social Control in Late Republic and Early Imperial Rome. In J. Edmonson, A. Keith (eds), *Roman dress and the fabrics of Roman culture*. Toronto, 21–46.

Egyptian Antiquities Organization, Museum Service, ed. (1982) *The Egyptian Museum, Cairo: A Brief Description of the Principal Monuments*. Cairo.

Eiling, U. (2001) *Philadelpheia*. Studien zur Wirtschafs- und Sozialgeschichte eines Dorfes im römischen Ägypten (1.-3. Jh n. Chr.). Marburg.

Elton, H. (1996) *Frontiers of the Roman Empire*. Bloomington.

Engelhardt, C. (1860) *Diary (Copy of unpublished manuscript)*.

Engelhardt, C. (1863/reprint 1969) *Thorbjerg Mosefund*. Kjöbenhavn.

Engelhardt, C. (1865/reprint 1970) *Nydam Mosefund*. Kjöbenhavn.

Engelhardt, C. (1869/reprint 1970) *Vimose Mosefund*. Kjöbenhavn.

Erdkamp, P. (ed.) (2002) *The Roman Army and the Economy*. Amsterdam.

Erdkamp, P. (ed.) (2007) *A Companion to the Roman Army*. Malden, MA.

Facella, M. and Speidel, M. A. (2011) From Dacia to Doliche (and back). A New Gravestone for a Roman Soldier. In E. Winter (ed.), *Von Kummuh nach Telouch – Archäologische und historische Untersuchungen in Kommagene*, Dolichener und kommagenische Forschungen IV, 207–216.

Feldtkeller, A. (2003) Nierenförmige Webgewichte – Wie Funktionieren Sie? *ATN* 37, 16–19.

Feugère, M. (1985) Nouvelles observations sur les cabochons de bronze estampés du cingulum romain. In M. C. Bishop (ed.), *The Production and Distribution of Roman Military Equipment. Proceedings of the Second Roman Military Research Seminary*. BAR Series 275. Oxford, 117–141.

Feugère, M. (2002) *Weapons of the Romans*. D. G. Smith transl. Stroud.

Fich, H., Fischer-Hansen, T., Moltesen, M. and Waaben, K. (1999) *Græsk Kunst*. Copenhagen.

Filer, J. M. (1997) If the Face Fits … A Comparison of Mummies and their Accompanying Portraits Using Computerised Axial Tomography. In M. L. Bierbrier (ed.), *Portraits and Masks. Burial Customs in Roman Egypt*. London, 121–125.

Filer, J. M. (1999) Ein Blick auf die Menschen hinter den Porträts. Eine Untersuchung ägyptischer Mumien mit Hilfe von Computertomographie und Gesichtsrekonstruktion. In K. Parlasca and H. Seemann (eds), *Augenblicke. Mumienporträts und ägyptische Grabkunst aus römischer Zeit, Exhibition Frankfurt January 30 to April 11, 1999*. Frankfurt/München, 79–86.

Fink, R. O. (1958) Hunt's. Pridianum: British Museum Papyrus 2851. *JRS* 48, 102–116.

Fink, R. O. *et al.* (1971) *Roman Military Records on Papyrus.* Philological Monographs of the American Philological Association 26, London.

Fischer, C.-H. (1997) Historische organische Farbstoffe. *Spektrum der Wissenschaft* 10/1997, 104–108.

Fischer, Th. (1988) Zur römischen Offiziersausrüstung im 3. Jahrhundert. *Bayrische Vorgeschichtsblätter* 53, 167–190.

Fittschen, K. and Zanker, P. (1994) *Katalog der römischen Porträts in den Capitolinischen Museen und den anderen kommunalen Sammlungen der Stadt Rom* (2nd revised edition). Mainz.

Fluck, C. and Vogelsang-Eastwood, G. (2004) *Riding Costume in Roman Egypt.* Leiden.

Foerst, G. (1978) *Die Gravierungen der Pränestinischen Cisten*, Archaeologica 7. Rome.

Foss, C. (1977) Late Antique and Byzantine Ankara. *Dumbarton Oaks Papers* 31, 27–87.

Franzoni, C. (1987) *Habitus atque habitudo militis*: Monumenti funerari di militari nella Cisalpina romana, no. 5. Roma

Fuentes, N. (1987) The Roman Military Tunic. In M. Dawson (ed.), *Roman Military Equipment: The Accoutrements of War*. BAR International Series. Oxford, 41–75.

Gansser-Burckhardt, A. (1942) *Das Leder und seine Verarbeitung in römische Legionslager Vindonissa*, I, Veroffentlichungen der Gesellschaft pro Vindonissa. Basel.

Gayet, A. (1904) *Fantomes d'Antinoë. Les Sépultures de Leukyoné et Myrithis.* Paris.

Gilliam, J. F. (1962) The Moesian 'Pridianum'. In Renard, M. (ed.), *Hommages à Albert Grenier*. Brüssel, 747–756.

Gilliver, K. (2007) The Augustan Reform and the Imperial Army. In P. Erdkamp (ed.), *A companion to the Roman Army*. Malden MA, 183–200.

Gleba, M. (2008) *Textile Production in Pre-Roman Italy.* Oxford.

Goldsworthy, A. (2003) *The Complete Roman Army.* New York.

Gostencnik, K. (2009) *Commercial textile production or household production for domestic use? The evidence of textile-tools and written sources in Roman Noricum.* (Unpublished paper presented at DressID: Study Group E Meeting. Work and Identity: The agents of textile production and exchange in the Roman period 2. Hallstatt, Austria, June, 2009.)

Gräf, J. (2010) Die Schwertgurte aus dem Thorsberger Moor. In Busch, H.-J. and Schalles (eds), *Proceedings of the XVI. International Roman Military Equipment Conference*. Xantener Berichte. Köln, 131–136.

Gräf, J. (in print) Römisch oder germanisch? Die Lederfunde aus dem Thorsberger Moor. In H.-J. Schalles (ed.), *Proceedings of the XVI. International Roman Military Equipment Conference*. Xantener Berichte.

Granger-Taylor, H. (1982) Weaving Clothes to Shape in the Ancient World: the Tunic and Toga of the Arringatore. *Textile History* 13, I, 3–25.

Granger-Taylor, H. (1998a) Evidence for Linen Yarn Preparation in Ancient Egypt – the Hanks of Fibre Strips and the Balls of Prepared Rove from Lahun in the Petrie Museum of Egyptian Archaeology, University College London (Uc 7421, 7509 and 7510). In S. Quirke (ed.), *Lahun Studies*, 102–107.

Granger-Taylor, H. (1998b) The Textile Material from Lahun. In S. Quirke (ed.), *Lahun Studies*, 100–101.

Granger-Taylor, H. (2008) A Fragmentary Roman Cloak Probably of the 1st Century CE and Off-Cuts from Other Semicircular Cloaks. *ATN* 46, 6–16.

Granger-Taylor, H. (forthcoming) The Textiles from Masada, with contributions by T. Vogel, E. Netzer, N. Ben Yehuda, Z. Koren, M. Ciszuk, P. Walton Rogers, K. Lund Rasmussen, J. van der Plicht and F. Nielsen. In J. Aviram, G. Foerster, E. Netzer and G. D. Stiebel (eds), *Masada IX – the Yigael Yadin Excavations 1963–1965*. Jerusalem.

Groenman-van Waateringe, W. (1997) Classical Authors and the Diet of Roman Soldiers: true or false? In *Roman Frontier Studies 1995. Proceedings of the XVIth International Congress of Roman Frontier Studies*, Oxbow Monographs 91. Oxford, 261–265.

Gschwind, M. (1997) Bronzegießer am raetischen Limes, Zur Versorgung mittelkaiserzeitlicher Auxiliareinheiten mit militärischen Ausrüstungsgegenständen. *Germania* 75:2, 607–638.

Haensch, R. (1997) *Capita provinciarum: Statthaltersitze und Provinzialverwaltung in der römischen Kaiserzeit*, Kölner Forschungen 7. Mainz am Rhein.

Hald, M. (1980) *Ancient Danish Textiles from Bogs and Burials*, Publications of the National Museum, Archaeological-Historical Series XXI. Copenhagen.

Hauken, T. (1998) *Petition and Response. An epigraphic Study of Petitions to Roman Emperors* Monographs from the Norwegian Institute of Athens Vol.2. Bergen.

Herz, P. (2007) *Finances and Costs of the Roman Army*. In (ed.) P. Erdkamp, 306–322.

Holliday, P. J. (1993) Narrative Structure in the François Tomb. In P. J. Holliday (ed.), *Narrative and Event in Ancient Art*. Cambridge, 175–197.

Horvat, J. *et al.* (2003) Poetovio. Development and Topography. In M. Šašel Kos and P. Scherrer (eds), *The Autonomous Towns of Noricum and Pannonia: Pannonia I*, Situla 41. Ljubljana, 153–189.

Hoss, S. (forthcoming) Studien zum römischen Militärgürtel im 1.–3. Jh. n. Chr.

Hoss, S. (2006) VTERE FELIX und MNHMΩN – Zu den Gürteln mit Buchstabenbeschlägen. *Archäologisches Korrezpondenzblatt* 2006/2, 237–253.

Hoss, S. (2010) The military belts of the equites. In Busch, H.-J. and Schalles (eds), *Proceedings of the XVI. International Roman Military Equipment Conference*. Xantener Berichte. Köln, 313–322.

Hübener, W. (1963–4) Zu den provinzialrömischen Waffenfunden. *Saalburg-Jahrbuch* XXI, 20–32.

Hudeczek, E. (2002) Flavia Solva, Entwicklung und Topographie. In M. Šašel Kos and P. Scherrer (eds), *The Autonomous Towns of Noricum and Pannonia: Noricum*, Situla 41, 203–212.

Hunt, A. S. (1925) Register of a cohort in Moesia. In *Raccolta di Scritti in Onore di como Lumbroso*. Mailand 265–272.

Ilkjær, J. (2003) Danske krigsbytteofringer. In L. Jørgensen (ed.), *Sejrens triumf. Norden i skyggen af det romerske Imperium*. København, 44–46.

James, S. (1999) The Community of Soldiers: a major identity and centre of power in the Roman Empire. In P. Barker, S. Jundi and R. Witcher (eds), *TRAC 98: Proceedings of the Eighth Annual Theoretical Roman Archaeology Conference Leicester 1998*. Oxford, 14–25.

James, S. (2001) Soldiers and civilians: identity and interaction in Roman Britain. In S. James and M. Millett (eds), *Britons and Romans: advancing an archaeological agenda*. CBA Research Report 125. York, 187–209.

James, S. (2004) *The Excavations at Dura-Europos Conducted by Yale University and the French Academy of Inscriptions and Letters 1928 to 1937. Final Report VII, the Arms and Armour and Other Military Equipment*. London.

Jarva, E. (1995) *Archaiologia on Archaic Greek Body Armour*. Studia Archaeologica Septentrionalia 3. Rovaniemi.

Jost, C. A. (2007) Vorbericht zu den Ausgrabungen 2002–2004 im Limeskastell Niederberg bei Koblenz. In *Forschungen zur Funktion des Limes. Beitrage zum Welterbe Limes* 2. Stuttgart, 49–55.

Junkelmann, M. (1992) *Die Reiter Roms III. Zubehör, Reitweise, Bewaffnung*. Mainz.

Jørgensen, E., Vang Petersen, P. (2003) Nydam mose – nye fund og iagttagelser. In L. Jørgensen (ed.), *Sejrens triumf. Norden i skyggen af det romerske Imperium*. København, 258–284.

Kehne, P. (2007) *War and Peacetime Logistics: Supplying Imperial Armies in East and West*. In P. Erdkamp (ed.), 323–338.

Keppie, L. (1983) *Colonisation and Veteran Settlement in Italy 47–14 BC.* British School at Rome. London

Keppie, L. (2003) Having been a soldier. In J. J. Wilkes (ed.), *Documenting the Roman Army. Essays in honour of Margaret Roxan*, Institute of Classical Studies. London, 31–53.

Koch, G. (1986) *The Material Culture of Kiribati.* Suva 1986

Koeppel, G. M. (1985) *Die historische Reliefs der römischen Kaiserzeit III. Stadtrömische Denkmäler unbekannter Bauzugehörigkeit aus trajanischer Zeit.* Bonner Jahrbücher 185, 141–213.

Koeppel, G. M. (1986) Die historischen Reliefs der römischen Kaiserzeit, IV. Stadtrömische Denkmäler unbekannter Bauzugehörigkeit aus hadrianischer bis konstantinischer Zeit. *Bonner Jahrbücher* 186, 1–90.

Koeppel, G. M. (1989) Die historischen Reliefs der römischen Kaiserzeit, VI. Reliefs von bekannten Bauten der augusteischen bis antoninischen Zeit. *Bonner Jahrbücher* 189, 17–71.

Koh, Bu-Ja (2007) Sambe: Korean Hemp Fabrics. In R. W. Hamilton and B. L. Milgram (eds), *Material Choices: Refashioning Bast and Leaf Fibers in Asia and the Pacific.* Los Angeles, 78–91.

Kolb, A. (2000) *Transport und Nachtrichtentransfer im Römischen Reich*, Klio – Beiträge zur Alten Geschichte. Beihefte NF 2. Berlin

Kraeling, C. H. (1956) *The Excavations at Dura-Europos: Conducted by Yale University and the French Academy of Inscriptions and Letters; Final Report 8; Part 1, the Synagogue* F. E. Brown, A. R. Bellinger, A. Perkins and C. B. Welles (eds). New Haven.

Krüger, J. *et al.* (1990) *Oxyrhynchos in der Kaiserzeit: Studien zu Topographie und Literaturrezeption.* Frankfurt am Main.

Kruse, T. (2005) Eine römische Silberschale in den Staatlichen Antikensammlungen München. *Chiron* 35, 113–136.

Künzl, E. (1994) Dekorierte Gladii und Cingula: Eine ikonographische Statistik. *JRMES* 5, 33–58.

Łajtar, A. (2006) *Deir el-Bahari in the Hellenistic and Roman Periods. A Study of an Egyptian Temple based on Greek Sources. The Journal of Juristic Papyrology* Suppl. IV.

Lauffer, S. (1971) *Diokletians Preisedikt.* Berlin.

Le Bohec, Y. (ed.) (1989) *La troisième légion Auguste.* Paris.

Le Bohec, Y. (1998) Heerwesen [III Rom]. *DNP* 5, 229–232.

Leander Touati, A.-M. (1991) Portrait and historical relief. Some remarks on the meaning of Caracalla's sole ruler portrait. In A.-M. Leander Touati, E. Rystedt and Ö. Wikander (eds), *Munuscula Romana*, Swedish Institute in Rome, Bind 17 af Acta Instituti Romani Regni Sueciae, Series in 4 Degree, 117–131.

Lee, A. D. (2007) *War in Late Antiquity: a social history. Ancient World at War.* Malden, MA.

Lendon, J. E. (1997) *Empire of Honour. The Art of Government in the Roman World.* Oxford

Lesquier, J. (1918) *L'armée romain d'Egypte d'Auguste à Diocletian.* Cairo.

Levick, B. (2004) The Roman Economy: Trade in Asia Minor and the Niche Market. *Greece and Rome* 51.2, 180–198.

Liapis, H. (2005) *The Monastery of Hosios Loukas in Boeotia.* Athens.

Lindblom, K. G. (1940) *The Sling, especially in Africa: Additional Notes to a Previous Paper.* Statens etnografiska museum. Stockholm.

Loeben, C. and Wiese, A. (2008) *Köstlichkeiten aus Kairo! Die ägyptische Sammlung des Konditorei- und Kaffeehaus-Besitzers Achille Groppi (1890–1949).* Basel–Hannover.

Lorimer, H. L. (1950) *Homer and the Monuments.* London.

Lund Hansen, U. (2003) Våbenofferfundene gennem 150 år – forskning og tolkninger. *Sejrens triumf. Norden i skyggen af det romerske Imperium* L. Jørgensen (ed.). København, 84–89.

Mackensen, M. (1987) *Die frühkaiserzeitlichen Kleinkastelle Nersingen und Burlafingen an der oberen Donau*, Münchener Beiträge zur Vor- und Frühgeschichte. München.

MacMullen, R. (1960) Inscriptions on Roman Armour and Supply of Arms to the State. *AJA* 64, 23–40.

MacMullen, R. (1963) *Soldier and Civilian in the Later Roman Empire*. Cambridge MA.

Mannering, U. (2000) Roman Garments from Mons Claudianus. In D. Cardon and M. Feugère 2000, 283–290.

Markle, M. N. III. (1982) Macedonian Army and Tactics under Alexander the Great. In B. Bar-Sharrar and E. N. Borza (eds), *Macedonia and Greece in Late Classical and Early Hellenistic Times, Studies in the History of Art 10*. Washington, 87–111.

Massing, J. M. (2006) In Arms and Amour: Battles in the Gilbert Islands (Kiribati). In *Pacific Arts* NS 1, 44–53.

Maxfield, V. A. (2000) The Development of the Roman Auxilia in Upper Egypt and the Eastern Desert during the Principate. In G. Alföldy, D. Dobson and W. Eck. (eds), *Kaiser, Heer und Gesellschaft in der Römischen Kaiserzeit. Gedenkschrift für Eric Birley*. Stuttgart 407–442.

Miks, C. (2007) *Studien zur römischen Schwertbewaffnung in der Kaiserzeit*. Rahden

Millar, F. (1963) The fiscus in the first two centuries. *JRS* 53, 29–42.

Miller, S. G. (1993) *The Tomb of Lyson and Kallikles: A Painted Macedonian Tomb*. Mainz am Rhein.

Mitthof, F. (2000) Soldaten und Veteranen in der Gesellschaft des römischen Ägypten (1.–2. Jh. n. Chr. In G. Alföldy, D. Dobson and W. Eck (eds), *Kaiser, Heer und Gesellschaft in der Römischen Kaiserzeit. Gedenkschrift für Eric Birley*. Stuttgart, 378–405.

Mitthof, F. (2001) *Annona Militaris. Die Heerversorgung im spätantiken Ägypten* Papyrologica Florentina 32. Florence.

Mitthof, F. (2003) review of R. P. Salomons *Papyri Bodelaine I,* Amsterdam 199. In *Gnomon* 75, 420–424.

Möller-Wiering, S. (2008) Die Textilien aus Illerup Ådal – erste Ergebnisse. In A. Abegg-Wigg and A. Rau (eds), *Aktuelle Forschungen zu Kriegsbeuteopfern und Fürstengräbern im Barbaricum, Internationales Kolloquium Schleswig 15.-18. Juni 2006, Schriften des Archäologischen Landesmuseums, Ergänzungsreihe 4*. Neumünster, 209–214.

Möller-Wiering, S. (2010) Evidence of War and Worship: Textiles in Roman Iron Age Weapon Deposits. In M. Gleba, U. Mannering, C. Munkholt, M. Ringgaard and E. Andersson Strand (eds), *NESAT X*, Ancient Textiles Series vol. 5. Oxford, 167–173.

Möller-Wiering, S. (2011) *War and Worship: Textiles from 3rd to 4th century AD Weapon Deposits in Denmark and Northern Germany* Ancient Textiles Series vol. 9. Oxford.

Montserrat, D. (1996) 'Your name will reach the hall of the Western Mountains': some aspects of mummy portrait inscriptions. In D. M. Bailey (ed.), *Archaeological Research in Roman Egypt. The Proceedings of the Seventeenth Classical Colloquium of the Department of Greek and Roman Antiquities, British Museum, 1–4 December, 1996*, 177–185.

Moock, D. W. von (1998) *Die figürlichen Grabstelen Attikas in der Kaiserzeit*. Mainz.

Morel, J.-M. A. W. and Bosman, A. V. A. J. (1989) An early Roman burial in Velsen I. In van Driel-Murray, C. (ed.), *Roman Military Equipment: the sources of evidence. Proceedings of the fifth Roman Military Equipment Conference*. BAR International series 476. Oxford, 167–191.

Moretti Sgubini, A. M. (2004) *Eroi Etruschi e Miti Greci: gli affreschi della Tomba François tornano a Vulci*. Celenzano.

Moxon, I. S. (2000) The Linen Breast-Plates in Herodotus 3.47. *Ars Textrina* XXXIV, 125–133.

Müller, A. (1873) *Programm des Königlichen Gymnasiums zu Ploen.* Ploen.

Müller, M. (1999) *Faimingen-Phoebiana II. Die römischen Grabfunde. Limesforschungen* 26. Mainz.

Nagy, M. (2007) *Lapidárium. Ausstellungskatalog des Ungarischen Nationalmuseums.* Budapest.

Netzer, E. (1991) *The Buildings, Stratigraphy and Architecture. Masada III. The Yigael Yadin Excavations 1963–1965 Final Reports.* Jerusalem.

Nicolay, J. A. W. (2007) *Armed Batavians. Use and Significance of Weaponry and Horse Gear from non-military contexts in the Rhine Delta (50 BC to AD 450). Amsterdam Archaeological Studies* 11. Amsterdam.

Nockert, M. (1991) *The Högom Find and other Migration Period Textiles and Costumes in Scandinavia. – Högom II* Archaeology and Environment 9. Umeå.

Oldenstein, J. (1976) Zur Ausrüstung römischer Auxiliareinheiten. *Berichte der Römisch-Germanischen Kommission* 57, 49–284.

Ortisi, S. (2007) The Roman Military in the Vesuvius Area. In L. de Blois, E. Lo Cascio (eds), *The Impact of the Roman Army (200 BC–AD 476). Econimic, Social, Political, Religious and Cultural Aspects.* Impact of Empire 6. Leiden, 343–353.

Paetz gen. Schieck, A. (2002) *Textile Bilderwelten. Wechselwirkungen zwischen Ägypten und Rom. Untersuchungen an 'koptischen' Textilien unter besonderer Berücksichtigung unbearbeiteter Sammlungsbestände in Nordrhein-Westfalen,* Dissertation.

Paetz gen. Schieck, A. (2003) *Aus Gräbern geborgen. Koptische Textilien aus eigener Sammlung* Exhibition. Krefeld.

Paetz gen. Schieck, A. (2005) *Die koptischen Textilien. Gewebe und Gewänder des ersten Jahrtausends aus Ägypten,* Kolumba. Essen.

Paetz gen. Schieck, A. (2010) Mumienporträts und ihre kulturellen Bezugssysteme – Formen der Selbstdarstellung und des Totengedenkens im römischen Ägypten. *Mannheimer Geschichtsblätter* 19, 81–98.

Paetz gen. Schieck, A. (2011) Über das Bildnis eines römischen Offiziers aus Ägypten, textile Überreste und militärische Rangabzeichen im 3. Jh. n. Chr, 79. Jahrestagung des Nordwestdeutschen Verbandes für Altertumsforschung e.V., Detmold am 1.9.2009. In J. Drauschke/R. Prien/S. Ristow (eds.), *Untergang und Neuanfang, Tagungsbeiträge der Arbeitsgemeinschaft Spätantike und frühes Mittelalter, Studien zur Spätantike und zum Frühmittelalter 3,* 305–333.

Paetz gen. Schieck, A. and Fuchs, R. (2011) Colour spectrometry – A non-destructive method of dye-analysis applied on Late Roman textiles from Egypt. In C. Alfaro Giner, J.-P. Brun, P. Borgard, R. Pierobon Benoit (eds.), *Purpureae Vestes III, Textiles y Tintes en la ciudad Antigua, Actas del III Symposium Internacional sobre Textiles y Tintes del Mediterráneo en el mundo antiguo, Neapel 14.–15.11.2008,* 109 – 118.

Paetz gen. Schieck, A. and Pásztókai-Szeőke, J. (2010) Számú épület falfestményén ábrázolt, nyílhegyben végződő clavival d´szített tunica értelmezése. In *Római Kori Falfestmények Brigetióból, Acta Archaologica Brigetionensia I, 3,* 106–113.

Page, D. (1955) *Sappho and Alcaeus.* Oxford.

Parlasca, K. (1966) *Mumienporträts und verwandte Denkmäler.* Wiesbaden.

Parlasca, K. (1969) *Ritratti di Mummie Serie B Vol. I.* Palermo.

Parlasca, K. (1977) *Ritratti di Mummie Serie B Vol. II.* Palermo.

Parlasca, K. (1980) *Ritratti di Mummie Serie B Vol. III.* Rome.

Parlasca, K. (1981) Bildnis eines römischen Offiziers. In J. Romano (ed.), *Das Museum für Altägyptische Kunst in Luxor, Katalog,* Mainz, 186–197.

Parlasca, K. (1999) Bedeutung und Problematik der Mumienporträts und ihr kulturelles Umfeld. In K. Parlasca and H. Seemann (eds), *Augenblicke. Mumienporträts und ägyptische Grabkunst aus römischer Zeit, Exhibition Frankfurt January 30 to April 11, 1999.* Frankfurt/München, 23–48.

Parlasca, K. (2003) *Ritratti di Mummie Serie B Vol. IV.* Rome.

Parlasca, K. and Seemann, H. (1999) *Augenblicke. Mumienporträts und ägyptische Grabkunst aus römischer Zeit, Exhibition Frankfurt January 30 to April 11, 1999.* Frankfurt/München.

Pausch, M. (2003) *Die römische Tunika.* Augsburg.

Pauli Jensen, X. (2008) Vimose revisited – Perspectives and preliminary Results. In A. Abegg-Wigg and A. Rau (eds), *Aktuelle Forschungen zu Kriegsbeuteopfern und Fürstengräbern im Barbaricum, Internationales Kolloquium Schleswig 15.–18. Juni 2006,* Schriften des Archäologischen Landesmuseums, Ergänzungsreihe 4. Neumünster, 137–149.

Petculescu, L. (1995) Military Equipment Graves in Roman Dacia. *JRMES* 6, 105–145.

Petersen, P. (1995) *Nydam Offermose.* Lyngby.

Petrie, F. (1917) *Tools and Weapons.* London.

Petrie, F. (1927) *Objects of Daily Use, British School of Archaeology in Egypt.* London.

Pfister, R. (1934) *Textiles de Palmyre découverts par le Service des Antiquités du Haut-Commissariat de la République Française dans la nécropole de Palmyra.*

Pfister, R. (1940) *Textiles de Palmyre. Découverts par le Service des Antiquités du Haut-Commissariat de la République Française dans la Nécropole de Palmyre III.* Paris.

Pfister, R. and Bellinger, L. (1945) In M. I. Rostovtzeff *et al.* (eds), *The Excavations at Dura Europos. Final Report IV Part II. The Textiles.* New Haven.

Pfrommer, M. (1998) *Untersuchungen zur Chronologie und Komposition des Alexandersmosaiks auf Antiquarischer Grundlage.* Mainz am Rhein.

Pfrommer, M. (2001) *Alexander der Grosse: Auf den Spuren eines Mythos.* Mainz.

Pontrandolfo, A. and Rouveret, A. (1992) *Le tombe dipinte di Paestum.* Modena.

Preisigke, F. (1922) *Namenbuch enthaltend alle griechischen, lateinischen, ägyptischen, hebräischen, arabischen und sonstigen semitischen und nichtsemitischen Menschennamen, soweit sie in griechischen Urkunden (Papyris, Ostraka, Inschriften, Mumienschildern usw) Ägyptens sich vorfinden.* Heidelberg.

Quirke, S. and Spencer, J. (1992) *The British Museum Book of Ancient Egypt.* London.

Rainbird, S. (1986) The Fire Stations of Imperial Rome. *PBSR* 54, 147–169.

Rathbone, D. (2007) Military Finance and Supply. In Ph. Sabin, H. van Wees and M. Whitby (eds), *The Cambridge History of Greek and Roman Warfare, Vol. II. Part I.* Cambridge, 158–176.

Rathbone, D. W. (1990) Villages. Land and Population in Greaco-Roman Egypt. *PCPS* 216, 103–142.

Rathmann, M. (2002) Straßen [V Römisches Reich]. *DNP* 12/2, 1134–1160.

Richardson, T. (1998) The Ballistics of the Sling. *Royal Armouries Yearbook* 3, 44–49.

Robertson, M. (1978) *Greek Painting.* London.

Robinson, H. R. (1975) *The Armour of Imperial Rome.* London.

Rößler, D. (1993) Das Kaiserporträt im 3. Jahrhundert. In K.-P. Johne (ed.), *Gesellschaft und Wirtschaft des Römischen Reiches im 3. Jahrhundert. Studien zu ausgewählten Problemen.* Berlin, 319–374.

Roth, J. P. (1999) *The Logistics of the Roman Army at War (264 BC–AD 235).* Leiden.

Ruffing, K. (1995) Einige Überlegungen zu Koptos: Ein Handelsplatz Oberägyptens in römischer Zeit. *MBAH* 14:1, 17–42.

Ruffing, K. (1996) Textilien als Wirtschaftgut in der römischen Kaiserzeit. In S. Günther, O. Stoll and K. Ruffing (eds), *Pragmata. Beiträge zur Wirtschaftsgeschichte der Antike im Gedenken an Harald Wuinkel* Philippika 17. Wiesbaden, 41–43.

Sabin, Ph., van Wees, H. and Whitby, M. (2007) *The Cambridge History of Greek and Roman Warfare. Vol. 1, Greece, the Hellenistic world and the rise of Rome. Vol. 2, Rome from the late Republic to the late Empire.* Cambridge.

Sacconi, A. (1971) A proposito dell'epiteto omerico ΛΙΝΟΘΩΡΗΞ. *Živa Antika* XXI, 49–54.

Saddington, D. B. (2007) Classes in The Evolution of the Roman Imperial Fleets. In P. Erdkamp (ed.), *A Companion to the Roman Army*, London New York, 201–234.

Salomons, R. P. (ed.) (1996) *Papyri Bodeleianae I*, Stud. Amst. 34, Amsterdam.

Sander, E. (1963) Die Kleidung des römischen Soldaten. *Historia* 13 (1), 144–166.

Sayar, M. H. (1998) *Perinthos-Herakleia (Marmara Ereglisi) und Umgebung: Geschichte, Testimonien, griechische und lateinische Inschriften.* Veröffentlichungen der Kleinasiatischen Kommission 9. Wien.

Schenke, G. (2001) Mumienporträts im römischen Ägypten: Totenbildnisse oder Privatporträts? *Cd'É* LXXVI, 281–289.

Schlabow, K. (1976) *Textilfunde der Eisenzeit in Norddeutschland.* Neumünster.

Schleiermacher, M. (1984) *Römische Reitergrabsteine. Die kaiserzeitlichen Reliefs des triumphierenden Reiters*, Abhandlung zur Kunst-, Musik- und literaturwissenschaft 338. Bonn.

Schmidt-Colinet, A. (1985) Neue Ausgrabungen in Palmyra: Das Tempelgrab einer Aristokratenfamilie. *Universitas, Zeitschrift für Wissenschaft, Kunst und Literatur* 469:6, 677–689.

Schmidt-Colinet, A. (1995) (ed.) *Palmyra – Kulturbegegnung im Grenzbereich*, Zaberns Bildbände zur Archäologie 27. Mainz.

Schmidt-Colinet, A. and Stauffer A. (2000) *Die Textilien aus Palmyra. Neue und alte Funde.* Mainz.

Schmidt-Colinet, A., Stauffer, M. and Al-Asad, K. (2000) *Die Textilien aus Palmyra.* Mainz.

Schweppe, H. (1976) Untersuchung alter Textilfärbungen. *Die BASF. Aus der Arbeit der BASF. Aktiengesellschft* 26, 29–31.

Schweppe, H. (1993) *Handbuch der Naturfarbstoffe. Vorkommen – Verwendung – Nachweis.* Hamburg.

Seiler-Baldinger, A. (1994) *Textiles: A Classification of Techniques.* Bathurst.

Seipel, W. (1998) *Bilder aus dem Wüstensand. Mumienportraits aus dem Ägyptischen Museum Kairo, Exhibition at the Kunsthistorisches Museum Wien, October 20, 1998–January 24.* Ostfildern.

Seyrig, H. (1937) Armes et costumes iraniens de Palmyre. *Syria* 18, 4–31.

Shaw, I. (1991) *Egyptian Warfare and Weapons.* London.

Sheffer, A. and Granger-Taylor, H. (1994) Textiles from Masada – a Preliminary Selection. In J. Aviram, G. Foerster and E. Netzer (eds), *Masada IV – The Yigael Yadin Excavations 1963–65.* Jerusalem, 149–256.

Sheridan, J. A. (1998) *Columbia Papyri IX – The Vestis Militaris Codex.* American Studies in Papyrology 39. Atlanta.

Silver, M. (1995) *Economic Structures of Antiquity.* Contributions in Economics and Economic History 159. London.

Simkins, M. (1984) *The Roman Army from Caesar to Trajan.* Oxford.

Southern, P. (2007) *The Roman Army: a social and institutional history.* Oxford.

Southern, P. and Dixon, K. R. (1996) *The Late Roman Army.* New Haven.

Spalinger, A. J. (2005) *War in Ancient Egypt: The New Kingdom, Ancient World at War.* Oxford.

Spaul, J. (2000) *Cohors. The evidence for and a short history of the auxiliary infantry unit of the Imperial Roman Army.* BAR International Series 841. Oxford.

Speidel, M. A. (1996) *Die römischen Schreibtafeln von Vindonissa.* Veröffentlichungen der Gesellschaft pro Vindonissa XII. Brugg.

Speidel, M. A. (2009) *Heer und Herrschaft im Römischen Reich der Hohen Kaiserzeit.* Stuttgart

Speidel, M. P. (1970) The captor of Decebalus. *JRS* 60, 142–153.

Speidel, M. P. (1976) Eagle-Bearer and Trumpeter. *Bonner Jahrbücher* 176, 123–163.

Speidel, M. P. (1992) The Weapons Keeper (*Armorum Custos*) and the Ownership of Weapons in the Roman Army. In M. P. Speidel (ed.), *Roman Army Studies 2*. Mavors 8. Stuttgart, 131–136.

Speidel, M. P. (1993) The fustis as a soldier's weapon. *Ant. Afr.* 29, 137–149.

Speidel, M. P. (1994a) *Die Denkmäler der Kaiserreiter*. Bonn.

Speidel, M. P. (1994b) *Riding for Caesar. The Roman Emperor's Horse Guard*. London.

Speidel, M. P. (1997) Late-Roman military decorations II: gold-embroidered capes and tunics. *Ant. Tard.* 5, 231–237.

Speidel, M. P. (1998) A Soldier of *Legio IIII Scythica* from Zeugma. In D. Kennedy (ed.), *The Twin Towns of Zeugma on the Euphrates*. Portmounth (*JRA*), 203–204.

Speidel, M. P. (1999) Bildnisse römischer Offiziere aus dem Fayum. In K. Parlasca and H. Seemann (eds), *Augenblicke. Mumienporträts und ägyptische Grabkunst aus römischer Zeit, Exhibition Frankfurt January 30 to April 11, 1999*. Frankfurt/München, 87–88.

Speidel, M. P. (2000a) Commodus and the King of the Quadi. *Germania* 78, 193–197.

Speidel, M. P. (2000b) Sold und Wirtschaftslage der römischen Soldaten. In G. Alföldy, B. Dobson and W. Eck (eds), *Kaiser, Heer und Gesellschaft in der römischen Kaiserzeit. Gedenkschrift für Eric Birley*. Heidelberger althistorische Beiträge und epigraphische Studien. Stuttgart, 22–58.

Speidel, M. P. (2002) The Framework of an Imperial Legion. In R. J. Brewer (ed.), *The Second Augustan Legion and the Roman Military Machine*. Cardiff, 125–143.

Speidel, M. P. (2006a) *Emperor Hadrian's speeches to the African Army – a new Text*. Romisch-Germanisches Zentralmuseum, Forschungsinstitut fur Vor- und Fruhgeschichte. Mainz.

Speidel, M. P. (2006b) *Ancient Germanic Warriors. Warrior Styles from Trajan's Column to Icelandic Sagas*. London.

Speidel, M. P. (2007) The Missing Weapons at Carlisle. *Britannia* 38, 237–240.

Stamm, R. (ed.) (2007) *Paula Modersohn-Becker und die ägyptischen Mumienportraits. Eine Hommage zum 100. Todestag der Künstlerin*, Exhibition Bremen. Köln.

Starr, C. (1941) *Roman Imperial Navy*. Ithaca.

Stauffer, A. (2002) Tessuti. In *Guerriero e Sacerdote: Autorità e Comunitá nell'età Del Ferro a Verucchio: La Tomba Del Trono* (ed.) P. Von Eles. Firenze, 192–220.

Steingräber, S. (1986) *Etruscan Painting. Catalogue Raisonné of Etruscan Wall Paintings*. New York.

Stephenson, I. P. (1999) *Roman Infantry Equipment: the later empire*. Gloucestershire.

Stiebel, G. D. and Magness, J. (2007) The Military Equipment from Masada. In J. Aviram, G. Foerster, E. Netzer and G. D. Stiebel (eds), *Masada VIII – The Yigael Yadin Excavations 1963–1965*. Jerusalem, 1–94.

Strecker, C. and Heinrich, P. (2007) Eine innovative Restaurierung – Eine neuartige Präsentation. Das altägyptische Perlennetz aus El-Hibe. In *Ägyptische Mumien. Unsterblichkeit im Land der Pharaonen, Große Landesausstellung Baden-Württemberg October 6, 2007 to March 24, 2008* Landesmuseum Württemberg. Stuttgart (ed.), 216–227.

Studniczka, F. (1887) Zur Herkunft der Mykenischen Cultur. *MKDAIAA* 12.

Sturm, A. (2003) Die Kleider von Alpirsbach – Ihre Geschichte und die Reproduktion. *Karfunkel* 48, 115–118.

Summer, G. (2002) *Roman Military Clothing. Vol. 1, 100 BC–AD 200*. Oxford.

Summer, G. (2003) *Roman Military Clothing Vol 2, AD 200–400*. Oxford.

Sumner, G. (2009) *Roman Military Dress*. Stroud.

Toynbee, J. M. C. (1971) *Death and Burial in the Roman World*. London.

Turcan, R. (1971) Les Guirlandes dans l'Antiquité Classique. *Jahrbuch für Antike und Christentum* 14, 92–139.

Tørnkvist, S. (1969) Note on Linen Corslets. *Opuscula Romana* VII, 81–82.

Ulbert, G. (1969) *Das frührömische Kastell Rheingönheim*. Limesforschungen 9. Berlin.

Ullemeyer, R. and Tidow, K. (1981) Textil- und Lederfunde der Grabung Feddersen Wierde. In *Einzeluntersuchungen zur Feddersen Wierde*, (ed.) Feddersen Wierde 3W Haarnagel, Wiesbaden, 77–152.

v. Premerstein, A. (1903) Die Buchfürung einer ägyptischen Legionsabteilung. *KLIO* 3, 1–46.

van Driel-Murray, C. (2002) The leather trades in Roman Yorkshire and beyond. In P. Wilson and J. Price (ed.), *Aspects of industry in Roman Yorkshire and the North*. Oxford, 109–123.

van Driel-Murray, C. (2003) Ethnic soldiers: The experience of the Lower Rhine Tribes. In Th. Grünewald and S. Seibel (eds), *Kontinuität und Diskontinuität. Germania inferior am Beginn und am Ende der römischen Herrschaft. Beiträge des deutsch-niederländischen Kolloquiums in der Katholieke Universiteit Nijmegen 27.–30. Juni 2001*, Ergänzungsband Reallexikon Germanische Altertumskunde 35. Berlin, 200–218.

Verboven, K. (2007) Good for business. The Roman army and the emergence of a 'business class' in the northwestern provinces of the Roman empire. In L. de Blois and E. Lo Cascio (eds), *The Impact of the Roman Army (200 BC–AD 476): Economic, Social, Political, Religious and Cultural Aspects*. Impact of Empire 6. Leiden/Boston, 295–313.

Vittinghoff, F. (1986) Römische Bürgerrechts- und Integrationspolitik in der hohen Kaiserzeit. In Eck, H. and Wolff (eds), *Heer und Integrationspolitik. Die römischen Militärdiplome als historische Quelle*. Passauer Historische Forschungen 2W. Köln, 535–555.

Vogelsang-Eastwood, G. (1999) *Tutankhamun's Wardrobe: Garments from the Tomb of Tutankhamun*. Rotterdam.

von Moock, D. W. (1998) *Die figürlichen Grabstelen Attikas in der Kaiserzeit*. Mainz.

Walker, S. (1997) Mummy Portraits and Roman Portraiture. In S. Walker and M. Bierbrier (eds), *Ancient Faces. Mummy Portraits from Roman Egypt*. A Catalogue of the Roman Portraits in the British Museum IV. London, 14–16.

Walker, S. and Bierbrier, M. (1997) *Ancient Faces. Mummy Portraits from Roman Egypt. A Catalogue of the Roman Portraits in the British Museum IV*. London.

Watson, G. R. (1956) The Pay of the Roman Army: Suetonius, Dio, and the quartum stipendium. *Historia* 5, 332–340.

Webster, G. (1979) *The Roman Imperial Army*. 2nd ed. London.

Wedenig, R. (1997) *Epigraphische Quellen zur städtischen Administration in Noricum*. Klagenfurt.

Weill, S. (2003) Danmarks mosefundpionér – Arkæologen Conrad Engelhardt og hans virke. In L. Jørgensen (ed.), *Sejrens triumf. Norden i skyggen af det romerske Imperium*. Copenhagen, 66–83.

Weitzmann, K. (1977) (ed.) *Age of Spirituality. Late Antique and Early Christian Art. Third to Seventh Century*. Exhibition. New York.

Wesch-Klein, G. (1998) *Soziale Aspekte des römischen Heerwesens in der Kaiserzeit*. Stuttgart.

Whittaker, C. R. (1994) *Frontiers of the Roman Empire: A social and economic study*. Baltimore.

Whittaker, C. R. (2002) Supplying the Army. Evidence from Vindolanda. In P. Erdkamp (ed.), *The Roman Army and the Economy*. Amsterdam, 204–235.

Widengren, G. (1956) Some Remarks on Riding Costume and Articles of Dress among Iranian Peoples in Antiquity. *Artica, Studia Ethnographica Upsaliensia* XI, 228–276.

Wierschoski, L. (2001) Die römische Heeresversorgung im frühen Prinzipat. *MBHA* 20/2, 37–61.

Wieser, M. (1996) Die Wiederzusammenführung von Gürtelbestandteilen des Museums Lauriacum in Enns und eine kurze Bemerkung zum Balteusbestandteil RVII 531. *Museumverein Lauriacum Enns* 34, 17–20.

Wild, J. P. (1976) The *Gynaecea*. In R. Goodburn and P. Bartholonew (eds), *Aspects of the Notitia Dignitatum*. Oxford, 51–58.

Wild, J. P. (1981) A Find of Roman Scale Armour from Carpow. *Britannia* 12, 305–306.

Wild, J. P. (2002) The Textile Industries of Roman Britain. *Britannia* 33, 1–42.

Willems, H. and Clarysse, W. (eds) (1999) *Keizers aan de Nijl. Exhibition Tongeren 1999–2000.*

Wilson, A. (2001) Timgad and Texile Production. In D. J. Mattingly and J. Salmon (eds), *Economies Beyond Agriculture in the Classical World*. London, 271–296.

Wilson, L. M. (1931) Textiles. In *The Excavations at Dura-Europos conducted by the Yale University and the French Academy of Inscriptions and Letters*. Preliminary Report of the Second Season of Work, October 1928–April 1929 (eds) P. V. C. Baur and M. I. Rostovzeff, Yale/New Haven, 178–180 pl. XVIII–XXI.

Woods, D. (1993) The Ownership and Disposal of Military Equipment in the Late Roman Army. *JRMES* 4, 55–65.

Yadin, Y. (1963a) *The Art of Warfare in Biblical Lands* Vols I & II. Jerusalem.

Yadin, Y. (1963b) *The Finds from the Bar-Kokhba Period in the Cave of Letters.* Jerusalem.

Yadin, Y. (1965) The Excavations of Masada, 1963–4, Preliminary Report. *IEJ* 15, 1–120.

Yadin, Y. (1966) *Masada: Herod's Fortress and the Zealot's Last Stand.* London.

Zhao, F. (2008) Eastern Influence on Local Textiles in Xinjiang during the 3rd–4th Centuries. In Zhao F. (ed.), *Western Imprints: Textiles from Han and Jin Dynasties in China*. Hong Kong, 77–92.